Toward New Sources of Competitiveness in Bangladesh

DIRECTIONS IN DEVELOPMENT
Trade

Toward New Sources of Competitiveness in Bangladesh

Key Findings of the Diagnostic Trade Integration Study

Sanjay Kathuria and Mariem Mezghenni Malouche

WORLD BANK GROUP

ISBN (paper): 978-1-4648-0647-6
ISBN (electronic): 978-1-4648-0648-3
DOI: 10.1596/978-1-4648-0647-6

Cover photo: © Mariem Mezghenni Malouche/World Bank; further permission required for reuse.
Cover design: Debra Naylor, Naylor Design, Washington, DC

Library of Congress Cataloging-in-Publication Data
Kathuria, Sanjay.
  Toward new sources of competitiveness in Bangladesh : a Bangladesh diagnostic trade integration study / Sanjay Kathuria, Mariem Malouche.
     pages cm. — (Directions in development)
  Includes bibliographical references and index.
  ISBN 978-1-4648-0648-3 (alk. paper) — ISBN 978-1-4648-0647-6 (alk. paper)
  1. Exports—Bangladesh. 2. Bangladesh—Commerce. 3. Bangladesh—Commercial policy. 4. Bangladesh—Economic policy. I. Malouche, Mariem, 1973- II. Title.
  HF3790.6.K38 2015
  382'.6095492—dc23

                                                                        2015021971

Contents

Boxes

Figures

Photos

Tables

Foreword

Bangladesh can be justly proud of its track record in reducing poverty and achieving progress on key human development indicators, such as child mortality, school enrollment, and female empowerment, to name a few. In mid-2015, reflecting a decade of robust growth, the World Bank reclassified Bangladesh from "low income" to "lower-middle-income."

Over the next decade, the most important development challenge for Bangladesh will be to provide more and better jobs to its workers, as more than 20 million people join the labor force.

Achieving this goal will require Bangladesh to connect more deeply to the world market for garments and other labor-intensive products. Opportunities exist, particularly as wages continue to rise in China, gradually reducing China's dominance in labor-intensive manufacturing.

To benefit fully from international demand and emerging opportunities for export-based job creation, Bangladesh will need to craft a proactive strategy. This comprehensive report lays out a path for doing so. It covers a lot of ground, including trade policy and institutions, logistics and infrastructure, and finance and foreign direct investment. It also anchors that thematic work in detailed studies of different sectors, such as shipbuilding, non-leather footwear, jute products, garments/polo shirts, bicycles, information technology, services, and pharmaceuticals.

We are confident that the depth and breadth of the report, combined with the high quality of its analysis, will contribute to the development debate in Bangladesh. In addition, policy makers and development partners will find a possible reform agenda, focused on areas critical to Bangladesh's development, that they can support.

The World Bank Group is already supporting the Government of Bangladesh in a broad range of areas related to private sector development, and, following the guidance of this report, expects to deepen this engagement, centering around job creation and trade and competitiveness.

We are grateful to the Government of Bangladesh for entrusting the World Bank Group to carry out this important diagnostic work, and to the Enhanced

Integrated Framework Secretariat at the World Trade Organization for funding and other substantive support.

Johannes Zutt
Country Director
  for Bangladesh, Bhutan, and Nepal
The World Bank Group

Anabel Gonzalez
Senior Director
Trade and Competitiveness
  Global Practice
The World Bank Group

Acknowledgments

This Diagnostic Trade Integration Study (DTIS) has been prepared in response to a request from the Government of Bangladesh under the Enhanced Integrated Framework (EIF) for Trade-Related Technical Assistance to Least Developed Countries. The EIF is a multidonor program that supports least developed countries in becoming more active players in the global trading system by helping them tackle supply-side constraints to trade. The ultimate objective of the study is to build the foundation for accelerated growth by enhancing the integration of the economy of Bangladesh into regional and global markets.

The World Bank thanks the Government of Bangladesh for placing its confidence in the World Bank to conduct this study. The main counterpart for the DTIS is the World Trade Organization (WTO) Cell in the Ministry of Commerce of Bangladesh. The European Union is the donor facilitator, which means it is taking the lead in mobilizing resources to fund the identified actions. The Government of Bangladesh has displayed strong ownership of the task, initiating its preparation and forming a national steering committee with concerned ministries, local think tanks, and the private sector to provide guidance to the work. The government's views and comments have been reflected at all stages of the report, from the concept-note stage to the final Action Matrix. The team particularly thanks Mr. Amitava Chakraborty, Director General (Additional Secretary), WTO Cell, and the team in the WTO Cell, Ministry of Commerce, including Mr. Nesar Ahmed (Director, WTO Cell), Md. Hafizur Rahman (Director, WTO Cell), Dr. Md. Moniruzzaman (Director, WTO Cell), Mr. Mohammad Zakir Hossain (Deputy Director, WTO Cell), and Mr. Mohammad Mashooqur Rahman Sikder (Deputy Director, WTO Cell).

Development partners, think tanks, the private sector, and other stakeholders have been consulted regularly at different stages in the preparation of the DTIS. Their views have been solicited through consultative workshops and one-on-one meetings. As an example, the team organized a consultative workshop with business leaders, development partners, members of the government, members of academia, and researchers in June 2010. One-on-one meetings were also held with a number of individuals. The team organized two interim consultative workshops in December 2012. A two-day validation workshop was organized jointly by the WTO Cell, Ministry of Commerce, and the World Bank on October 22–23, 2013, in Dhaka. The prioritized recommendations of the Action Matrix were discussed in the validation workshop. The team has benefited from consultations with Dr. Mirza Azizul Islam (former Adviser to the Government of Bangladesh, Ministry of Finance); Dr. Md. Mozibur Rahman (CEO, Bangladesh Foreign Trade Institute [BFTI]); Dr. Mostafa Abid Khan (Director, BFTI); Dr. M. K. Mujeri (Director General, Bangladesh Institute of Development Studies); and Dr. Zaidi Sattar, Dr. Sadiq Ahmed, and Dr. Ahsan Mansur (Policy Research Institute [PRI], Bangladesh).

The report has been prepared by a core World Bank team led by Sanjay Kathuria (Lead Economist) and Mariem Mezghenni Malouche (Senior Economist), including Nadeem Rizwan (Research Analyst). The contributing team included several World Bank Group staff members and consultants, including Charles Kunaka (Senior Trade Specialist, World Bank); Peter Kusek (Senior Investment Policy Officer, IFC); Michael Friss Jensen, Olivier Cadot, Nihal Pitigala, Hugh Baylis, Zaidi Sattar, and PRI Bangladesh; Dr. Selim Raihan (Dhaka University) and Rupa Chanda (Indian Institute of Management, Bangalore); Kay Dausendschoen (FutureShip); Glenn Surabian and Yasuo Konishi (Global Development Solutions); and Atdhe Veliu. Support was also received from Martha Denisse Pierola (Economist), Jose Daniel Reyes (Economist), Mohammad Anis (Energy Specialist), Iffath Sharif (Senior Economist), Ayesha Vawda (Senior Education Specialist), Tanya Primiani (Investment Policy Officer, IFC), and Sanjana Zaman (Research Analyst). The team thanks the development partners for their comments and cooperation. The team acknowledges comments received from World Bank Group colleagues, including peer reviewers Ndiame Diop (Lead Economist, MNSED), Philip Schuler (Senior Economist, AFTP1), Vincent Palmade (Lead Economist, SASFP), and Reynaldo Bench (Senior Port Specialist, TWITR); Salman Zaidi (Lead Economist); Zahid Hussain (Lead Economist); Vinaya Swaroop (Sector Manager, SASEP); Gladys Lopez-Acevedo (Lead Economist); Martin Maxwell Norman (Senior Private Sector Development Specialist); Manju Haththotuwa (Senior Private Sector Development Specialist); Arbind Modi (Principal Operations Officer, IFC); Sherif Muhtaseb (Senior Operations Officer, IFC); Hosna Ferdous Sumi (Associate Operations Officer, IFC); Raihana Rabbany (Consultant, IFC); Rodrigo Cubero and Seng Guan Toh (IMF); and Sadiq Ahmad and Zaidi Sattar (PRI). Mariem Mezghenni Malouche, Lalita Moorty, and Md. Abul Basher led the initial preparation of the concept note for the report. The team thanks Mehar Akhtar Khan and Kamrun Nahar Chowdhury for support with desktop publishing, logistics, and organizing the workshops in Dhaka. Rita Soni and Muhammad Shafiq helped with contracting and Sandra Gain and Michael Alwan edited the report. The team also thanks colleagues in the International Finance Corporation (in particular, Masrur Reaz and Paramita Dasgupta) for supporting a number of the sector studies, which greatly helped to increase the coverage of the DTIS, and Christiane Kraus, Chief Coordinator for the Enhanced Integrated Framework at the World Trade Organization. Finally, the team acknowledges the support of the World Bank management team led by Country Director Johannes Zutt (and previous Country Director Ellen Goldstein) throughout the process of preparation.

About the Authors

Sanjay Kathuria is Lead Economist in the World Bank's South Asia Regional Cooperation and Integration Unit, based in Washington, D.C. Until August 2012, he was the World Bank's Lead Economist for Bangladesh, based in Dhaka. In 23 years at the World Bank, he has worked in South Asia, as well as in the Latin American and the Caribbean and Europe and Central Asia regions. Prior to joining the World Bank, he was a Fellow at the Indian Council for Research on International Economic Relations in New Delhi. He graduated from St. Stephen's College, and he received his master's from the Delhi School of Economics and his PhD from Oxford University. His research interests include economic growth, economic integration, international trade and trade policy, competitiveness, technology development, fiscal policy, and financial sector development. He has published several books and academic and popular articles on those topics. Recent books and reports include coauthor of *Consolidating and Accelerating Exports in Bangladesh* (World Bank 2012); lead author of *Macedonia, FYR: Moving to Faster and More Inclusive Growth: A Country Economic Memorandum* (World Bank 2009); and editor of *Western Balkan Integration and the EU: An Agenda for Growth and Development* (World Bank 2008).

Mariem Mezghenni Malouche is a Senior Economist at the World Bank in Washington, D.C. Her areas of interest include trade and competitiveness, economic integration, trade policy, nontariff measures, export diversification, trade finance, and diaspora. She joined the World Bank in 2004 as an economist in the Middle East and North Africa (MENA) and later the International Trade department. She earned a PhD in international economics from Université Paris-Dauphine, France, and a master's degree in business from University of Tunis III with the highest honors. She is a coauthor of *Streamlining Non-Tariff Measures: A Toolkit for Policy Makers* (World Bank 2012); coeditor of *Non-Tariff Measures: A Fresh Look at Trade Policy's New Frontier*; and coeditor of *Trade Finance during the Great Trade Collapse* (World Bank 2011). She participated in and contributed to a number of country-level policy dialogue, development policy loans, and reports in MENA, South Asia, and Sub-Saharan Africa, notably in Bangladesh, Kazakhstan, Lao PDR, Libya, Mauritius, Morocco, and Tunisia.

Abbreviations

6FYP	Sixth Five-Year Plan
ADB	Asian Development Bank
AEO	Authorized Economic Operator
API	active pharmaceutical ingredients
ASEAN	Association of Southeast Asian Nations
ASYCUDA	Automated SYstem for CUstoms DAta
BASIS	Bangladesh Association of Software and Information Services
BB	Bangladesh Bank
BEZA	Bangladesh Economic Zones Authority
BFTI	Bangladesh Foreign Trade Institute
BGMEA	Bangladesh Garment Manufacturers and Exporters Association
BIDS	Bangladesh Institute of Development Studies
BITM	BASIS Institute of Technology and Management
BIWTA	Bangladesh Inland Water Transport Authority
BJRI	Bangladesh Jute Research Institute
BKMEA	Bangladesh Knitwear Manufacturers and Exporters Association
BOI	Board of Investment
BPDB	Bangladesh Power Development Board
BPO	business process outsourcing
BSTI	Bangladesh Standards and Testing Institution
BTC	Bangladesh Tariff Commission
BTMA	Bangladesh Textile Mills Association
BUILD	Business Initiative Leading Development
BWH	bonded warehouse
CAP	corrective action plan
CPA	Chittagong Port Authority
CPD	Centre for Policy Dialogue
DEDO	Duty Exemption and Drawback Office
DFID	Department for International Development (United Kingdom)

DGDA	Directorate General of Drug Administration
DTIS	Diagnostic Trade Integration Study
dwt	dead weight tonnes
EEF	Equity Entrepreneurship Fund
EIF	Enhanced Integrated Framework
EPA	Economic Partnership Agreement
EPB	Export Promotion Bureau
EPZ	export processing zone
ERP	effective rate of protection
ESCAP	Economic and Social Commission for Asia and the Pacific (United Nations)
EU	European Union
FDI	foreign direct investment
FERA	Food and Environment Research Agency
FTA	free trade agreement
FY	fiscal year
GDP	gross domestic product
GIZ	Gesellschaft für Internationale Zusammenarbeit, the German Society for International Cooperation
GSP	Generalized System of Preferences
GT	gross tonnes
HS	Harmonized System
ICD	inland container depot
ICT	information and communications technology
IDLC	Industrial Development Leasing Company
IFC	International Finance Corporation
ILO	International Labour Organization
IMF	International Monetary Fund
IPS	Instant Power Supply
IT	information technology
ITC	International Terrestrial Cable
ITES	information technology enabled services
ITES-BPO	Information technology enabled services–business process outsourcing
IWT	inland waterways transport
JICA	Japan International Cooperation Agency
L/C	letter of credit
LCS	Land Customs Station

LDC	least developed country
LPI	Logistics Performance Index
MOAG	Ministry of Agriculture
MOC	Ministry of Commerce
MOF	Ministry of Finance
MOI	Ministry of Industries
MRA	Mutual recognition agreement
MW	megawatts
NBR	National Board of Revenue
NLC	National Logistics Committee
NTB	nontariff barrier
NTM	nontariff measure
OEM	original equipment manufacturer
PMO	Prime Minister's Office
PPP	public-private partnership
PRI	Policy Research Institute
R&D	research and development
RCA	revealed comparative advantage
RMG	ready-made garment
SAFE	Safety Advancement for Employees
SBW	special bonded warehouse
SITC	Standard International Trade Classification
SMEs	small and medium enterprises
SPS	sanitary and phytosanitary
TA	technical assistance
TBT	Technical Barriers to Trade
TEU	20-foot equivalent container unit
TIR	Transports Internationaux Routiers (International Road Transport)
Tk	Taka
TRIPS	Trade Related Aspects of Intellectual Property Rights
TVET	technical and vocational education and training
UNIDO	United Nations Industrial Development Organization
UPS	uninterruptable power supply
US$	U.S. dollar
USITC	U.S. International Trade Commission
VAT	value-added tax

WB   World Bank
WTO   World Trade Organization

Government Fiscal Year
July 1–June 30

Current Equivalents
Currency unit = Bangladesh taka (Tk)
US$1 = Tk 77.8 (March 2015)

Key Messages

Bangladesh's ambition is to build on its solid growth and poverty reduction achievements and accelerate growth to become a middle-income country by 2021, continue its high pace of poverty reduction, and share prosperity more widely among its citizens.

One of the country's greatest development challenges is to provide gainful employment to the more than two million people who will join the labor force each year over the next decade. Moreover, only 58.1 million of the country's 103.3 million working-age people are employed. Bangladesh needs to use its labor endowment even more intensively to increase growth and, in turn, absorb the additional labor.

The Commission on Growth and Development (2008) suggests that all 13 country cases of sustained high growth over the postwar period were marked by full exploitation of the knowledge, resources, and deep and elastic demand that the global economy offered. Bangladesh will need to do the same and exploit the international market more intensively, building on the pivotal role that exports have already played in providing gainful employment and access to imports.

Bangladesh's exports have exhibited strong growth and doubled their world market share between 1995 and 2012, owing to success in garments, catering largely to the European Union and the United States. Since 2009, Bangladesh has become the world's second largest garment exporter, making it unique among least developed countries (LDCs) in its high share of manufactures in total exports, which reached 90.5 percent in 2013 compared with about 26.2 percent for LDCs.

Garment exports can continue to grow in existing and newer markets. Newer products will emerge more slowly. Thus, more rapid export growth will initially rely on capturing higher market shares in Bangladesh's existing strengths, that is, basic garments, in current markets and penetrating newer and dynamic markets, such as China, India, and Japan and the countries of the Association of Southeast Asian Nations (ASEAN). In addition, many firms are starting to produce higher-value garments, and this will expand the target market for Bangladesh. Other products are emerging, such as jute goods, footwear, seafood, and information technology enabled services (ITES), and some of these may over time become part of a larger product cluster.

To achieve the above and sustain and accelerate export growth will require actions centered on four pillars. The first pillar is *breaking into new markets* through (a) better trade logistics to reduce delivery lags, as world markets become more competitive and newer products demand shorter lead times, to generate new sources of competitiveness and thereby to enable market diversification and (b) better exploitation of regional trading opportunities in nearby growing and dynamic markets, especially East Asia and South Asia. The second pillar is *breaking into new products* through (a) more neutral and rational trade policy and taxation and bonded warehouse schemes; (b) concerted efforts to spur domestic investment and attract foreign direct investment and to contribute to export promotion and diversification, including by easing the energy and land constraints; and (c) strategic development and promotion of services trade. The third pillar is *improving worker and consumer welfare* by (a) improving skills and literacy, (b) implementing labor and work safety guidelines, and (c) making safety nets more effective in dealing with trade shocks. The fourth pillar is *building a supportive environment*, including (a) sustaining sound macroeconomic fundamentals and (b) strengthening the institutional capacity for strategic policy making aimed at the objective of international competitiveness to help bring focus and coherence to the government's reform efforts.

Detailed studies of a number of growing export sectors confirmed the cross-cutting findings highlighted above and added other, sector-specific issues. In shipbuilding, enforcement of standards for domestic ships would help bring the domestic and export market segments closer and help exporting yards to achieve better scale economies. More credible enforcement of standards in pharmaceuticals would help people's health and reduce the disincentives of firms, including foreign firms that practice self-enforcement. Training to upgrade skills is a critical need in many sectors, including shipbuilding, ITES, and bicycles. Foreign direct investment (FDI) could play a much larger role in many sectors, especially those with technology upgrading needs, such as pharmaceuticals, bicycles, and shipbuilding. Improvements in access to finance and easing of Bangladesh Bank–monitored current account transactions would relieve constraints across all sectors. Additional submarine cables would help the reliability of Internet services for the ITES sector.

A neutral trade policy needs to be defined by consumer interests, not just the interests of domestic producers and exporters. Currently, distortions affect critical areas that affect consumer welfare, such as medicines and consumer products, and producer interests have tended to dominate over consumer interests. For example, allowing trade and FDI in drug supply would enhance the choices and quality of medicines and enable a more effective health strategy. In addition, societal demands for better regulation of imports to address an expanding array of issues, such as public safety, food safety, and plant and animal health, will increase, and this will need to be done in a credible and efficient manner that respects the balance between safety and access to a variety of imports.

Trade regime signals are critical for defining domestic production structures and shaping labor and capital usage. Bangladesh needs to increase the share of labor-intensive manufacturing in its gross domestic product (GDP) and a stronger export orientation will play a critical role here. Increasing basic skills will be critical for Bangladesh to remain competitive in exports, improve worker productivity, and enable sustainable wage increases. For skill flows, development of cognitive and noncognitive skills through a focus on the quality of primary and secondary education, along with industry-specific skills, will bring immense dividends.

An example of outward orientation would be the following. If it were to capture 20 percent of China's current garment exports, Bangladesh's total exports would more than double, increasing by US$29 billion and, based on current parameters, create 5.4 million new jobs and 13.5 million new indirect jobs. These would be virtually enough to absorb all new entrants into the labor force over the next decade.

With the implementation of the four-pillar agenda, a virtuous circle of export-led growth can be put in place, with multiple sources of strength. This will help improve the overall competitiveness of the economy and provide sources of strength other than low wages.

The ultimate goal of export-led growth is poverty reduction and the enhanced welfare of Bangladesh's citizens. Rapidly growing exports and the millions of new jobs accompanying them, along with skill upgrading, will increase productivity and wages, which over the long term is the only sustainable way to improve living standards. It will also begin a discourse to move beyond wage-based competitiveness. Improving skills will allow the effective participation of people in growth. Improving labor standards and worker safety is also part of this agenda and, in the wake of recent tragic incidents in the garment sector, has become a part of the preconditions for garment exports.

Bangladesh is well placed to take on some its strongest development challenges, provided it displays the right leadership. Its track record on growth and employment is strong. To grow faster, absorb more labor, and continue its pace of poverty reduction, the country will need to build on that record and improve on it. The good news is that a number of reforms are relatively low-hanging fruits, may be implemented in the short to medium term, and can bring large payoffs.

The example of Vietnam shows that accelerated, export-oriented development is possible, even in the context of the current global environment. Vietnam moved from being one of the poorest countries in the world to a lower-middle-income one in the space of 25 years, with FDI and trade playing a dominant role in the economy. Vietnam's exports and imports each form 90 percent of GDP, and, with 88 million people compared with Bangladesh's 150 million, Vietnam exports four times as much as Bangladesh today.

Bangladesh will need strong leadership to support its multisector competitiveness agenda. In many cases, it will require taking on strong domestic interests that may not welcome competition, either through imports or FDI. In other cases, it will require cohesion and coordination between different ministries or departments, such as the National Board of Revenue; the Ministries of Commerce,

Finance, and Industry; the Roads Division, and so on. If the Sixth Plan and Vision 2021 goals are to be achieved, this leadership has to be exercised.

Reference

Commission on Growth and Development. 2008. *Strategies for Sustained Growth and Inclusive Development*. Washington, DC: World Bank.

CHAPTER 1

Overview

This Diagnostic Trade Integration Study (DTIS), prepared at the request of the Government of Bangladesh, analyzes the internal and external constraints to further integration with the world economy, keeping in view the end goals of job creation and poverty reduction, as well as enhancement of citizens' welfare. The DTIS seeks to identify policies as well as gaps in physical and institutional infrastructure that need to be overcome to consolidate Bangladesh's strengths in existing markets as well as help diversify export products and export markets. At the same time, it spells out the links between these policies and consumer and worker welfare, focusing additional attention on import policies, skill enhancement, and labor safety. To illustrate and anchor these policy constraints to further integration, the DTIS includes industry and service sector studies.[1] Although the DTIS is comprehensive in its coverage of issues and sectors, as requested by the Government of Bangladesh, it is not intended to be an exhaustive study of industries and services. The identified policies and constraints are summarized at the end of this chapter, as well as in the Action Matrix presented in appendix A.

Bangladesh aims to accelerate growth to become a middle-income country by 2021, continue its high pace of poverty reduction, and share prosperity more widely among its citizens. It seeks to increase the growth rate of its economy to about 7.3 percent per year over the Sixth Plan period, fiscal year 2011 to fiscal year 2015 (FY2011–FY2015), and reduce the poverty headcount by about 10 percentage points. It also seeks to pay closer attention to the wider prosperity of its citizens and improve access to and quality of health, education, and nutrition services.

One of the country's greatest development challenges is to provide gainful employment to the 2.1 million people who will join the labor force each year over the next decade and to improve the utilization of existing labor. Although Bangladesh has the eighth largest population in the world and the third largest in South Asia after India and Pakistan, only 58.1 million of its 103.3 million working-age people are employed. Moreover, the working-age population is growing at a higher rate than the overall population, at 2.5–2.8 and 1.4 percent per year, respectively. This presents a potentially major demographic dividend, but it also represents a major challenge to lift incomes and citizens' welfare. Bangladesh needs to use its labor endowment even more intensively to increase growth and, in turn, to absorb the incoming labor. In this context, the emphasis of the Sixth Five-Year Plan (6FYP) on export-oriented manufactures, with their job potential, seems appropriate.

Imperative to Engage with the World Economy

The Government of Bangladesh recognizes that export-led growth and a broadening of the country's export structure are pivotal to its growth ambitions. In the 6FYP, trade is considered a strong source to accelerate growth and provide high-productivity and high-income jobs. The government recognizes that a dynamic manufacturing sector will benefit from greater outward orientation, particularly based on the experience of other successful Asian exporters, such as China, India, the Republic of Korea, Thailand, and Vietnam. The government has emphasized product and market diversification and regional and global integration. The 6FYP projects "…the share of exports in relation to gross domestic product (GDP) to rise by 7.7 percentage points to 23.9 percent of GDP by the end of the 6FYP, reflecting a leading role that [the] export sector is envisaged to play in increasing domestic activity" (General Economics Division 2011, volume 2, 85). This strategy recognizes the pivotal role that higher export orientation has already played in the impressive export and job creation of the garment export sector.

But current policies place limits on the extent of labor-intensive growth. At present, policies are heavily skewed toward favoring production for the domestic market, which limits growth because the market is limited. Because of protection, production is not necessarily competitive: many sectors have high effective rates of protection. Production for exports, by contrast, is necessarily competitive, usually implying in the Bangladeshi context that it is highly labor-intensive and the potential market, in practical terms, is immense.

Addressing Bangladesh's prime development objective of more and better jobs will require the following:

- A neutral trade policy that seeks to exploit the world market and favors exports as much as domestically oriented production
- A regime that proactively encourages foreign direct investment (FDI)
- Infrastructure improvement, especially relating to energy and trade logistics

Ensuring consumer and worker welfare is not only an end in itself, but will also help sustain export growth and better jobs. It would entail the following:

- Improving skills and literacy to allow a move up the quality ladder and enable higher productivity and wages
- Implementing labor and work safety guidelines
- Taking into account consumer interests in trade policy, balancing issues such as food safety and animal health with efficient access to imports

The Growth Commission Report (Commission on Growth and Development 2008) highlights the deep link between sustained growth and the world market. It finds that all 13 country cases of sustained high growth over the postwar period were marked by full exploitation of the knowledge, resources, and deep and elastic demand that the global economy offered. Thus, if Bangladesh were to capture 20 percent of China's current garment exports, Bangladesh's total exports would more than double, increasing by US$29 billion and, based on current parameters, creating 5.4 million new jobs and 13.5 million new indirect jobs. These jobs would be virtually enough to absorb all the new entrants into the labor force over the next decade. It is certainly doable, given the strengths that Bangladesh has, but would need sustained implementation of the agenda highlighted in this report.

Strong Record on Growth, Poverty Reduction, and the Current Account

Bangladesh has posted a robust and resilient economic performance over the past decade, accompanied by a sustained decline in poverty. Real GDP grew at a healthy rate of around 6 percent per year (table 1.1) over the past decade, accelerating by a percentage point compared with the previous one. GDP growth was remarkably stable, with a low standard deviation of 0.7 percent during this decade (half of what it was a decade earlier). This robust growth was

Table 1.1 Key Macroeconomic Indicators, FY2006–FY2014

Indicator	FY2006	FY2007	FY2008	FY2009	FY2010	FY2011	FY2012	FY2013	FY2014
Output and prices									
Real GDP growth (%)	6.7	7.1	6.0	5.0	5.6	6.5	6.5	6.0	6.1
Gross investment (% GDP)	26.1	26.2	26.2	26.2	26.2	27.4	28.3	28.4	28.7
CPI inflation (average)	7.2*	9.4	12.3	7.6	6.8	10.9	8.7	6.8	7.3
External accounts									
Exports (US$, millions)	10,526	12,178	14,111	15,565	16,205	22,924	24,288	27,018	30,177
Annual % change	21.6	15.7	15.9	10.3	4.1	41.5	5.9	11.2	11.7
Garments/total exports (%)	75.1	75.6	75.8	79.3	77.1	78.1	78.6	79.6	81.2
Imports (US$, millions)	14,746	17,157	21,629	22,507	23,738	33,658	36,985	37,290	40,616
Annual % change	12.2	16.3	26.1	4	5.5	41.8	9.9	0.8	8.9
Remittances (US$, millions)	4,802	5,979	7,915	9,689	10,987	11,650	12,843	14,456	14,228
Annual % change	24.8	24.5	32.4	22.4	13.4	6	10.2	12.6	−1.6
Current account balance (% GDP)	1.1	1.2	0.7	2.4	3.2	0.7	−0.3	1.6	0.9
Gross official reserves (US$, millions)	3,484	5,077	6,151	7,471	10,750	10,912	10,325	15,315	18,248
Gross official reserves (months of GNFS imports)	2.8	3.4	3.4	3.7	5.1	3.9	3.3	4.7	5.4

Sources: Bangladesh Bureau of Statistics, Bangladesh Bank, Export Promotion Bureau, Ministry of Finance, International Monetary Fund, and World Bank staff estimates.
Note: CPI = consumer price index; FY = fiscal year; GDP = gross domestic product; GNFS = goods and non-factor services; * = 1995–96 base.

accompanied by a uniform and steady decline in poverty headcount rates between 2000 (48.9 percent) and 2010 (31.5 percent) and a continuous decline in the number of poor people—from nearly 63 million in 2000 to 47 million in 2010, despite a growing population.

The Bangladesh Poverty Assessment shows that during 2000–10, poverty reduction was closely linked to the growth in labor income and changes in demographics (World Bank 2013). The most important driver of poverty reduction was growth in labor income. An increase in the share of the adult population in the country (that is, within each household as well) was also a significant factor, implying a declining dependency ratio.

How did Bangladesh grow in such a sustained fashion? Economic growth has accelerated since the 1990s, largely because of the accumulation of physical capital and increase in the size of the labor force and, to a smaller extent, because of an increase in total factor productivity (World Bank 2007, 2012b). Underpinning this were several economic reforms: sound macroeconomic management, targeted trade policy reforms that enabled the garment sector to thrive, similarly focused policies that facilitated takeoffs in other specific sectors (for example, frozen foods in European markets), import and financial sector liberalization, and investment in human development and social protection. Remittances and garment exports were the twin drivers of growth in the economy—remittances through their effect on consumption and construction, as well as easing the foreign exchange constraint and garment exports through providing sustained direct and indirect employment for millions of workers in garments, input and ancillary suppliers, and other measures. In addition, the manufacturing sector has been the largest single contributor to growth in the past two decades. As a result, the share of manufacturing in total GDP increased from 9.8 percent in FY1980 to 18.7 percent in FY2014. Modest investment rates notwithstanding, capital deepening has played an important role in agriculture and industry.

Bangladesh has proven to be relatively resilient to global economic shocks (figure 1.1). Its growth continued to be resilient despite several external shocks that slowed exports, remittances, and investment growth, including the end of the Agreement on Textiles and Clothing in 2005 and the 2008–09 global financial crisis. Bangladesh's resilience owes largely to strong fundamentals at the onset of the crisis, relatively underdeveloped and insulated financial markets, as well as preemptive policy response. Although slow growth in Europe and the United States, its two main export markets, has dampened Bangladesh's export growth, exports have nevertheless recovered and continue to grow at a reasonable pace.

The current account and balance of payments have been stable, thanks to remittances. Bangladesh relies heavily on imports for capital goods, oil, intermediates, and even a variety of consumer goods. Exports are not sufficient to pay for all imports, but the current account has been positive since FY2006, owing to growing remittances, which have proved critical to the stability of the balance of payments. Despite some concerns in FY2011 and FY2012 about oil imports and their impact on the balance of payments, the external sector has by and large proved stable over the years. Reserves have grown and stood at more than five

Figure 1.1 Resilient Growth Performance: GDP Growth, FY1981–FY2014

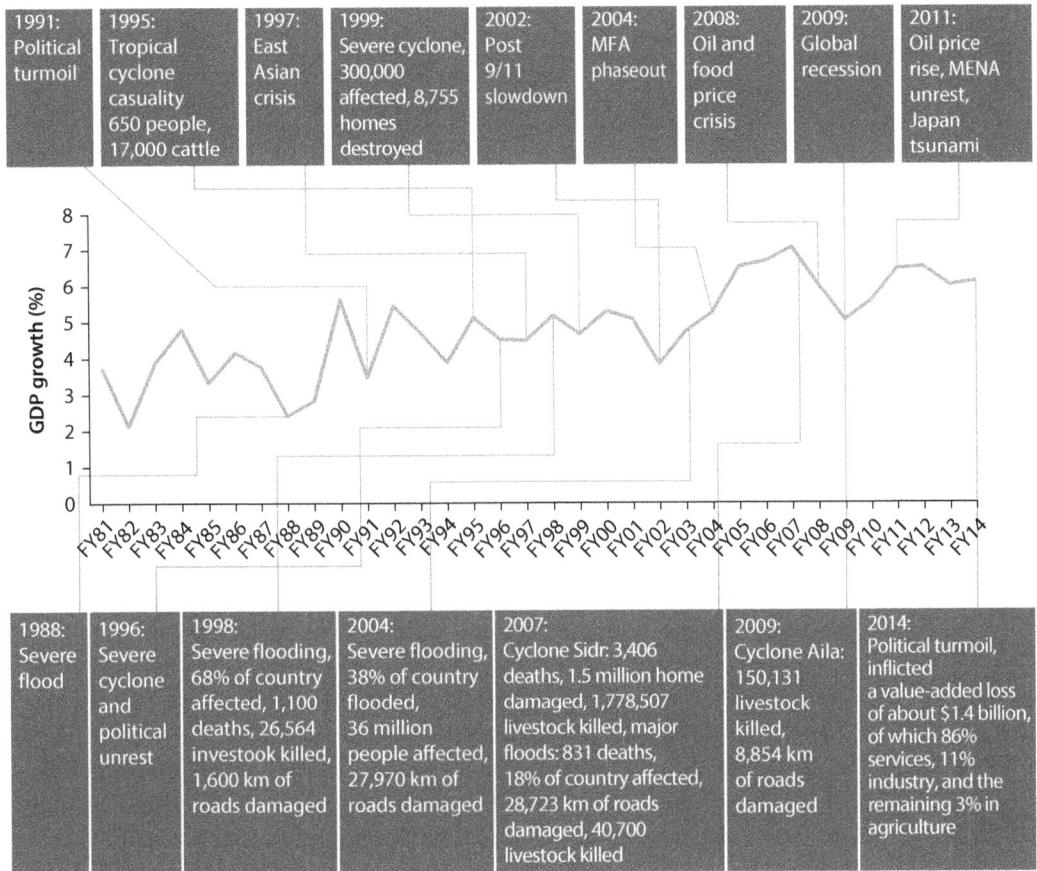

| 1991: Political turmoil | 1995: Tropical cyclone casuality 650 people, 17,000 cattle | 1997: East Asian crisis | 1999: Severe cyclone, 300,000 affected, 8,755 homes destroyed | 2002: Post 9/11 slowdown | 2004: MFA phaseout | 2008: Oil and food price crisis | 2009: Global recession | 2011: Oil price rise, MENA unrest, Japan tsunami |

| 1988: Severe flood | 1996: Severe cyclone and political unrest | 1998: Severe flooding, 68% of country affected, 1,100 deaths, 26,564 investook killed, 1,600 km of roads damaged | 2004: Severe flooding, 38% of country flooded, 36 million people affected, 27,970 km of roads damaged | 2007: Cyclone Sidr: 3,406 deaths, 1.5 million home damaged, 1,778,507 livestock killed, major floods: 831 deaths, 18% of country affected, 28,723 km of roads damaged, 40,700 livestock killed | 2009: Cyclone Aila: 150,131 livestock killed, 8,854 km of roads damaged | 2014: Political turmoil, inflicted a value-added loss of about $1.4 billion, of which 86% services, 11% industry, and the remaining 3% in agriculture |

Source: Bangladesh Bureau of Statistics.
Note: FY = fiscal year; GDP = gross domestic product; MENA = Middle East and North Africa; MFA = Multi-Fiber Arrangement.

months of goods and services imports in FY2014. Macroeconomic pressures that had developed on account of energy subsidies have also eased recently, supported by more restrained fiscal and monetary policies (see IMF 2013).

Emerging Issues in Export Growth and Its Sustainability

Bangladesh's unique manufacturing performance raises a puzzle. Bangladesh appears to have mastered labor-intensive mass manufacturing as displayed in its many large garment factories; the high share of manufactures in exports is unique at its income level. Yet, this success has so far not led to the creation of another large, labor-intensive cluster. Garments dominate the export basket. This raises some potential issues about the sustainability and volatility of export growth.

Although growing over time, the role of trade in the overall economy is still low. Trade could play a more significant role in promoting faster GDP growth and poverty reduction. Imports as a percentage of GDP stand at 21 percent, while exports accounted for 17.4 percent of GDP in FY2014, which is significantly lower than Indonesia, Thailand, or Vietnam (exports and imports are each about 90 percent of GDP).[2] Higher volumes of trade can increase the efficiency of domestic production and contribute to greater labor intensity in the economy. Thus, if the share of trade in GDP is higher (with the same net exports balance), then, even with constant GDP levels, it could mean an increase in overall employment in the economy. In addition, trade policy could be used in a more deliberate way to enhance consumer welfare.

The positive current account in most years in a low-income economy speaks to the lack of investment opportunities. A low-income economy usually draws on foreign savings to supplement domestic national savings to increase the overall rate of investment. Yet, in the case of Bangladesh, the current account has been positive in most years since FY2006, indicating the lack of sufficient investment opportunities and an inadequate climate for investment. This means that acceleration of export growth, which will demand a significant increase in overall investment, will require a concerted policy effort.

The macro economy is stable, but institutional weaknesses and several vulnerabilities loom large. Despite recent weakening in the pace of economic activity and ongoing political tensions, Bangladesh's macroeconomic position has remained stable, with declining inflation supported by prudent monetary and fiscal policy. Nevertheless, the ongoing political uncertainty, together with frequent general strikes and associated violence, has added to the long-standing energy and infrastructure deficits in dampening investment, posing a nontrivial threat to sustaining the recent average 6 percent growth, let alone raising it to 7 percent in the near future. Moreover, deep-rooted weaknesses in institutional capacity underlie the failure to speed up implementation of top priority infrastructure projects and are not easily addressed. Bangladesh's near and medium-term macroeconomic outlook is subject to several vulnerabilities—the central risk being the prolongation and intensification of the ongoing political turmoil. No clear end to the instability is currently in sight. Although street violence may abate in the near future, the contours of a political settlement acceptable to all significant stakeholders continues to elude political observers. Without such a settlement, Bangladesh is likely to pass through phases of instability punctuated by street violence of the kind experienced in the second half of 2013 as well as the first half of 2015. A protracted slowdown in the European Union could hurt exports, compounding the challenges arising from real exchange rate appreciation of the taka (with the U.S. dollar strengthening against the euro), undermining export competitiveness in Bangladesh's main export markets in Europe. Garment exports are particularly vulnerable. This will be amplified if preferential access to the European Union is withdrawn or truncated for lack of progress in upgrading labor and factory safety standards in the garment industry. There are also concerns about financial weaknesses in state-owned banks and some private banks. These have potential fiscal and financial stability implications. On the flip side, although international financial linkages are growing, Bangladesh's vulnerability to global financial volatility is still small.

The energy shortage is an overarching constraint affecting virtually all segments of the economy. In 2012, the demand-supply gap of electricity was around 5,000 gigawatt-hours (Ministry of Finance 2013). Bangladesh ranks nearly last among its Asian competitors (only above Nepal) in the prevalence of power outages. Power outages are a key reason why manufacturing productivity in Bangladesh is much lower than in China and Vietnam. The use of captive generation to compensate for outages adds to costs (World Bank 2012b). The sector studies done for this DTIS corroborate this, from sectors as varied as information technology enabled services (ITES) to shipbuilding (Kathuria and Malouche 2016b). A comparison of the World Bank's Investment Climate Assessment between 2002 and 2007 revealed that the value lost because of electrical shortages increased from 2.9 to 12.3 percent of sales (World Bank 2012b). Although access to reliable sources of electricity tops the list of concerns for the region as a whole, the losses that Bangladeshi firms suffer are much higher compared with 5.4 percent of sales lost in Pakistan and 5.5 percent in India.

The overall low use of labor in the economy is a concern and increasing labor-intensive, export-oriented manufacturing will need to be part of the solution. Of Bangladesh's 103.3 million working-age population, only 58.1 million were employed in 2013, reflecting a low 33.5 percent female participation in the labor force. Moreover, the labor force will grow faster in the coming years, with 2.1 million people entering the prime working-age population annually over the next decade. Increasing the employment rate (utilization of the working-age population) and providing jobs for the growing labor force will be a major challenge. Part of the solution will involve a re-orientation of the economy away from its anti-export bias and improvements in trade infrastructure to shorten lead times, among other initiatives.

Bangladesh will need to focus more attention on skills development: skills are emerging as a major constraint, even in the garment sector, as well as other, more skill-intensive sectors. Although educational access has increased significantly over the past decade, particularly at the lower levels of education and especially for females, currently 96 percent of the labor force has less than secondary education and 66 percent has less than primary education. According to the World Bank (2013), just one-third of primary graduates acquire the numeracy and literacy skills they are expected to master by the time they graduate. Moreover, among the labor force, the percentage of persons having professional education, such as engineering and medicine, is very small (only 0.17 percent of the labor force has such degrees). A World Bank survey of 1,000 garment firms in 2011 found that skills were the major disadvantage of firms located outside Dhaka. High rejection rates in a 2010 United Nations Industrial Development Organization (UNIDO) survey also point to the low average skills of garment workers. In sectors such as ITES, shipbuilding, and pharmaceuticals, part of this DTIS, higher skills are in constant demand (Kathuria and Malouche 2016b; World Bank 2012a, 2012b).

The low level of literacy and years of schooling of the labor force make skill acquisition more difficult. About 37.6 percent of the population of the country remains illiterate; the average years of schooling among the labor force was 4.8 years in 2010. Compared with many other Asian countries, Bangladesh has a rather low level of literacy. Moreover, the average years of schooling is also low compared with countries that are currently competing with Bangladesh's garment sector. The lower time spent in school complicates the process of learning and skill acquisition. In contrast, Sri Lanka has provided a skills environment that allows garment firms to move up the value chain quickly. Bangladeshi firms' choice is restricted to only primary school graduates and high school dropouts.

Labor issues, such as wages, workplace safety, and compliance with labor standards, can generate major reputational risk for Bangladesh's overall garment exports and will need to be carefully managed. Labor standards and safety issues can affect future exports and Bangladesh's overall reputation in the exporting sector. Concerns have been heightened following a series of fatal incidents, and the government has been pressured to take measures to improve workers' safety. International buyers and governments have reacted strongly to these events (box 1.1). On June 27, 2013, the United States suspended Generalized System of Preferences (GSP) trade privileges for Bangladesh over concerns about safety problems and labor rights violations in the garment industry. Whatever measures the government will implement under domestic and international pressure, the important issue will be enforcement and commitment to ensure better and safer practices. Continued improvement in labor conditions in the garment sector, in coordination with international business and development partners, will be important.

Box 1.1 Rana Plaza Momentum for Reforms: Implementation Will Be Key

The fallout from the April 24, 2013, collapse of the eight-story Rana Plaza multipurpose building in Savar, Dhaka, has had domestic and international repercussions. The death toll exceeded 1,100, mostly female garment workers who worked on the upper floors of the building in several garment factories supplying about 30 Western clothing retailers. Analysis suggests that the building was not built to code; was not fit to sustain the additional weight of the three highest floors, which were added after the original building was built; and was not suited to carry the weight of people and equipment that a garment factory requires or to withstand the vibrations of the backup generators that were installed in the upper-floor factories. A few people have been jailed for complicity in this situation, including the building owner and some factory owners (who urged factory workers to return to their work places a day after large cracks were found in the building and a structural engineer pronounced the building to be unfit for use) and others have been suspended, including public officials who authorized the building's construction.

In the meantime, international clothing retailers that source products in Bangladesh as well as the European Union are paying more attention to ensure safety compliance and improve

box continues next page

Box 1.1 Rana Plaza Momentum for Reforms: Implementation Will Be Key *(continued)*

supply chain transparency. The Accord on Fire and Building Safety (http://bangladeshaccord
.org), consisting of more than 180 global apparel brands (mostly European), has agreed on a
legally binding plan to inspect all Bangladeshi garment factories that supply the companies,
and publicly disclose the names of these factories as well as inspection reports and agreed
remediation measures. As of September 2014, 1,103 factories had been inspected, resulting in
the highlighting of 52,605 safety issues. The brands also agreed on 500 corrective action plans
(CAPs) with the factory owners. The inspection reports and CAPs are being published online.

A group of 26 American retailers, which have formed the Alliance for Bangladesh Worker
Safety, announced a nonbinding five-year initiative, developed with the help of the Bipartisan
Policy Center. This initiative seeks to improve factory safety in the Bangladeshi garment
industry[a] by inspecting 100 percent of Alliance member factories, developing common safety
standards, sharing inspection results transparently, and ensuring that all alliance factories
actively support the democratic election and successful operation of Worker Participation
Committees in each factory. Until March 2015, the Alliance had conducted initial inspections
of 580 factories (100 percent), of which 19 have been partially or fully closed. Almost 300 CAPs
have been finalized with the factories. The Alliance plans to complete final inspection (after
implementation of remediation measures) of all these factories by July 2017.

As initial inspection of all the factories has been completed, international buyers can move
toward implementation of remediation measures and coordinate among themselves while
doing so, to help minimize additional burden and the possibility of remediation fatigue among
factory owners. Financing of the remedial work is also becoming a growing concern, as in
some cases buyers are allegedly not getting involved as promised.

Although Bangladesh is still considered the leading apparel sourcing destination alternative to China, its popularity as a top destination for sourcing in the next five years dropped
after the Rana Plaza incident, leading to order cancellations of around US$110 million from 37
factories, according to a newspaper report.[b] The potential impact on Bangladesh's garment
industry, which accounts for almost 80 percent of export earnings, and therefore on gross
domestic product, could be significant. Under pressure to respond to the Savar tragedy, the
Government of Bangladesh has made considerable progress in improving labor safety and
working conditions by amending the Labor Law, revising the minimum wage for garment
workers from Tk 3,000 (US$38) to Tk 5,300 (US$68), and strengthening the labor inspection
system. The government has also inspected 282 factories that are not under the purview of the
Western initiatives. While there is progress in improving workplace compliance, more needs to
be done to fulfill the commitment of raising it to international standards.

a. "Reuters Insight Inspection Intensifies Bangladesh Garment Industry's Woes," *The Bangladesh Chronicle*, June 27, 2014.
b. "Safety Compliance a Make or Break for Many Garment Factories," *The Dhaka Tribune*, April 30, 2014.

Enabling Exports and Imports to Play a More Prominent Role in the Economy

Bangladesh needs not just to raise the rate of growth of exports, but also to move
beyond the low-wage paradigm. Growth acceleration will require Bangladesh to
become more export-oriented. Thus far, it has enjoyed strong success in exports,

primarily based on low-skill, low-wage competitiveness in garments, which dominate the export basket. However, this strategy does not guarantee continued growth in exports, given the pressures of global competition and the possible emergence of future competitors with a better wage-productivity combination. In any case, the living standards of workers can only rise if their real wages go up—and to enable sustained real wage increases, worker productivity and therefore skills need to improve. To capitalize on developments in educational access, Bangladesh will need to make structural changes in the economy, create more and higher-productivity jobs, and improve education and skill development to derive maximum benefit from the demographic dividend.

Thus, this DTIS identifies several other sources of competitiveness so that low-wage labor is not the only comparative advantage of Bangladesh. The report emphasizes the great potential for Bangladesh to increase its trade competitiveness and investment attractiveness.

Although growth in garment exports can be sustained in the near future with the right supporting environment, greater product diversification is a desirable policy goal. Product diversification can reduce export volatility as well as the risk to aggregate exports of relying on a single product line. A diversification goal also anticipates an eventual slowdown in the growth of garment exports and an increasing contribution from other sectors. It helps to put flesh on the longer-term goal of structural transformation and rising employment in higher-wage and higher-productivity sectors, including higher-value garments (World Bank 2012a).

However, such diversification will not be easy, since it involves developing capabilities that revolve around product types. The product space literature (see chapter 2) suggests that Bangladesh's strengths are still centered on the garments and footwear cluster and that exports of bicycles and ships, for example, are in the periphery and not part of a larger cluster. Although a number of export products have emerged and some, such as jute products and frozen foods, have become quite large, the dominance of garments continues: their share of total exports rose even further, from 74.2 to 81.2 percent between FY2005 and FY2013.

Several sector studies were conducted as part of this DTIS, to illustrate and understand the constraints to diversification (Kathuria and Malouche 2016b). These studies seek to anchor the thematic analyses of the DTIS (Kathuria and Malouche 2016a), but are not meant to be exhaustive in coverage. A number of common themes emerged that support the thematic analysis on constraints to export and trade development. In addition, some sector-specific constraints to exports also came up; these are detailed in chapter 4, and some are highlighted in the following section.

The agenda laid out in this DTIS is ambitious, given its objectives and the linkages of those objectives with the country's development goals. The DTIS analyzes the internal and external constraints to further integration with the world economy, keeping in view the end goals of job creation, poverty reduction, and enhancement of citizens' welfare. The DTIS highlights policies as well as gaps in physical and institutional infrastructure that will consolidate Bangladesh's strengths in existing markets, as well as help diversify export products and export markets. At the same time, it spells out the linkages between these policies and consumer and worker welfare, which focuses additional attention on import policies, skill enhancement, and labor safety.

Prioritization of the agenda is essential. Given the vast agenda, implementation will require prioritization and sequencing, keeping in view capacity constraints. There is no exact science of sequencing, but some priorities can be identified, based on the diagnostics and international experience.

An initial focus on market diversification as well as worker safety issues, in partnership with the private sector, will provide high payoffs. This follows from the diagnosis that market diversification with existing products is likely to be the most important source of export growth in the short-to-medium term (see chapter 2). Given the recent accidents in garment factories, improved labor safety and work conditions have become necessary to sustain and accelerate growth in garments and overall exports.

Product diversification may face higher fixed costs and will require overcoming potential resistance, and policy moves in this space will likely be gradual. Bangladesh has not yet built up a product cluster other than garments and footwear, with exports of other products being relatively low as well as on the periphery of the product space (chapter 2, figure 2.3 and box 2.1). Developing another major cluster like garments will take more time and involve more investments. And although rationalizing trade policy and improving the environment for foreign investment are critical inputs for product diversification, they face potential resistance from domestic producer interests. Policy changes are likely to be gradual to allow time for adjustment.

Other elements of the agenda include building a supportive macroeconomic environment, easing energy constraints, and improving worker and consumer welfare; these are mostly part of ongoing efforts. The continuation of a sound macroeconomic environment is a necessary condition for sustained export growth. Easing energy constraints is a critical part of Bangladesh's overall development program and is no less critical for the export agenda. Improving skills will enable productivity and wage increases and hence worker welfare. All of these are ongoing priorities in Bangladesh, but would nevertheless benefit from reiteration and being part of the export agenda as well. Finally, consumer welfare is directly affected by import policy, including tariff and nontariff measures, and may need additional effort beyond that aimed at reducing the anti-export bias. To implement this agenda, leadership will be critical and should be part of the immediate priorities.

This DTIS has identified a four-pillar strategy that could contribute to accelerated development of the export sector, a priority for jobs and growth (see the Action Matrix in appendix A and chapters 2–4); enhance worker and consumer welfare; and enable sources of competitiveness beyond low-wage labor. Some of these areas, such as the macroeconomic environment, skill development, the energy constraint, and the creation of effective safety nets, are not explored in any depth in Kathuria and Malouche (2016a), being outside the scope of the DTIS. However, some of the key issues and remedies in these areas are summarized in the following chapters (referring to other pieces of analysis) for the sake of completeness, and also mentioned in the Action Matrix (appendix A). Many of them also come up in the sector analyses Kathuria and Malouche (2016b). The following could be considered priority action areas, while detailed measures are listed in the Action Matrix.

Pillar 1. Breaking into New Markets

A. *Improving trade facilitation.* Improving trade logistics will help reduce delivery lags and thereby enable Bangladesh to become more competitive globally, reaching out to more emerging and dynamic markets. It would also help in the quest to diversify into products with shorter lead times, including higher-value garments. Key actions include the launching of a National Logistics Strategy; establishment of the rail inland container depot (ICD) at Tongi, on the outskirts of Dhaka; development of the Inland Water Transport sector; improvement in the efficiency of Dhaka-Chittagong road connectivity; and working closely with the Government of India to improve the efficiency of common land border posts. Reducing trade finance costs by leaving title documents open and not assigning them to a local bank and making current account transactions, such as payments for samples and consultants, etc., hindrance-free, would also facilitate exports.

B. *Promoting economic integration with Asia.* Exploiting market diversification opportunities would involve taking advantage of Bangladesh's location in the fastest-growing region in the world and between India and China. Given geography and potentially lower trading costs, the possibilities for greater exports to Asia are immense. Granting transit rights and concluding road transport agreements with Bhutan, India, Myanmar, and Nepal would foster regional trade going through Bangladesh and have potential spillover effects on Bangladesh's own trade. Economic relations with India in particular can be deepened significantly. Bangladesh can increase its exports to India several fold through mutual recognition agreements (MRAs) for harmonization of standards, mutual reduction of nontariff barriers (with an efficient dispute resolution mechanism), harmonization of border clearance procedures, and signing of the International Road Transport (TIR) Convention by both countries, with a view to allowing transit traffic.[3] China and Japan are major potential markets as well and FDI from all three countries can help bring exports back to the source countries as well as other destinations.

Pillar 2. Breaking into New Products

A. *Rationalizing trade policy to level the playing field.* (a) Rationalizing trade taxation and moving toward eliminating the anti-export bias, as seen, for example, in high and varying rates of effective protection, will mean that it is not just garments that enjoy a more neutral tariff regime. Critical actions will include reducing overall tariff protection and simplifying the import tax regime such that cross-sector tariff distortions are reduced and para-tariffs are eliminated or applied equally on domestic production. Such goals can be achieved without risking revenue generation. (b) Ensuring efficient imports for exports will progressively make the private sector's production and export decisions less dependent on domestic availability of inputs. In practice, given the poor functioning of duty drawback, the best answer seems to lie in ensuring well-functioning bonded warehouse schemes that are in principle available to all sectors and high-performing operators. Such schemes have been critical to explain the initial success of Korea's exports. Reviewing mandatory standards to ensure a smooth flow of imports would also be useful. (c) Formulating and adopting a strategy for trade in services will help in better understanding specific services, trends, and markets in services trade and boost the ITES sector.

B. *Improving the environment for domestic and foreign investment.* Attracting much larger FDI flows would help in upgrading technology and improve market linkages, and develop an area where Bangladesh has had only narrow success. To accomplish this, Bangladesh needs to improve allocation of serviceable land for business use, including through the 2010 Export Processing Zone Act; more proactively welcome FDI and promote it through high-level missions to potential FDI sources, such as China, India, and Japan; and reduce discretionary practices, increase transparency, and enforce standards more strictly so that foreign as well as domestic firms that enforce strict compliance and standards are not penalized. Enforcing standards would also help bridge the gap between the domestic and foreign markets. Resolving energy constraints will help all segments of the economy and provide a major boost to investment. It would be critical for Bangladesh to implement sustainable solutions that are able to provide unsubsidized power at competitive prices. Critical actions involve both the public and private sectors, including increasing generation capacity in low-cost, base-load power plants; commissioning of the large, gas-fired and dual-fuel combined-cycle power plants awarded to the private sector; converting the Bangladesh Power Development Board's simple-cycle plants to combined-cycle plants; and accelerating moves to imported power from Bhutan, Myanmar, and Nepal and India's northeastern states. These actions would help move attention away from the measures that have been taken by the government so far, which have focused on shorter-term solutions, raised costs and subsidies, and added to fiscal vulnerabilities. Many of the recommended measures, as well as those relating to skills, logistics, and trade policy, would also improve the environment for domestic and foreign investment.

Pillar 3. Improving Worker and Consumer Welfare

A. *Improving skills and literacy.* Improving skills and literacy will allow increased productivity of workers, wage increases, and a reduced level of waste. This will enable, among other things, the production of higher-quality products, garments and nongarments. It will require articulating a comprehensive vision for skill development, reskilling the current labor force through greater access to nonformal training and skill-building, and improving the quality of foundational education.

B. *Implementing labor and work safety guidelines.* Minimizing the chances of further tragedies in the garment and other export sectors in Bangladesh has become a precondition for sustained export growth. This will require strong and credible government action and a partnership with the private sector, domestic and international. Seriousness of intent on the part of the government will play a critical role in trade relations with the European Union and the United States, the major players in post–Rana Plaza events.

C. *Making safety nets more effective in dealing with trade shocks.* Starting preparation of a safety net and labor strategy that recognizes possible winners and losers in trade liberalization could help reduce opposition to a neutral trade policy. Apart from cash transfers, a key part of this strategy should prioritize finding mechanisms that link poor safety net beneficiaries to more productive employment opportunities with a particular focus on youth. The swelling youth cohorts offer opportunities and challenges. Investment in appropriate skills development to meet global and domestic demand has the potential to harness substantial gains from globalization, whereas training and retraining of workers will help to ensure their resilience to trade shocks.

Pillar 4. Building a Supportive Environment

A. *Sustaining sound macroeconomic fundamentals.* Continuing its record of sound macroeconomic management will help Bangladesh keep inflation at bay and help price competitiveness. Implementing the ongoing International Monetary Fund (IMF) program will help anchor the macroeconomic framework.

B. *Building institutions for trade policy coherence and implementation.* Implementing the multi-sector competitiveness agenda outlined above will require strong leadership, such as through an empowered inter-ministerial Cabinet Sub-Committee on Trade, and is a top priority. This body can also take on the more gradual process of institution building to ensure that institutions are working coherently and in a coordinated manner toward the objective of trade competitiveness. Important steps here will include the National Board of Revenue and Ministry of Commerce (MOC) jointly formulating tariff policy, with due consultation; strengthening the in-house economic capacity of MOC; and linking MOC's policy making and trade negotiation roles more strategically with think tanks. Further steps will include making the Export Promotion Bureau more effective by augmenting its in-house capacity; enabling greater private sector participation; targeting market diversification in key markets, such as China, India, and Japan; and allowing private sector providers to provide quality services in areas under government regulation.

Sector-Specific Issues

Detailed studies of a number of growing export sectors confirmed the cross-cutting findings highlighted above and added other, sector-specific issues. In shipbuilding, enforcement of standards for domestic ships would help bring domestic and export market segments closer and help exporting yards to achieve better scale economies. More credible enforcement of standards in pharmaceuticals would help people's health and also reduce the disincentives for firms, including foreign firms that practice self-enforcement. Training to relieve skill shortages was identified as a critical need in many sectors, including shipbuilding, ITES, and bicycles. FDI could play a much larger role in many sectors, especially those with technology upgrading needs, such as pharmaceuticals, bicycles, and shipbuilding. Making improvements in access to finance and easing Bangladesh Bank-monitored current account transactions would relieve constraints across all sectors. Additional submarine cables would increase the reliability of Internet services for the ITES sector. The energy constraint was ubiquitous, almost taken as a given in all sector discussions.

Conclusions

To achieve its development objectives, Bangladesh will need a fundamental policy shift that is geared toward international competitiveness and is neutral between the interests of the domestic producer, exporter, and consumer.

A virtuous circle of export-led growth can be put in place, which would lead to more effective integration with the world economy. A virtuous circle would consist of improving logistics and linkages with neighbors, implementing a more neutral trade policy that corrects the anti-export bias, ensuring trouble-free imports for exports, putting in place a hospitable FDI regime and a cohesive policy establishment geared to competitiveness, and improving the quality of primary and secondary education and industry-specific skills. The virtuous circle would enable sustained, labor-intensive export growth and allow effective participation of people in that growth.

Implementing the four-pillar agenda will help improve the overall competitiveness of the economy and provide sources of strength other than low wages.

The ultimate goal of export-led growth is poverty reduction and the enhanced welfare of Bangladesh's citizens. Rapidly growing exports and the millions of new jobs accompanying them, along with skill upgrading, will help increase productivity and wages, which over the long term is the only sustainable way to improve living standards. Improving labor standards and worker safety is also part of this agenda and, in the wake of the tragic incidents in the garment sector, has become a part of the preconditions for garment exports. Rationalization of trade policy that balances consumer and producer interests will contribute significantly to citizen welfare. For example, allowing a due role for trade and FDI in drug supply will enhance the choice and quality of medicines and enable a more effective health strategy. To complement this, the quality system would need to be improved and the list of mandatory standards reviewed, to determine whether they meet legitimate regulatory objectives and can be effectively enforced. The objective is to ensure that imports flow smoothly while respecting the legitimate needs for import regulation, such as for food safety.

Openness brings opportunities, but also vulnerability to global shocks. Appropriate safety nets should be an important part of the globalization process. Globalization allows countries to benefit from the knowledge and technologies that have been developed anywhere in the world, whether embodied in machinery, intermediates, FDI, or people. At the same time, it greatly increases the need for governments to ensure that citizens are able to benefit from these opportunities: workers must be able to acquire the needed skills; firms need to be able to access credit to finance profitable investment opportunities; and farmers need to be connected to markets (Porto and Hoekman 2010). Greater openness also increases the vulnerability of countries to global shocks, with potentially major adverse consequences for the poorest households that do not have the savings needed to survive a period of unemployment or sharp falls in the prices of their outputs (and thus incomes) resulting from global competition. Therefore, it is important that countries have in place mechanisms to assist those adversely affected by trade shocks. These mechanisms should be targeted toward those households that are most vulnerable and have to manage shocks. Governments should more systematically assess, ex ante, possible trade-related, poverty-distributional outcomes of policy changes. This will help in the design of better complementary or transitional policies as well as compensation mechanisms and targeted programs to ensure that firms and workers can benefit from the new opportunities generated by trade openness. Policies and actions to achieve these objectives require actions by labor and finance ministries and are not necessarily part of the mandate of trade ministries.

Bangladesh is well placed to take on some of its strongest development challenges and begin a discourse to move beyond wage-based competitiveness. Its track record on growth and employment is strong. To grow faster, absorb more labor, and continue its pace of poverty reduction, it will need to build on that record and improve on it. The good news is that a number of reforms are relatively low-hanging fruits, may be implemented in the short-to-medium term, and can bring large payoffs.

The example of Vietnam shows that accelerated, export-oriented development is possible, even in the context of the current global environment. Vietnam moved from being one of the poorest countries in the world to a lower-middle-income one in the space of 25 years, with FDI and trade playing a dominant role in the economy: exports and imports each form 90 percent of GDP and, with 88 million people compared with Bangladesh's 150 million, Vietnam exports four times as much as Bangladesh today.

Bangladesh will need strong leadership to support its multisector competitiveness agenda. In many cases, it will require taking on strong domestic interests that may not welcome competition, either through imports or FDI. In other cases, it will require cohesion and coordination between different ministries or departments, such as the National Bureau of Revenue; the Ministries of Commerce, Finance, and Industry; and the Roads Division. If the Sixth Plan and Vision 2021 goals are to be achieved, this leadership has to be exercised.

Notes

1. The two other books published as part of this DTIS are on thematic assessments (Kathuria and Malouche 2016a) and sector analyses (Kathuria and Malouche 2016b).

2. In 2012, comparable countries had ratios of exports and imports to GDP of 31.6 and 29.4 percent (Indonesia), 78 and 75 percent (Thailand), and 89.8 and 90.2 percent (Vietnam), respectively.

3. The TIR (Transports Internationaux Routiers) is a system of bonds, operated in nearly 70 countries, that guarantees that any customs and other duties will be paid on goods transported in transit trucks. Its objectives are the improvement of transport conditions and the simplification and harmonization of administrative formalities in international transport, particularly at frontiers.

References

Commission on Growth and Development. 2008. *Strategies for Sustained Growth and Inclusive Development*. Washington, DC: World Bank.

General Economics Division. 2011. *6th Five-Year Plan FY2011–FY2015*. Dhaka: General Economics Division, Planning Commission, Government of Bangladesh.

IMF (International Monetary Fund). 2013. *Bangladesh: Second Review under the Three-Year Arrangement under the Extended Credit Facility and Request for Modification of Performance Criteria*. Washington, DC: IMF.

Kathuria, Sanjay, and Mariem Mezghenni Malouche, eds. 2016a. *Strengthening Competitiveness in Bangladesh—Thematic Assessment: A Diagnostic Trade Integration Study*. Washington, DC: World Bank.

———. 2016b. *Strengthening Competitiveness in Bangladesh—Sector Analyses: A Diagnostic Trade Integration Study*. Washington, DC: World Bank.

Ministry of Finance. 2013. *Power and Energy Sector Roadmap*. Dhaka: Government of Bangladesh.

Porto, G., and B. M. Hoekman. 2010. *Trade Adjustment Costs in Developing Countries: Impacts, Determinants and Policy Response*. Washington, DC: World Bank.

World Bank. 2007. "Bangladesh: Strategy for Sustained Growth." Bangladesh Development Series Paper 18, Poverty Reduction and Economic Management Sector, South Asia Region, World Bank, Washington, DC.

———. 2012a. "Consolidating and Accelerating Exports in Bangladesh: A Policy Agenda." Bangladesh Development Series Paper 29, Poverty Reduction and Economic Management Sector, South Asia Region, World Bank, Washington, DC.

———. 2012b. *Bangladesh: Towards Accelerated, Inclusive and Sustainable Growth—Opportunities and Challenges*. Vol. 2. Report 67991, Poverty Reduction and Economic Management Unit, South Asia Region. Washington, DC: World Bank.

———. 2013. "Bangladesh Poverty Assessment—Assessing a Decade of Progress in Reducing Poverty 2000–2010." Bangladesh Development Series Paper 31, World Bank Office, Dhaka.

CHAPTER 2

Bangladesh's Export Performance

Bangladesh's exports have performed impressively, based on the growth of its garment sector. This chapter discusses the dimensions of export growth in Bangladesh, including product and market concentration. It then addresses the often-voiced concern that Bangladesh is too heavily reliant on garments and draws on international experiences to understand the prospects for continued export growth in garments and the potential for product and market diversification.

Future export growth will likely rely first on market penetration with existing products. Garments can continue to grow with the right supporting environment, not only in the current lower-quality segment, but also moving up in the quality space, which will provide further room within the sector. For product diversification, the product space literature suggests that Bangladesh has not developed another large cluster apart from garments and footwear. This would make the move to other clusters, such as light engineering, more difficult, but a cohesive set of supportive government policies could provide impetus to that shift. Services such as information technology enabled services (ITES) can also grow and lead to skilled job creation. To diversify markets, Bangladesh enjoys some natural advantages, such as its location between some of the fastest growing economies in the world, and this advantage can be exploited much more proactively. More details on trade outcomes and performance can be found in Kathuria and Malouche (2016, chapter 1).

Characteristics of Export Growth

Bangladesh's export growth, especially in manufactured products, has been impressive so far. Although it is still a least developed country (LDC), Bangladesh is unique in the unusually high share of manufactured exports in its export basket relative to its income level, which illustrates its strengths in mass manufacturing and labor availability. As measured by the ratio of exports plus imports to gross domestic product (GDP), trade openness in Bangladesh increased from 18 percent on average in the 1980s to 35 percent in the 2000s. Its exports grew on average by 15.2 percent annually during fiscal year 2004 to fiscal year 2014 (FY2004–FY2014). Its world market share doubled from 0.08 percent in 1995 to 0.16 percent in 2013. During 2005–10, Bangladesh gained world market share in most of its top 25 export products. Exports remained strong during the 2008–09 crisis, owing to the so-called Walmart effect, driven by low-value garment exports.

Concentration of export markets and products is very high. Bangladesh's exports are heavily concentrated at the sector and even the product level, where five products account for more than 50 percent of sales in the U.S. and European Union markets. Twenty-one of the top 25 products are clothing articles. In general, product concentration in Bangladesh is much higher than in its comparators. Similarly, with regard to markets, the European Union and the United States together account for about two-thirds of the country's total exports. Exports have been boosted by duty-free access to Australia, Canada, China, the European Union, Japan, and Norway. The United States does not provide duty-free access for Bangladesh's key exports and only a few goods qualify under the U.S. Generalized System of Preferences (GSP) (these privileges were suspended in June 2013). Before the suspension, only 0.6 percent of the country's goods exported to the United States qualified under the GSP, so that import duties on Bangladesh's exports to the United States amounted to US$824 million in 2014 (USITC Trade Database). At present, 96 percent of Bangladesh's exports to the United States consist of ready-made garments (RMGs) and textile products, which are bought by retail groups such as Walmart, Gap, and Target.

Bangladesh's transactions data show that existing products have not exploited new markets sufficiently. The contribution of the intensive margin component in Bangladesh is particularly high compared with its peer countries (table 2.1). Bangladesh's performance is more modest when it comes to growth of old products in new markets or growth of new products in old and new markets, reinforcing the observation of sluggish export diversification across products and markets.

Table 2.1 Comparative Decomposition of Export Growth, 2008–12
Percent

Margin	Components of export growth	Bangladesh	India	Pakistan	Sri Lanka
Intensive	Increase of old products in old markets	263.2	100.6	110.4	120.1
	Decrease of old products in old markets	−159.9	−58.1	−70.4	−83.4
	Extinction of exports of existing products to existing markets	−29.9	−19.2	−33.2	−24.5
Extensive	Increase of new products in new markets	0.1	0.0	0.1	0.0
	Increase of new products in old markets	5.6	0.0	1.7	5.4
	Increase of old products in new markets	20.9	10.0	24.8	15.6

Note: The decomposition is first computed on a year-by-year basis over 2008–12 and then averaged for the period.

Growth in Garments and Product and Market Diversification

Future strong growth will be able to build on the success in RMGs. The garment sector in Bangladesh has 4,222 running factories and employs about four million workers,[1] with indirect employment estimated at around 10 million. Among low- and middle-income countries, Bangladesh is the second largest exporter of clothing after China. The garment sector, mostly knit and woven garments, generates 80 percent of export revenues, with exports concentrated in basic garments and growth being mostly volume-driven. Bangladesh is also relatively diversified at the product level compared with other LDCs, where many countries are single-commodity exporters.

Substantial evidence demonstrates that Bangladesh's garment exports can continue to grow. There is a body of literature that indicates that long periods of export growth in developing countries can be attributed to consolidation and growth of existing products. The garment industry has grown at an annual average rate of 16.5 percent since the abolition of the Multi-Fiber Arrangement in 2005. This period includes the opening up of world garments trade to full competition, as well as the global economic crisis that started in 2008. There is room to grow. Japan is actively seeking to diversify its garments import base away from a focus on China to "China plus." Chinese investors are seeking to source from Bangladesh, given rising wages in China. Growing diversification away from garments by large countries, such as China and India, gives Bangladesh an opportunity not only to increase its world market share in garments, but also to find markets in these countries. Despite recent increases, wages in Bangladesh remain very competitive.

Evidence from other countries indicates that Bangladesh's current level of per capita income should allow continued dynamism in garment exports for the foreseeable future. Figure 2.1 shows that real per capita exports of garments in Thailand grew until the country reached a per capita GDP of about US$2,000 (in constant 2000 U.S.$). The same threshold was reached in the Philippines at about US$1,000 and in Sri Lanka at about US$1,150. By this reasoning, Bangladesh's garment sector should be able to continue to grow and capture world market share. Figure 2.1 indicates the steep trajectory of Bangladesh's success in garments—its per capita GDP of US$482 (in constant 2000 US$), well below the apparent threshold, could allow this trajectory to be sustained (provided the investment conditions improve to enable even larger volumes of production). The composition of exports also shows that before reaching the threshold where per capita garment exports start to decline, a country's basket has a relatively diversified mix of basic and higher-value garments. This is because the increasing upward pressure on wages and benefits erodes competitiveness in basic garments.

The external environment is not a major issue in the growth of garments or exports in general. The global economic crisis, if anything, boosted Bangladesh's garment sector, as buyers worldwide switched to less expensive garments—the so-called Walmart effect. In addition, the ongoing rise in Chinese wages and currency has made Bangladesh a favorable investment destination. Other often-cited

Figure 2.1 Per Capita Income and Per Capita Garment Exports of Selected Countries

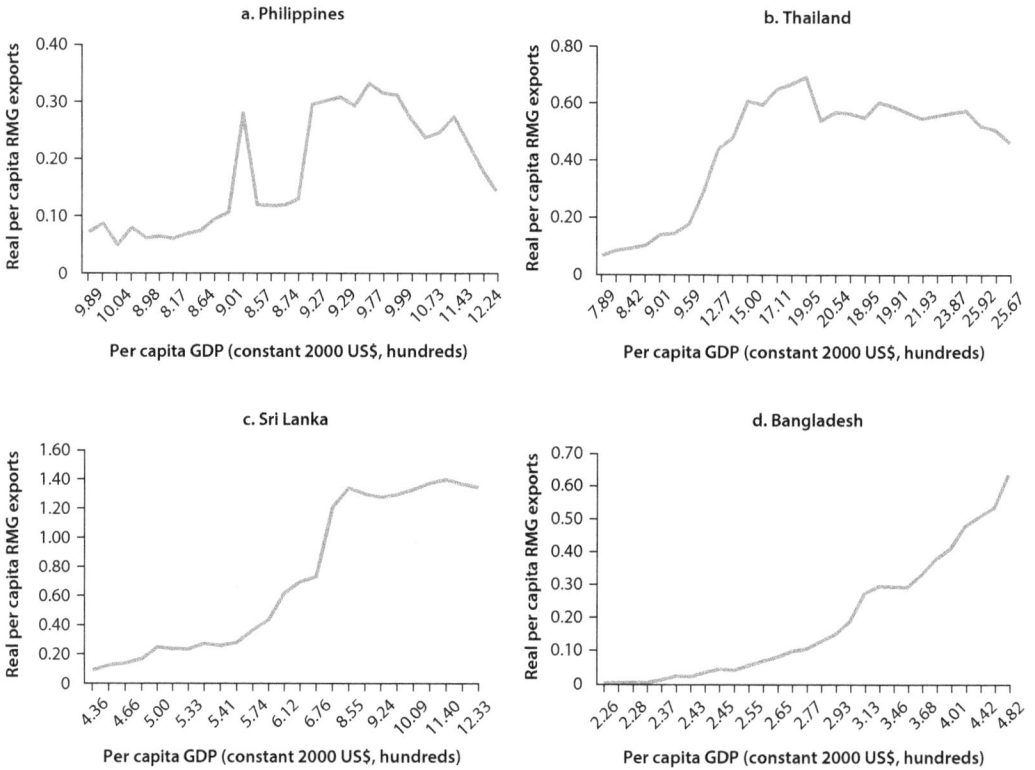

a. Philippines

Per capita GDP (constant 2000 US$, hundreds)

b. Thailand

Per capita GDP (constant 2000 US$, hundreds)

c. Sri Lanka

Per capita GDP (constant 2000 US$, hundreds)

d. Bangladesh

Per capita GDP (constant 2000 US$, hundreds)

Source: World Bank 2012.
Note: GDP = gross domestic product; RMG = ready-made garment.

constraints relate to trade barriers, such as tariffs in the United States. Another issue is the relative preferences given to some African countries. The African Growth and Opportunity Act has allowed duty- and quota-free access for a number of goods, including garments from African countries, into the U.S. market since 2000. However, Bangladesh is a major player in garments and these preferences do not seem to affect its ability to compete worldwide. This is evidenced by the continuous growth of the garment sector and the fact that many garment firms report an inability to service all the orders they receive on account of power, logistics, and skill constraints.

Capturing 20 percent of China's garment export markets would more than double Bangladesh's total exports, but this will not happen automatically. There is a lot of room for the garment sector in Bangladesh to grow and capture an increasing share of the world market. Bangladesh's share of world garment trade has risen gradually to 6.5 percent. Vietnam has been catching up and is now close to Bangladesh, with a market share of 4.9 percent. If Bangladesh can address the key constraints hindering exports, it could take some of the market being gradually vacated by China: 20 percent of China's garment exports would more than double Bangladesh's total exports and absorb almost all the new entrants into the labor force over the next decade.

Bangladesh has been the world's second largest exporter of garments since 2009, followed by Turkey and Vietnam, which has closely tracked Bangladesh's rapid rise (figure 2.2).

If Bangladesh fails to act soon enough, other competitors could march ahead and take the markets China is vacating. China is either vacating some price competitive product segments or investing abroad in more competitive locations, offering great opportunities for Bangladesh. Bangladesh could potentially become an important player in manufacturing based on a strong comparative advantage in labor-intensive industries, with wages half those in India and less than one-third those in China or Indonesia. This comparative advantage, matched with a large population, has translated into strong price competitiveness in the garment sector and, with the right policies, could possibly translate into competitive positions in other manufacturing industries. Unskilled wage rates vary between US$50 and US$100 per month in garments, about half the going wage

Figure 2.2 World Market Share in Clothing, Bangladesh and Comparators, 1988–2012

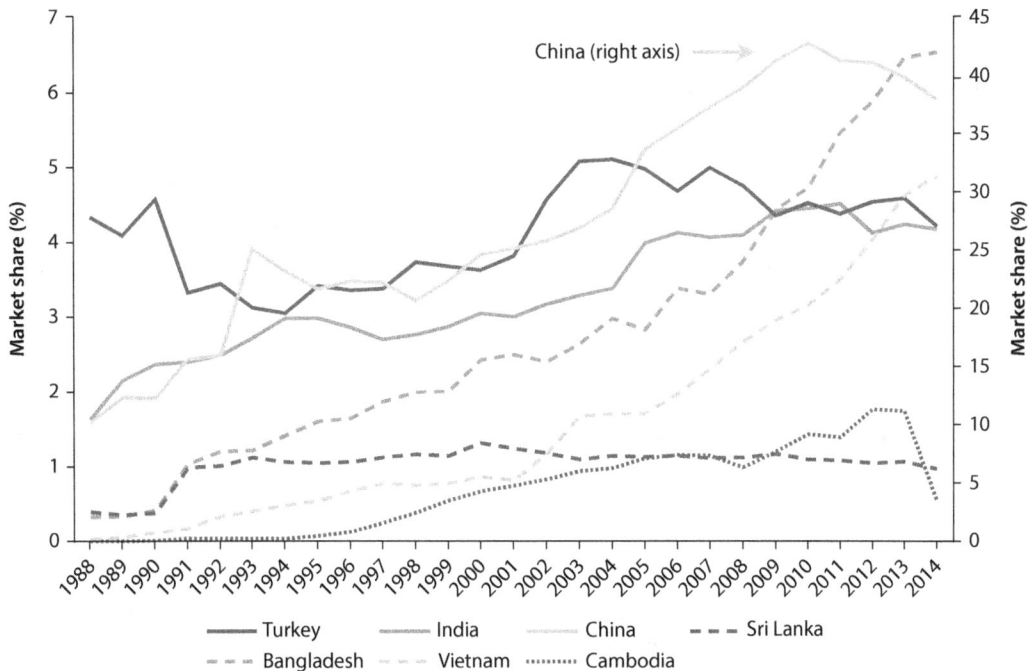

Source: United Nations Comtrade data.

in export processing zones (EPZs) in Sub-Saharan Africa and even less than average garment wages in Chinese EPZs. Bangladesh's competitors are becoming expensive too. Chinese wages are rising above US$150–250 per month with rising income and skills, serious shortages of labor in China's coastal areas, and adoption of labor regulations.[2]

There appears to be diversification potential in different goods, but despite starts, Bangladesh has not yet achieved scale in products other than garments. The product space literature (see box 2.1 and figure 2.3) suggests that Bangladesh's strengths are still centered on the garments and footwear cluster and that exports of bicycles and ships, for example, are on the periphery. Although a number of export products have emerged and some, such as jute products and frozen foods, have become quite large, the dominance of garments continues, with their share of total exports going up further, from 74.2 to 81.2 percent between FY2005 and FY2014. Moreover, a large, labor-intensive cluster has not yet emerged: jute goods

---

Box 2.1 Product-Related Capabilities and Discovery of New Products

Structural transformations are not smooth movements along a continuum, but a messy process beset by market failures. Hausmann and Klinger (2007) argue that every product requires capabilities that are specific to it, from labor training and physical assets to regulatory requirements, property rights, and infrastructure. Exporting mangoes requires different capabilities (such as a decent sanitary and phytosanitary regime) from producing synthetic apparel, but the capabilities for producing mangoes are likely to be similar to exporting vegetables. The ease with which an economy can move to producing new exports depends on what its installed capability looks like. The hypothesis is that countries that build up competence in producing a certain good can redeploy their human, physical, and institutional capital more easily if they seek to produce goods that are "near" to those they are currently producing. Location of firms in the denser parts of the forest (see figure 2.3) creates more opportunities for diversification and technological upgrading, because market failures are less binding when firms have to make smaller adjustments to move to produce nearby goods that require similar capacities. The central part of the map has a large number of products that are clustered together, particularly related to industries such as chemicals, machinery, and metals. Peripheral products include petroleum, agriculture, cereals, and labor-intensive products. The ease with which a country can transform itself economically can be predicted by whether its exports in which it has comparative advantage are located in the denser part of the product space or on the periphery.

Bangladesh has reinforced its revealed comparative advantage (RCA) in garments, located on the periphery of the forest. Figure 2.3 shows the product space for Bangladesh in 1990 and 2010, indicating the sectors in which Bangladesh has acquired or lost RCAs over time (outlined and colored dots indicate exports with an RCA[a] greater than 1), and provides a glimpse of the pace of structural transformation in the economy. Bangladesh's product space of 1990 is

box continues next page

Box 2.1 Product-Related Capabilities and Discovery of New Products *(continued)*

relatively similar to its 2010 one, with not much movement along the product space (for example, from garments to machinery or electronics, which are more knowledge intensive). Bangladesh did increase the number of products (defined at the SITC [Standard International Trade Classification] four-digit level) with RCA greater than 1, from 47 in 1990 to 65 in 2010, mostly garment and textile products. The location of garments on the periphery of the product space indicates that moving to another sector would require different capabilities than those used for garments. Interestingly, the two products with the highest RCAs are processed raw jute and jute woven fabric. The product space for Vietnam reveals how Vietnam has caught up with and even passed Bangladesh over the same period. Starting with around the same level of exports as Bangladesh in 1990, Vietnam exported four times more than Bangladesh in 2010. It expanded its garment exports but also built capabilities in new products, such as electric wire, furniture, electronics, and machinery. Sri Lanka, another garment exporter in the region, was able to maintain its competitiveness in garments and strengthen its global competitiveness in chemicals and medical instruments, as well as foodstuffs. Malaysia was able to diversify away from garments over the same period and improved its competitiveness in electronics, chemicals, medical instruments, and machinery, a denser area of the forest.

a. The concept of RCA is defined as Balassa's (1965) measure of relative export performance by country and industry, defined as a country's share of world exports of a good divided by its share of total world exports. The index for country i and good j is $RCAij = 100(Xij /Xwj)/(Xit /Xwt)$, where Xij is exports by country i (w = world) of good j (t = total for all goods). An RCA index greater than 1 indicates that a country's share of exports in a sector exceeds the global export share of the same product.

---

were 2.3 percent and leather 1.7 percent of total exports in FY2014. However, because footwear is in the dominant cluster, the product space literature would suggest that it could grow.

Bangladesh could also diversify into services, leading to skilled job creation. Bangladesh has untapped potential for diversifying into services exports. Given the large and growing size of the global information technology enabled services–business process outsourcing (ITES-BPO) market, even a small share for Bangladesh could result in significant benefits in generating employment, raising incomes, and diversifying exports. This sector is thriving in neighboring India and Sri Lanka, but is limited in Bangladesh.

International experience shows that export diversification comes naturally along the process of economic development. The product space literature provides one way to judge the near-term possibilities of diversification. However, to the extent that governments are proactive in providing a supporting environment, they can speed the process along. This DTIS is an attempt in that direction and provides a menu of policy options that Bangladesh can use to accelerate and, in time, diversify its exports.

Market diversification is likely to present the most important source of trade expansion in the short and medium term. Bangladesh is fortunately placed, between the world's fastest growing and potentially largest economies, which are now changing from competitors to markets for Bangladesh's exports. Currently,

Figure 2.3 What Bangladesh, Sri Lanka, and Vietnam Export: Product Space, 1990 and 2010

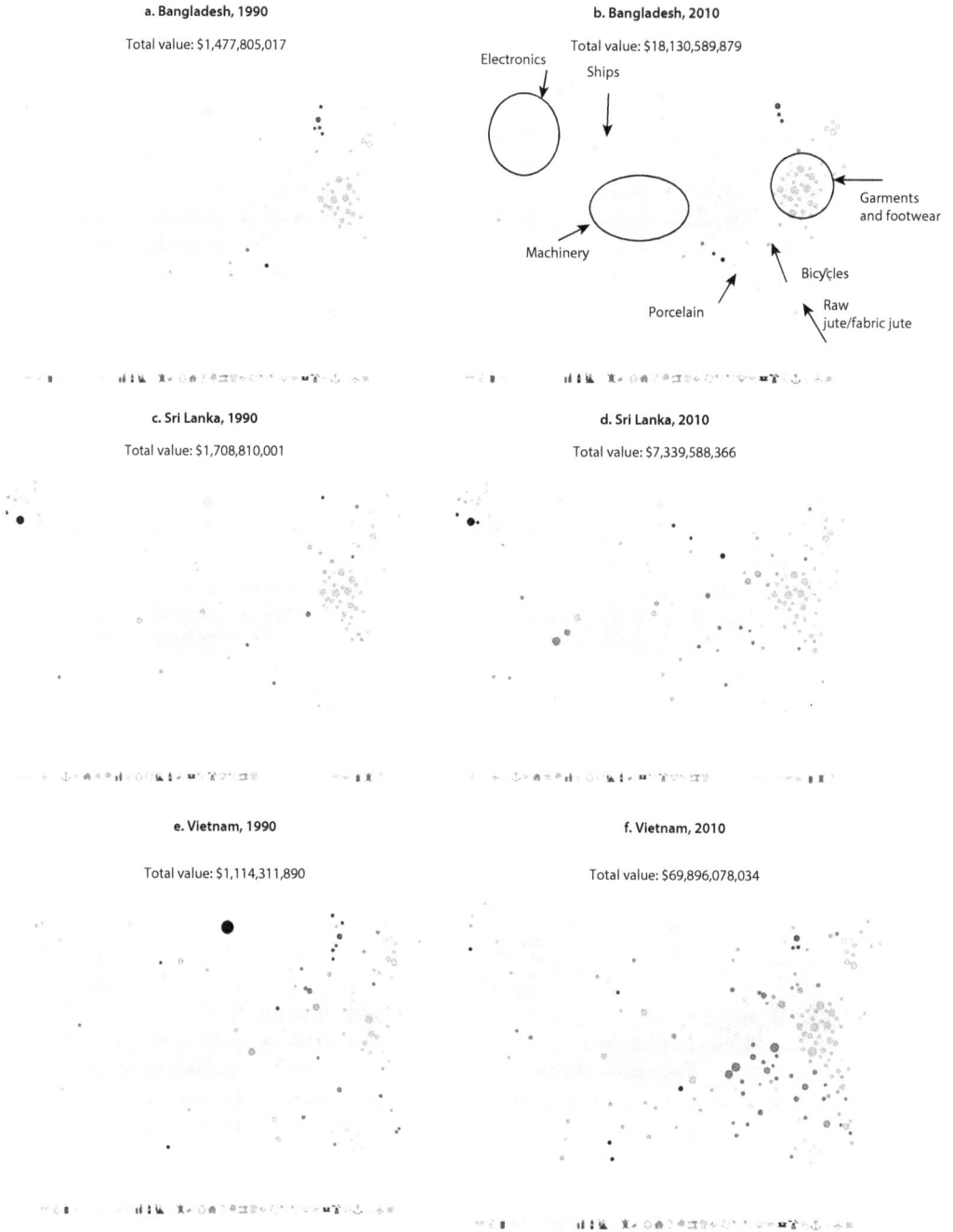

a. Bangladesh, 1990

Total value: $1,477,805,017

b. Bangladesh, 2010

Total value: $18,130,589,879

Electronics

Ships

Machinery

Porcelain

Bicycles

Garments and footwear

Raw jute/fabric jute

c. Sri Lanka, 1990

Total value: $1,708,810,001

d. Sri Lanka, 2010

Total value: $7,339,588,366

e. Vietnam, 1990

Total value: $1,114,311,890

f. Vietnam, 2010

Total value: $69,896,078,034

Source: Generated from http://atlas.media.mit.edu/.
Note: Colors indicate different sectors; outlined circles indicate exports with revealed comparative advantage greater than 1; $ = US$.

the shares of China, India, and the Association of Southeast Asian Nations (ASEAN) countries in Bangladesh's exports are only 2.5, 1.5, and 1.5 percent, respectively. Bangladesh needs to make the most of the growth of the Asian giants. In doing so, it will be helped by the fact that it costs less time and money to export to Asian markets than to the European Union and the United States.

Future export growth will likely rely first on capturing new markets and increasing market share in existing markets, with existing products. Bangladesh's exports achieved strong growth and doubled their world market share between 1995 and 2012, owing to the success in garments, catering largely to the European Union and the United States. Garments can continue to grow in existing and newer markets. Newer products will emerge more slowly. Thus, more rapid export growth will initially rely on capturing higher market shares in Bangladesh's existing strengths, that is, basic garments, in current markets and penetrating newer and dynamic markets such as China, India, Japan, and the ASEAN countries. In addition, many firms are starting to produce higher-value garments and this will expand the target market for Bangladesh. Other products are emerging, such as jute goods, footwear, seafood, and ITES, and some of these may over time become part of a larger product cluster. The relative growth of existing products in new markets is shown in table 2.1, whereas new products are emerging much more slowly.

Notes

1. Bangladesh Garment Manufacturers and Exporters Association, http://www.bgmea .com.bd/home/pages/aboutus.
2. According to the Institute of Global Labour and Human Rights, Bangladesh's garment wages are the lowest, at only 21 cents per hour. Wages in other competing countries are Cambodia (24 cents per hour), India (55–68 cents per hour), Pakistan (37 cents per hour), Sri Lanka (46 cents per hour), Thailand (56 cents per hour), and Vietnam (52 cents per hour).

References

Balassa, Bela. 1965. "Trade Liberalisation and Revealed Comparative Advantage." *The Manchester School* 33 (2): 99–123.

Hausmann, R., and B. Klinger. 2007. "Structural Transformation and Patterns of Comparative Advantage in the Product Space." CID Working Paper 128, Center for International Development, Harvard University, Cambridge, MA. http://www.cid.harvard.edu /cidwp/128.htm.

Kathuria, Sanjay, and Mariem Mezghenni Malouche, eds. 2016. *Strengthening Competitiveness in Bangladesh—Sector Analyses: A Diagnostic Trade Integration Study.* Washington, DC: World Bank.

World Bank. 2012. "Consolidating and Accelerating Exports in Bangladesh: A Policy Agenda." Bangladesh Development Series Paper 29, Poverty Reduction and Economic Management Sector, South Asia Region, World Bank, Washington, DC.

CHAPTER 3

Four-Pillar Strategy to Spur Faster, Export-Led Growth

The distinguishing feature of economies that have proved to be successful global-izers, such as the Republic of Korea; Singapore; and Taiwan, China, is that their governments put in place consistent, long-term strategies centered on export competitiveness and encompassing all issues relevant to productivity growth—credit, infrastructure, energy, facilitation, education, and the business and regulatory environment, apart from a sound macroeconomic environment and competitive exchange rates. Bangladesh has not yet translated the vision of export orientation of its Sixth Five-Year Plan (6FYP) into implementation of a coherent and coordinated trade competitiveness strategy.

Infrastructure issues continue to be the most binding constraints on investment. Bangladesh ranks last among its Asian competitors in the high prevalence of power outages. Currently, 76 percent of the country's power plants use natural gas as the primary energy source. Inadequate electricity supply is a major problem even in cases where the private sector has installed captive gas-based generators; the unreliability of gas-based supply to run these poses a major challenge. Power outages are a key reason for manufacturing productivity in Bangladesh being much lower than in China and Vietnam. Transportation has become another critical constraint. This Diagnostic Trade Integration Study (DTIS) did not investigate the important constraint of power shortages in Bangladesh, as this is already a well-known and much-analyzed theme. Instead, it focused on trade logistics. As elaborated in this chapter, some persistent bottlenecks clearly need to be urgently addressed to expand exports.

The chapter discusses the main challenges and selected priority actions. A four-pillar strategy is outlined that includes prospects for penetrating new markets, especially in South Asia and Asia more broadly; trade facilitation measures; reduction and eventual elimination of distortions in the trade regime; a more proactive foreign direct investment (FDI) policy; and stronger institutional capacity. This will be followed, in chapter 4, by an illustrative discussion of some sector-specific measures to enhance trade potential, based on detailed studies of seven key industries or sectors. As explained in chapter 1, the DTIS did not investigate solutions relating to the skills constraint, dealing with trade shocks, or sustaining sound macroeconomic fundamentals. These topics are the subject of ongoing analysis or programs in the World Bank and the International Monetary Fund (IMF), as well as other development partners. Nonetheless, for the sake of completeness and to provide a marker, the discussion below summarizes key concerns relating to these themes, including energy constraints. More detailed analysis underpinning this summary can be found in Kathuria and Malouche (2016a).

Pillar 1: Breaking into New Markets

Improving Trade Facilitation

The costs of trade-related transport and logistics and their timeliness and reliability are core elements of trade competitiveness. Research has clearly demonstrated that high trade transaction costs are among the most important obstacles that developing countries currently face in exploiting the trade opportunities presented by the world trading system (Hoekman and Nicita 2011; Wilson, Mann, and Otsuki 2003). These costs are often fixed and disproportionately affect small firms, farmers, and the poor, prohibiting their participation in trade and limiting inclusiveness. Thus, the costs associated with inefficient trade facilitation, weak logistics, and trade finance have a direct bearing on poverty reduction. Trade facilitation also lowers import costs, which have a direct impact on the prices paid by the poor for the goods they consume (World Bank 2012c).

Bangladesh's cost advantage resulting from low labor cost is reduced or sometimes wiped out by disadvantages on the trade facilitation side. High logistics costs can be seen as an implicit tax that biases the economy away from exports. Efficient logistics are important for enhancing Bangladesh's competitive edge in exports. Efficient logistics reduce costs and delays for exports and expedite imports for consumption and domestic production. In particular, superior logistics performance offers a competitive advantage in an era of increasing globalization, more production sharing across countries, and shortened product lifecycles. To date, low wages have benefitted Bangladesh's ready-made garment (RMG) exports and have partially compensated for poor logistics performance. But to ensure the general growth of exports, logistics performance in Bangladesh will need to improve considerably.

Despite some progress, Bangladeshi logistics performance lags in customs, infrastructure, competence of logistics service providers, and tracking and tracing (figure 3.1). There are ongoing reforms in customs and there has been considerable expansion of the road network and performance improvements at the main trade gateway, the Port of Chittagong. However, the 2014 Logistics Performance Index (LPI) suggests that Bangladesh performs below the regional average for South Asia in logistics, ranked above only Bhutan and Afghanistan, landlocked countries, and below other countries at similar income levels. The analysis of trade facilitation in Kathuria and Malouche (2016a, chapter 6) identifies options for

Figure 3.1 Bangladesh's Logistics Performance, 2014

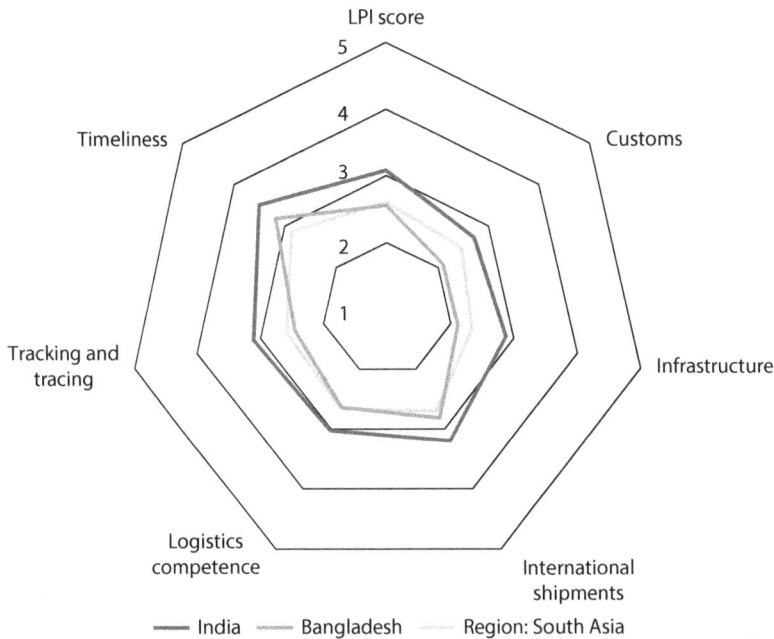

Source: World Bank 2014.
Note: LPI = Logistics Performance Index.

tackling four interrelated issues that are critical to Bangladesh's logistics efficiency. The four issues are the limited use of containers on the Dhaka-Chittagong corridor; customs and border management modernization; air transport capacity and connectivity; and regional transit and connectivity.

Inefficiencies in Handling Containers

Containers are not used much in the domestic movement of cargo in Bangladesh despite the rapid growth of containerization worldwide. Movement of containers inland is limited, and the trend is in the wrong direction. Although Bangladesh joined the containerization revolution in 1981, it has not fully exploited the benefits of containerization. Approximately half the cargo passing through the Port of Chittagong is containerized, but less than 15 percent of the containers are moved inland. The rest are stuffed and unstuffed either in the port or in privately operated inland container depots (ICDs) outside the port but within its vicinity. The containers that move inland are transported mostly by rail, with only a few transported by road. In 2009, rail moved approximately 3 and 5 percent of loaded import and export containers, respectively. Inland waterways within Bangladesh are generally not used to ship containers, although the authorities see great potential in utilizing waterways.

Transit times can be as high as 12 hours when they should be less than four hours with free-flowing traffic. Transit times by rail, the only other mode of transport, are even longer, close to 20 hours. The stripping of containers adds to handling costs as the goods are then loaded into trucks instead of the more efficient route of transporting containers. As a result, a large number of trucks moves cargo between Dhaka and Chittagong. The Dhaka-Chittagong highway is congested from the high volume of traffic, as well as from bottlenecks at specific locations, such as bridges and intermediate centers. Congestion increases transit time and decreases reliability on the corridor. The long transit times by road and rail discourage shipping lines from shipping containers to the ICD in Dhaka. In addition, customs regulation imposes that containerized cargo may only be removed from the port by rail (to the ICD in Dhaka) or to bonded facilities in the export processing zones (EPZs). As the volume of containers removed by rail is small, current practice is that containers are stripped in the port and then the goods are loaded into covered trucks for removal. A substantial proportion of the export and import containers are stuffed and stripped in the port itself (around 60 percent).[1]

Increasing the volume of containers moved by rail and inland waterways is a key to better integration in the domestic logistics system. This would require arresting a two-decade decline in railway capacity (figures 3.2 and 3.3) and improving inland waterway infrastructure. The latter would help in two respects: (a) avoiding congestion at Chittagong port and (b) moving containers using a cheaper mode than roads and railways. Improvements in infrastructure at the Pangaon Container Terminal and the introduction of customs facilities will help reduce cargo dwell time, as cargo would be cleared inland; this is already the case with railway-borne cargo. The government has reportedly authorized the construction of privately owned inland container terminals that

Figure 3.2 Dhaka-Chittagong Corridor: Number of Containers Carried by Rail

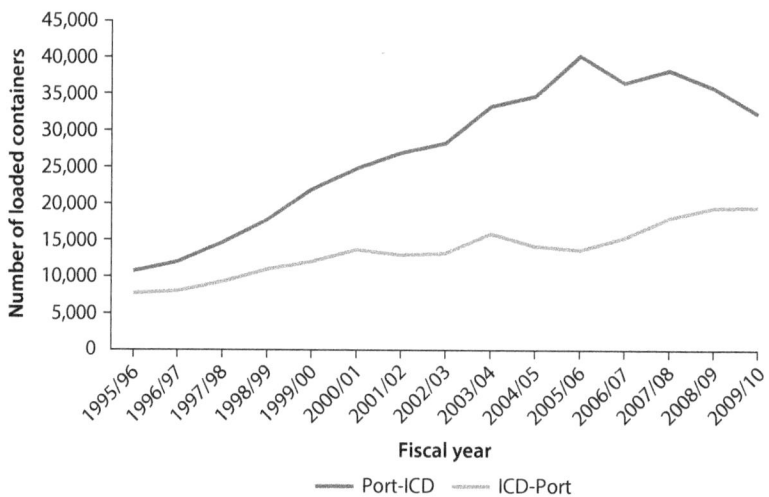

Source: Estimates using data from Bangladesh Railway.
Note: ICD = inland container depot.

Figure 3.3 Proportion of Chittagong Containers Moved In and Out by Rail

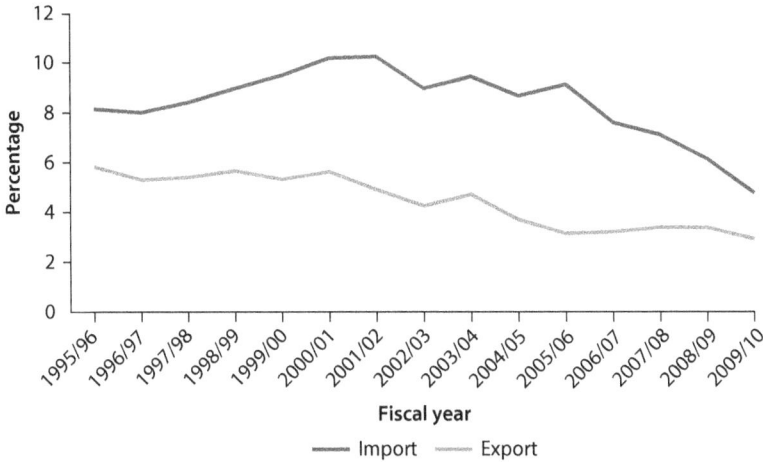

Source: Estimates using data from Bangladesh Railway.

will operate the same way. A few such facilities are already being developed near Dhaka and Narayanganj. However, a major constraint with the inland waterway system is the slow speed of movement.

Dhaka-Chittagong Corridor

The poor performance of the Dhaka-Chittagong corridor has been identified as one of the constraints to further expansion of the industry, including the garment sector. The Dhaka-Chittagong corridor is the most important trade link in the country and serves more than two-thirds of the country's import and export flows. It has multimodal transport possibilities, as it is composed of road, rail, and inland waterway links. Within the corridor, road transport handles just over half the traffic, followed by inland waterways, with 43 percent, and rail, with just over 6 percent[2] (railways are presently the most important mode for container movement inland). In 2012, Bangladesh Railway operated unit trains of 76–80 20-foot equivalent unit (TEU) containers twice a day between Chittagong and the Dhaka ICD in Kamalapur.[3]

The inefficiency of the Dhaka-Chittagong corridor is partly because of the low use of railways for freight. Generally, railway capacity is limited by short train length caused by track configuration and loop lengths, and long headways are needed for the signaling and loop configuration. For freight train operations, there is the additional constraint of the wagon braking systems that limit maximum speed to 29 kilometers per hour. Despite the high level of demand and the potential for future growth, Bangladesh Railway has not increased the frequency of unit train operation. Yet, unit train operation is Bangladesh Railway's only profitable service and has helped to offset some of the losses from passenger services. The reasons for not increasing the container service include the following:

- There is heavy demand on those sections that serve passenger traffic from the northeast, for example, between Tongi and Bhairab Bazaar and between Laksam and Chakisasma. This demand is compounded by the limitations of a single track between Tongi and Chinki Astana. The government is building another track with financing from the Asian Development Bank. This should remove a major operational bottleneck on the railways, although a shortage of wagons and locomotives will still constrain improvements in capacity.
- Government policy favors passenger services over freight services. Most of Bangladesh Railway's capacity is dedicated to interurban passenger train movements.[4]
- Lack of commercial incentives for management is satisfied with rationing capacity to collect a premium (formal and informal) for the service.
- Rail ICD capacity has difficulty handling three trains a day in each direction.

Trucking, Waterways, and Airfreight

Trucking services are highly distorted and inefficient in the non-garment industry. The garment industry has encouraged the emergence of modern trucking services based on contracts for services at an agreed price. Although these services tend to be expensive, they offer a predetermined quality of service, for which they charge a premium. However, non-RMG trucking services suffer from poor quality and low reliability. Many operators use old fleets. In addition, there is a high level of vehicle overloading. In an effort to mitigate competition, the operators typically have to go through transport brokers to obtain loads, especially on the Benapole-Dhaka route. The market is distorted, because the brokerage industry or clearing and forwarding agents control access to and competition for services. Moreover, one of the major constraints faced in this secondary market is the lack of access to financing that could be used to modernize fleets and improve access to new business.

In addition to road transportation, water transport has a large but unutilized potential in Bangladesh. More than 10 percent of the population of Bangladesh has direct access to the inland waterways transport system (IWT). Although inland waterways are cheaper than other modes of transport, they suffer from poor performance. Generally, the volume of cargo moved by the IWT has stagnated over the past decade. This mode is slow (16–20 hours between Chittagong and the ICD to the south of Dhaka). Although this is somewhat faster than the current rail service for inbound containers, it is slower than road transport, especially when door-to-door movement is considered. The IWT has great potential to move higher volumes of cargo, especially between Dhaka and Chittagong and between India and Bangladesh. It could help relieve some of the pressure on low railway capacity and congested roads.

Airfreight has been growing steadily but with many problems experienced on the ground, in particular with respect to the management of the air cargo terminal in Bangladesh. Through hubs in the Middle East and East Asia, Bangladesh is connected to the rest of the world. Airfreight is used mostly by the garment industry, usually at the buyer's request, and sometimes in the case of a missed ocean shipping date. For normal shipments, one of the practices is to use a sea-air combination: ship by sea to Dubai and airfreight from Dubai to Europe and the United States. Air charters are also used, especially during the period of high demand from July to October. However, clearing and forwarding agents report problems with ground handling and management of the air cargo terminal at the airport in Dhaka, performed by a subsidiary of the national carrier, Biman Airlines. The terminal area is often congested, partly because of increasing cargo volumes, but also because of poor performance in the handling and clearance processes. Furthermore, although agents pay Biman for all services, they often have to hire their own labor for the same purpose, which increases the costs of airfreight logistics. Another complicating factor is the absence of a simplified customs clearance procedure, even for small consignments or samples, or a *de minimis* provision. All packages are treated the same, resulting in clearance times that take one to five days, even for garment samples.

Customs Processes

The government is taking steps to automate further customs processes. It introduced the Automated SYstem for CUstoms DAta (ASYCUDA) World[5] in 2013, starting at the Port of Chittagong. The plan is to interconnect all the customs stations so that declarations can be lodged from anywhere. In addition, the National Board of Revenue is working to introduce a single-window system, starting at Chittagong Customs House. Already, ship agents can file vessel manifests electronically, although hard copies still have to be submitted. However, presently most of the land customs stations are not automated and use manual systems. Bangladesh has an extensive network of land customs stations. The most dominant one is Benapole, which is on the main land trade route with India. Clearance times are typically two to three days at the smaller stations and within five to six days at Benapole. At Benapole, 80 percent of declarations are assessed within a day of being lodged, whereas it takes up to five days to clear 80 percent of goods for release after declaration. The clearance times at the land customs stations are affected by several practices that increase time and cost. The main one is the transloading of cargo between trucks registered in Bangladesh and those registered in India. This practice has several consequences, including the need to provide warehousing space and equipment to handle and store goods and labor to handle the goods.

Informal payments are still common to facilitate clearance of goods. In part because of this, as well as lack of internal capacity, Bangladesh customs relies on the services of pre-shipment inspection companies. Although it is claimed that pre-shipment inspection improves revenue collection reporting on the declarations[6] and cargo clearance time by one to two days on average, the program has not been without controversy (Arnold 2010). On paper, 10 percent of pre-shipment inspection and 100 percent of non-pre-shipment inspection shipments were supposed to be subject to physical examination. However, the actual physical examination rate for pre-shipment inspection shipments was much higher (close to 50 percent). There were 8,000 disputes pending in the courts relating to the certifications by the pre-shipment inspection agencies—a small proportion of the total declarations. The disputes were usually about classification and valuation of imports and what was regarded as poor performance by the pre-shipment inspection companies (Mahmud and Rossette 2007; Uzzaman and Abu Yusuf 2011).

Bangladesh does not have an effective institutional mechanism to promote trade facilitation and logistics upgrading. The existing mechanism has been effective in meeting trade facilitation obligations under the World Trade Organization (WTO) framework, but some of the constraints now faced are much more about the interface between the physical infrastructure and meeting regulatory requirements for the movement of goods. Like other countries, Bangladesh has many agencies that play a role in trade facilitation and logistics. These include customs, chambers of commerce, the land port authority, port operators, railways, roads, inland waterways, clearing and forwarding agents, security services, and so forth. The lack of proper coordination is evident in the manner in which transit issues have been pursued, where a holistic assessment of the costs and benefits of transit has not gained enough traction. This is also reflected in the poor coordination among agencies at the border, which increases costs and clearance time and reduces reliability. In other countries, such as Pakistan, coordination of trade facilitation reforms is pursued through a National Trade Facilitation Committee.

Logistics to Reduce Lead Times and Enhance Competitiveness

A coherent and comprehensive National Logistics Strategy would help improve the efficiency of the transit regime. The government of Bangladesh can help improve the efficiency of the movement of goods by reducing the lead time and the cost of logistics for imports and exports through the Dhaka-Chittagong corridor. Such a strategy would potentially have important implications on infrastructure development and the quality and performance of logistics services. It would entail a set of coordinated reform pillars to (a) improve road and rail capacity; (b) improve customs procedures at the Port of Chittagong; (c) complement the phaseout from the services of pre-shipment inspection companies by adopting and implementing an appropriate roadmap, including capacity-building for customs officers; (d) enhance air shipment capacity; and (e) prepare for implementation of a single-window system.

Bangladesh should broaden the coverage and strengthen the capacity of the National Trade Facilitation Committee to play a more proactive role in guiding trade facilitation and logistics reforms in the country. Good logistics are important for enhancing the country's competitive edge in exports. To date, low wages have benefitted Bangladesh's RMG exports and have partially compensated for poor logistics performance. However, to ensure continued, rapid growth of exports, logistics performance will need to improve considerably. Moreover, while the focus to date has largely been on international trade facilitation reforms, recent empirical evidence suggests that measures to improve logistics performance at the subnational level to facilitate connections to international trade corridors and supply chains are as important, if not more so. In geographically large or dispersed countries such as Bangladesh, the performance of internal corridors is a key priority for reducing poverty in lagging regions and addressing rising concerns about development disparities across regions (Kunaka 2010).

The plan to establish a rail ICD at Tongi should be implemented as soon as possible. The existing Dhaka rail ICD in Kamalapur operates more efficiently than the container yard in Chittagong Port, but its location in the congested city center restricts access. The rail service provides a cost-effective means for repositioning of empties through lower backhaul tariff. There are no serious delays for the southbound movement from Dhaka to Chittagong and the ICD provides sufficient storage for empties. However, the benefits to exporters are limited, since the ICD does not currently operate as a dry port with a through bill of lading. The shipping lines continue to charge exporters for the round-trip movement of the boxes, even if they are loaded in both directions. Further, the lines require a bank guarantee for movement of empties from the ICD to the factory for stuffing of cargo. Given their interest in controlling how the boxes are used and coordinating their repositioning, the shipping lines have little incentive to offer attractive rates for backhaul-loaded movement. It is left to the freight forwarders to encourage the loading of the empties stored at the ICD with export cargo. They are able to move the boxes to the factory under a company guarantee rather than a bank guarantee and they can negotiate lower rates with the shipping lines for loaded southbound movement. The relocation of the ICD to Tongi should encourage this business.

Development of the IWT sector will require strengthening the regulatory oversight of transport services. Two bodies have regulatory responsibilities for IWT in Bangladesh: the Department of Shipping, which is responsible for the safety and overall regulation of the sector, and the Bangladesh Inland Water Transport Authority (BIWTA). BIWTA is responsible for dredging services, navigational aids, management of inland ports, and regulation of transport operations, among other functions. Often, the separation and allocation of responsibilities between the Department of Shipping and BIWTA is not clear. With proper regulation, inland water transport can help Bangladesh reduce the environmental impacts of transport operations, as it is more efficient and generates lower carbon emissions than other modes. Priorities for improving use of the IWT should also include improving service performance by dredging channels, improving IWT port capacity near Dhaka, and acquiring more efficient vessels (see also Kathuria and Malouche 2016b, chapter 1, on shipbuilding). Some of the improvements can be made by the private sector.

The government should complement the phasing out of pre-shipment inspection by implementing an Authorized Economic Operators (AEO)[7] program. After years of postponement, the government finally phased out pre-shipment inspection as of July 2013, as announced by the minister of finance in the fiscal year 2014 (FY2014) budget statement. Chief among the actions taken was a significant increase in and training of customs staff. An AEO program for Bangladesh would help address several objectives, including faster clearance of some goods and, as a corollary, freeing customs and other border management resources to target those consignments that pose the most risk. Typically, an AEO program is developed and implemented in phases, reflecting the capacity of the authorities and private sector readiness to participate in such a program. An AEO regime can be introduced for selected supply chain participants, such as with the established garment manufacturers. In addition, the management of risk should be automated as much as possible, based on international best practices. The ASYCUDA World system that is being developed has the capability to enhance risk management in a flexible manner.

Promoting Economic Integration with Asia

Bangladesh has not been sufficiently able to penetrate new and growing markets, such as China and India, or use its proximity to the broader Asia region, which is increasingly the world's economic center of gravity. Bangladesh's export market concentration largely reflects the preferential access its garment sector has enjoyed in the European Union (EU) market and strong demand from the U.S. market. It will continue to benefit from this preferential access following the European Union's adoption of new Rules of Origin for its Generalized System of Preferences[8] scheme, which became effective in January 2011.

Major gains would derive from integration with East Asia. Bangladeshi merchandise exports would be 52 percent higher and the country could gain around US$1.8 billion from broader South Asia–East Asia integration. Export growth to East Asia has significantly greater potential. A recent formal analysis that used computable general equilibrium modeling confirms that broader South Asia–East Asia integration that includes all members of South Asia would provide large gains to exports and trade and overall welfare for Bangladesh (Francois, Wignaraja, and Rana 2009). In fact, such analyses considerably understate growth impacts, because the models incorporate limited dynamic effects from cross-border investment flows in support of trade. This type of cross-border investment could be a much larger factor for Bangladesh and such opening to investment could raise economy-wide productivity and scale economies of domestic firms and industries.

Bangladesh has significant import complementarities with China, India, and members of the Association of Southeast Asian Nations (ASEAN). The complementarities are comparable to Eastern European countries' complementarities with developed EU members (France, Germany, and the United Kingdom) prior to joining the European Union.[9] Bangladesh maintains the highest levels of import complementarity with China, India, Indonesia, Malaysia, Singapore, and Thailand, owing to the high degree of sourcing of textiles for the RMG sector. Although prospects for increasing existing exports to East Asia may be weak on the basis of export complementarity, dynamic, medium-term impacts may give rise to new export industries, such as the export of processed foods that are currently domestically oriented.

Bangladesh has the potential to increase trade with South Asia, particularly India. Under the South Asian Free Trade Area, Bangladesh and other least developed countries (LDCs) have secured duty-free, quota-free access to India. This scenario could increase Bangladesh's exports to India by 134 percent; if Bangladesh also offers free trade status to India (in effect, a free trade agreement, FTA), its exports to India could rise by 182 percent, since inputs used in exports would become cheaper. However, estimated gains from trade facilitation between Bangladesh and India would be much larger than the gains from trade liberalization. Because of the size and proximity of the countries, a Bangladesh-India FTA plus improved connectivity[10] could raise Bangladesh's exports to India by about 297 percent (for details, see De, Raihan, and Kathuria 2012). Improvements in connectivity would provide the largest payoff in merchandise trade and the spillovers could facilitate trade with third countries. Note that these are static estimates and hence can be considered as lower bounds of potential gains. Dynamic gains can be much larger and can be realized by encouraging new trade in goods and services, especially through FDI in goods, infrastructure services, and other services.

In this context, the experience of the India-Sri Lanka FTA is salutary. It shows that, beyond the exchange of preferences, the agreement provided a boost of confidence to the private sector, resulting in substantial new investments by India in Sri Lanka's service sectors. In addition, the liberalization of air travel between the two countries resulted in major growth in Indian tourism in Sri Lanka. Bilateral trade has increased fivefold since the FTA became effective in 2001.

Stronger and deeper regional cooperation would benefit the poor disproportionately. Lagging border regions of Bangladesh, among the poorest in South Asia, need to be part of the new market expansion to help reduce poverty. In Bangladesh, the border districts tend to have lower than average per capita income, higher than average poverty, and poorer human development. Regions that share a border with India are not well connected to the national economy and lack the market linkages and infrastructure to formalize trade. Alternative bilateral and regional mechanisms, including cross-border bazaars and related facilities, can operate in parallel with FTAs to extend local market opportunities. Cross-border trade—defined as the flow of goods and services up to 30 kilometers across international land borders—is important for the prosperity of border communities.

Challenges

Major constraints lie in the policy choices of the countries, such as differences in axle load limits between Bangladesh and India, with which Bangladesh shares its longest border (table 3.1). Axle load limits in Bangladesh are consistently lower than those in India, for the same class of trucks. This could be a reflection of weaker pavements in Bangladesh; or it could reflect a regulatory legacy where the limits have not kept pace with recent trends in trucking technology. In fact, the differences in axle load limits are cited as one reason for denying India transit rights across Bangladeshi territory. This may be only one reason and possibly not

Table 3.1 Gross Vehicle Weight Limits in Bangladesh and India
tonnes

Vehicle type	Bangladesh	India
3 axle (1 front, 2 back)	22	25
4 axle (steering + 3 axles)	25	31
5 axle (3 prime mover, 3 trailer)	38	44
6 axle (3 prime mover, 3 trailer)	41	44[a]
7 axle (3 prime mover, 4 axle)	44	—

Source: World Bank staff estimates, data from various sources.
Note: — = not available.
a. Nominal weights are 45.4 and 54.2 tonnes, but 6-axle vehicles are restricted to 44 tonnes.

the main reason for denying such transit rights. Various other political, social, and economic considerations are also pertinent. Whole industries and a large number of people are already engaged in transloading of cargo at the borders. These stakeholders would be affected by a change in policy, regardless of the economic inefficiencies involved in the status quo.

Trade disputes are particularly frequent between Bangladesh and India. The private sector frequently complains that nontariff barriers (NTBs) on the Indian side severely hamper Bangladeshi export opportunities. Bangladeshi media frequently report on such NTBs, in particular concerns over the complicated technical regulations and standards when exporting processed food to India. Similarly, the Indian side has recorded complaints against Bangladeshi NTBs. Working level discussions to reduce trade-restricting NTBs and an effective dispute resolution mechanism would help to chip away at the barriers.

Problems are most commonly found at the major land customs stations, such as Petrapole-Benapole and Akhaura-Agartala, the largest ports between mainland India (i.e., to the west of Bangladesh) and Bangladesh and Bangladesh and northeastern India, respectively. Access roads to land border crossing points are often narrow and do not have enough space for vehicles to be parked on the roadside. This creates congestion and delays, which result in high truck demurrage charges to Bangladeshi exporters. Moreover, while there have been some increases in the border closing times, differences in border closing days on the Bangladesh and India sides continue to constrain trading. No documents are processed in Bangladesh on Fridays, and except for special consignments, such as perishables, none in India on Sundays. Both sides process documents on Saturdays. Thus, two of seven potential trading days are lost in the week.

Regional Opportunities to Enhance Exports

Because of the shape of the borders in the region, Bangladesh could serve as a transit country for trade between mainland India and northeastern states in India and for Nepal and Bhutan. Currently, movement of vehicles is not possible across Bangladesh's borders, whether for transit or for goods bound for Bangladesh. Goods have to be offloaded at the border and transferred to vehicles from the other country. This practice is inefficient. The same also applies to railways where locomotives have to be changed. Recently, however, the Governments of India and Bangladesh have been discussing how Indian traffic could cross from the mainland to the northeast states across Bangladesh. The intention is primarily to allow traffic between West Bengal and the landlocked Indian states in the northeast. Such transit would halve travel distance to about 500 kilometers.

The adoption by the Governments of India and Bangladesh of a trade transit agreement has the potential to transform the trade facilitation environment in South Asia. The immediate problem is a very specific one that requires a practical transit solution that would allow India's cargo to cross from its mainland to its northeastern states across Bangladesh on a few identified road corridors with significant traffic potential. In practice, a phased approach could be adopted and could include (a) a bilateral road transport agreement between India and Bangladesh to allow trucks to cross and deliver goods in each other's territory, and (b) agreement on a road infrastructure cost recovery mechanism that applies to both countries. The proposal has the potential to transform the trade facilitation environment in South Asia if the framework can be extended to accommodate traffic to and from Nepal and Bhutan, which may then be able to access Bangladeshi ports, especially Mongla.

Harmonization and cooperation at the border will be a major boost to speed up flows of goods. India has built or is planning integrated check posts at several borders with Bangladesh. Bangladesh could take a number of measures to improve overall efficiency at the land border posts. Some of the measures could be short-term measures, including the following:

- Increase and harmonize border working hours. Presently the land ports do not operate fully on Friday in Bangladesh and on Sunday in India. Two days of clearance are therefore lost each week.
- Allow pre-arrival clearance of goods. Some countries have realized significant gains from allowing the processing of documents to start before goods get to the border. The goods can be cleared as soon as they arrive, and customs and other agencies are able to carry out any physical verification they may desire.
- Increase capacity for handling transloaded goods. In the interim before phasing out the transloading of goods, capacity for handling such cargo should be increased.

Current practices are designed around significant use of manual labor and the involvement of hundreds of people at each border post in the transloading business. Some of the processes can be automated to expedite the movement of goods. India and Bangladesh could also agree on modalities for the penetration of trucking services into each other's territory.

Bangladesh and India should also sign the International Road Transport Convention. One of the likely benefits for India and Bangladesh would be the potential spillover effects beyond the South Asia region. Nepal and Bhutan are landlocked and need access to seaports and harmonized agreements to reduce time and costs. They could more easily access the ports of Bangladesh, in particular, which are closest. A functional regional transit system would unlock significant benefits for the South Asia region.

The Association of Travel Agents of Bangladesh and the main exporters are pressing for an open skies policy, which would reduce costs and provide more airfreight capacity for the garment sector. More generally, liberalization leads to increased air service levels and lower fares, which in turn stimulate additional traffic volumes and can bring about increased economic growth and employment. For example, Sri Lanka has concluded a number of open skies agreements since 2005, including with Malaysia, Singapore, Switzerland, Thailand, and the United States. Open skies has been rolling out in stages in ASEAN since 2009, helping to make Southeast Asia home to the world's fastest expanding low-cost airlines.

Moreover, trade disputes might be addressed by the conclusion of bilateral mutual recognition agreements (MRAs). An MRA states that technical regulations, standards, and conformity assessment procedures undertaken on one side of the border are essentially equal to the ones undertaken on the other side. Thus, goods produced in one country can be freely marketed in the other. MRAs facilitate trade by enabling manufacturers to have their products tested and certified in the country of origin, for compliance with the regulatory requirements of the importing country. By eliminating the time delays and costs associated with obtaining regulatory approval in the importing country, MRAs benefit the parties' businesses by delivering significant savings in time and money. Under MRAs, one government agrees to recognize the results of another's testing, inspection, sanitary and phytosanitary standards (SPS) certification, or other procedures.

Development partners could fund a road map of mutual recognition of food-related border procedures. The elements of this road map would consist of examining the concurrent Indian and Bangladeshi legislation; assessing the standards and conformity assessment procedures applied; promoting mutual trust and bilateral cooperation in food production and trade; working toward mutually recognizing the critical elements of each other's regulations; holding technical discussions about the necessary steps for achieving mutual recognition; identifying and supporting necessary reforms; and establishing regular contacts and communication concerning standards, technical regulations, and conformity assessments in India-Bangladesh border trade.

Finally, broader markets in Asia should also be targeted. For example, China, India, Japan, Korea, and the countries of ASEAN are major world markets with little Bangladeshi penetration. Targeted promotion to these markets by the Export Promotion Bureau (EPB), in cooperation with the Bangladesh Garment Manufacturers and Exporters Association (BGMEA) and the Bangladesh Knitwear Manufacturers and Exporters Association (BKMEA) (in the first instance), for example, could reap some dividends. This activity could have synergies with efforts by the Board of Investment (BOI) to promote FDI into Bangladesh from these markets. The building of a Bangladeshi brand could be a longer-term objective. Improving trade facilitation will also be critical to improve Bangladesh's competitiveness in global and regional markets.

Pillar 2: Breaking into New Products

Rationalizing Trade Policy to Level the Playing Field

Trade policy has served Bangladesh well so far, resulting in sustained export growth. Dollar exports have doubled over the past six years. Bangladesh is now the second largest exporter of garments and could benefit significantly from China's rising wages and the ongoing move to cheaper garment producers. Bangladesh also has an unusually high share (at its income level) of manufactured exports in its export basket, which illustrates its strengths in mass manufacturing and labor availability.

Challenges

The economy has become increasingly open since independence. Bangladesh went through a phase of heavy controls on exports and imports, price controls, and state trading (1972–75), followed by gradual market-based reforms, including domestic deregulation in agriculture, trade, and services; denationalization; abolition of most elements of state trading; and introduction of bonded warehouse facilities for the emerging garment sector. Since 1990, trade liberalization has been stepped up, albeit it was interspersed with periodic reversals. Trade policy reform included a substantial scaling down and rationalization of tariffs, removal of trade-related quantitative restrictions, elimination of import licensing, unification of exchange rates, and the move to a managed float exchange rate regime. In 1994, Bangladesh was declared to be conforming to the IMF's Article VIII, marking convertibility on the current account.

Yet, significant inconsistencies, stemming from lingering trade protectionism for some industries, and a focus on revenue targets raise questions about the overall efficacy of trade policy and the sustainability of export growth. Trade policy often responds to protectionist pressures, reminiscent of the import-substituting trade regime that prevailed before the 1990s. Revenue or protectionist considerations have usually dominated over trade policy issues. Thus, trade policy in Bangladesh has been skewed, where consumers and export sectors other than garments have not been conscious beneficiaries of such policies. Any protectionist measures should be justified by economy-wide, positive spillovers and should also be temporary. However, in recent years, border taxes have increased and grown more complex and have led to high and varied rates of effective protection. Overall, the trade policy regime has translated into reduced incentives to export and diversify and has led to higher domestic prices.

The tax treatment of imports in Bangladesh is complex. While the average customs duty has come down over the past decade from 70.6 percent in FY1992 to 13.2 percent in FY2015, a proliferation of para-tariffs has resulted in a complex import tax regime and substantially increased the rate of border protection. Supplementary duties and regulatory duties seem to have become standard instruments for raising revenue or offering protection to domestic import-substituting industries. Such tariff changes that raise overall protection and also increase its dispersion across products potentially set back the agenda for trade diversification.

The combination of tariffs and para-tariffs gives an average nominal protection rate of 26.9 percent in FY2015, up from 20.1 percent in FY2009 (albeit with a decline in FY2015 compared with the 28.1 percent rate of FY2014).

Inter- and intra-sector variation in border taxation abounds. Border taxation varies substantially at the sector level for tariffs and para-tariffs.[11] It varies substantially between and within sectors, potentially reinforcing distortions to individual decisions, opportunities for rent-seeking, and the consequent need for enforcement. In general, tariff rates are more dispersed (less concentrated) than para-tariff rates, reflecting tariff escalation (see figures 3.4 and 3.5).

Consumer goods are overly protected in Bangladesh and there is a growing wedge between input and output tariffs. The government levies a significant supplementary duty and regulatory duty on top of the 25 percent tariff for final goods, mostly on products that are produced domestically. Thus, tariff escalation is the highest at the last stage of processing—from intermediate goods to final goods (figure 3.6). The wedge between the average nominal protection rate on inputs and final consumer goods has been rising since FY2009 and appears

Figure 3.4 Decomposition of Border Taxation at the Sector Level, FY2011

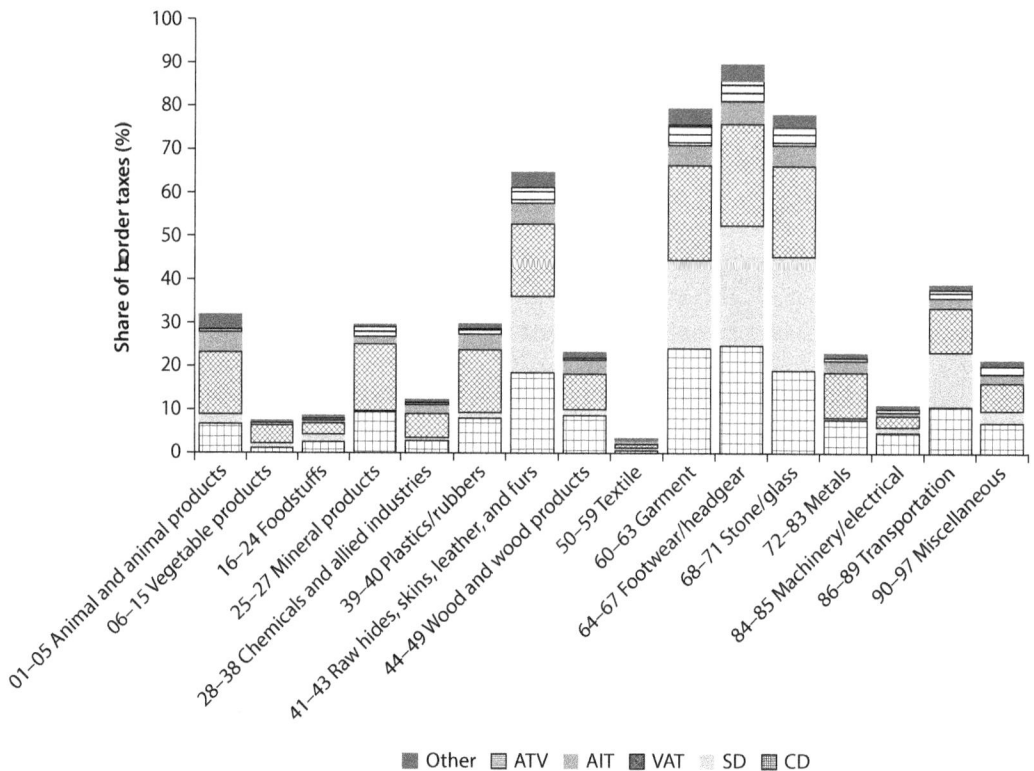

Source: Calculations using National Board of Revenue data.
Note: AIT = advanced income tax; ATV = advanced trade value-added tax (a tax levied nominally at 3 percent of the value-added tax inclusive price of commercially imported goods); CD = customs duty; SD = supplementary duty; VAT = value-added tax.

Figure 3.5 Intra-Sector Concentration of Tariff and Para-Tariff Rates, FY2011

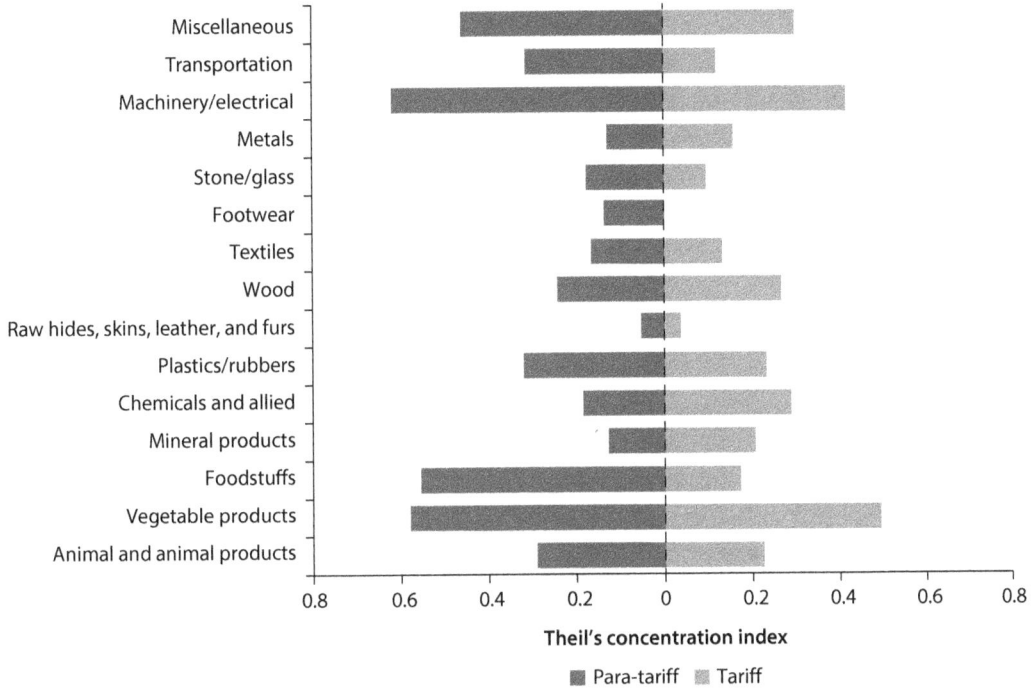

Source: Calculations using National Board of Revenue data.
Note: The length of bars measures the concentration of tax rates measured by Theil's concentration index. A long bar means that, within a given sector, a small number of subsectors shoulder a disproportionate share of the tax burden; a short bar means that the tax burden is spread relatively evenly within the sector.

Figure 3.6 Average Tariffs on Import Categories, FY2000–FY2013

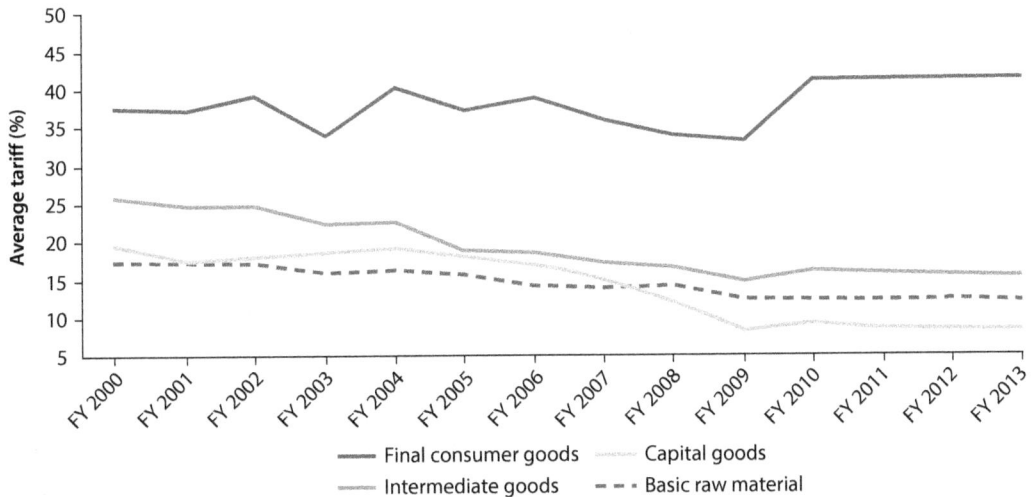

Source: Calculations using National Board of Revenue data.
Note: FY = fiscal year.

designed to offer higher protection to domestic industries primarily engaged in consumer goods production. Tariff escalation appears to be the outcome of pre-budget consultations with producer groups only, without consultation with other stakeholders, such as consumers who could suffer welfare losses through higher prices or reduced choice.

There has been no critical evaluation of the impact of protection. In general, higher tariffs on a product encourage its domestic production and discourage exports, since the former is protected by the tariff and the latter is a far more competitive marketplace. The low protection for intermediate and capital goods arguably discourages domestic production of these goods; high protection for consumer goods encourages domestic production. If there is no sunset clause or expiration date for protection and the impact of protection on the protected sector and the rest of the economy is not evaluated, as is the case in Bangladesh, this can lead to economic inefficiencies.

The escalating structure of protection results in high effective rates of protection (ERPs) for domestic production,[12] which biases incentives against exports. The analysis confirmed especially high ERPs in sectors such as footwear, some agrifood products, bicycles, and ceramics. Pharmaceuticals fall in a unique category, with ERPs only modestly positive (but this is not the full picture, since competing imports are not allowed; see chapter 4). By contrast, output destined for exports receives no protection and export ERPs are typically zero when imported inputs are duty exempt via mechanisms such as duty drawback or are exempt from duty and other import taxes altogether through special bonded warehouse (SBW) arrangements. Often, cash subsidies compensate for duty drawback or SBW. Comparing export ERPs with the high domestic protection, incentives to export are stifled (see chapter 4).

High import tariffs also affect consumers' welfare through prices. Simulations that use household expenditure surveys show that tariffs add 7.5 percent to the cost of living of the median Bangladeshi household. Adding up all the border taxes can increase living costs by up to 15 percent for the median household. Moreover, the taxes seem to fall heavily on middle-income households while sparing the richest (figure 3.7). Replacing the current array of tariff and para-tariff measures by a flat, combined border tax at a uniform 10 percent would raise consumers' real incomes by 11.3 percent on average—enough to lift 11.2 million people, 7.4 percent of Bangladesh's population (and 17.2 percent of Bangladesh's poor population, i.e., those living below US$1.25 a day), above the poverty line.[13] Although these numbers seem large, they illustrate the significant prevalence of imports in household expenditure baskets, as well as the high tariffs on many consumer goods.

Nontariff measures (NTMs) are also prevalent and may affect firms' competitiveness and household incomes. Private sector surveys, such as those conducted by the International Trade Center, have repeatedly shown that NTMs are costly and burdensome and make products less competitive in the destination market.[14] NTMs can also penalize domestic firms that need to buy critical inputs from abroad, thus reducing national competitiveness. The heavy reliance on

Figure 3.7 Consumption-Weighted Tariffs as a Function of Household Income, by Centile, FY2011

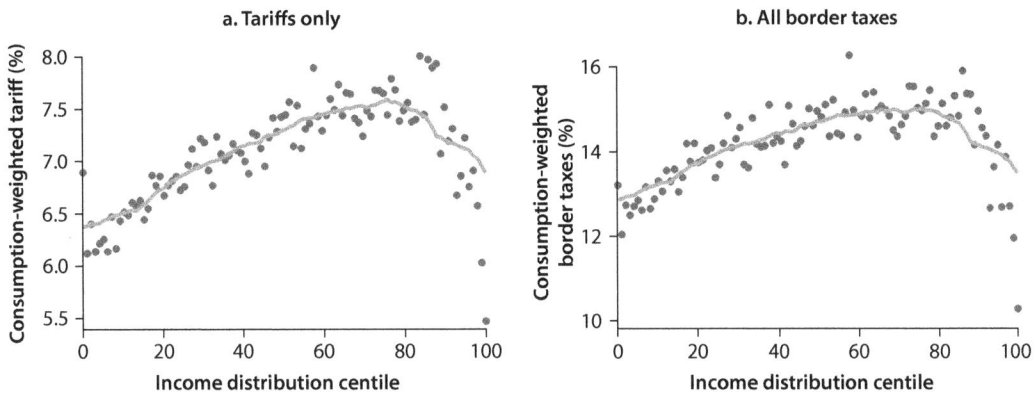

a. Tariffs only

b. All border taxes

Source: Calculations based on Bangladeshi tariff data and Bangladesh's household survey.
Note: The authors approximated income with total consumption. For readability, the data are aggregated by centile of the distribution of income. Thus, the point to the extreme left of the diagram is the consumption-weighted tariff affecting the lowest centile of Bangladesh's income distribution. For example, given the expenditure pattern of households in that centile, they face, on average, a tariff of 6.2 percent.

pre-shipment inspection until June 2013 and overly restrictive standards also increase the price of imports and hurt consumers' welfare.

Bangladesh's trade policy is still heavily influenced by considerations of revenue and assistance to local industries rather than trade competitiveness. Import policy is legally set in the Import Policy Order issued by the Ministry of Commerce in consultation with Customs. However, the National Board of Revenue, which does not have export promotion as its policy goal, seems to have the final authority on tariff setting (see also Kathuria and Malouche 2016a, chapter 4, on institutions). But at the same time, border tax exemptions are widespread and translate into significant revenue losses. The import tax structure is marked by a large number of exemptions of all kinds, including some that benefit single companies or are under non-transparent, special order labels. An analysis of customs transaction data at the tariff line level shows that the exemptions figure is almost 30 percent of the total number of transactions and 44 percent of total trade value. These exemptions add up to significant revenue shortfalls—13 percent of collected revenue in FY2011—especially in the foodstuffs sector where less than half the nominal taxes are actually collected.

In the future, as import duties go down, Bangladesh's ability to harness economic opportunities from global trade will depend on its management of the quality of the products it exports and imports. Bangladesh faces a quality challenge for its exports and imports. For exports, buyers and importing countries will set more stringent standards and technical regulations in the future. The success of Bangladesh's attempts to develop and diversify its exports will depend on how it meets this quality challenge. Simultaneously, in the future, the population of Bangladesh will demand better regulation of imports to address an expanding array of issues, such as public safety, food safety, and plant and animal health.

Meeting the quality challenge in the export and import markets will help maximize trade, accelerate growth, and reduce poverty. Imports need to flow smoothly to support the import needs of the export sectors and the needs of the domestic population.

A large number of quality-related laws and regulations in Bangladesh influences trade and unduly disturbs the free flow of imports. The problematic laws and regulations may be divided into three broad groups. The first group consists of mandatory standards on a range of products, including food and agricultural products, chemical products, textiles, electrical and electronic products, and engineering products. The second group consists of SPS measures, notably food safety laws and regulations and plant health laws and regulations. The third group includes a number of special rules stated in the Import Policy Order (Ministry of Commerce 2012).

In Bangladesh, services trade is more restricted than the world average, in particular in telecommunications and transportation services. Bangladesh has the second most restrictive services trade policies in the South Asia region, with an average Services Trade Restrictiveness Index of 44, well above the world average of 28.[15] Services trade restrictiveness is usually associated with low-quality, high-cost services, while openness has a positive impact on overall competitiveness, in particular on multi-factor productivity growth (Triplett and Bosworth 2004; Inklaar, Timmer, and van Ark 2008; Van der Marel 2011). Policy reforms in the services sectors played a major role in the transformation of the manufacturing sector in India, allowing greater foreign and domestic competition with improved regulation. Lack of liberalization in some sectors is seriously constraining the quality and capacity of some services, such as air-freight services, but also productivity gains in the manufacturing sector, a cornerstone of Bangladesh's economy. Productivity gains from services liberalization are more pronounced for domestic and small firms. Recent empirical studies that analyze the impact of services liberalization in Eastern Europe and Central Asia indicate that small and medium enterprises (SMEs) are the principal beneficiaries (Tarr 2012).

Trade Policy Reforms to Reduce Anti-Export Bias and Balance Consumer Interests

The gains from a balanced trade policy are multifaceted. For low- and middle-income countries, exports are not only important for their well-established static and dynamic gains, such as scale economies, competition, and knowledge transfer. Exports are also a main source of foreign currency, which is necessary to finance imports of capital goods and other inputs. Indeed, the gains to trade are as much derived from imports as from exports. Openness to imports also acts as a disciplining force on domestic markets, leading to lower-cost, higher-quality inputs and intermediate goods for producers. Access to a variety of products also encourages innovation and technological change. The smooth flow of imports is particularly critical for exporters who need to be competitive globally and are constantly competing with other players. Imports need to flow smoothly to support the import needs of the export sectors and the needs of the domestic population. Imports benefit consumers by decreasing prices and increasing product variety. Services imports have also become a pillar of countries' export competitiveness agenda by making services, as inputs to industry, more efficient and cost effective.

While garment exports growth can continue, the government needs to level the playing field so as not to discourage diversification. A more harmonized and simpler import tax regime would reduce distortions and ensure a level playing field among and within sectors and firms, favoring the development of new export sectors and SMEs. Bangladesh could deal with para-tariffs in several ways, all of which aim to phase in a more trade-neutral tariff structure: (a) eliminate para-tariffs and put everything in the import tariff to boost transparency; (b) lower para-tariff rates; and (c) ensure that para-tariffs apply to domestic production as well as imports, which would help reduce the distortionary impact of para-tariffs. Successful implementation of the National Board of Revenue's reform agenda will be critical to help the government shift trade policy from a focus on revenue generation to a long-term national competitiveness strategy. The objectives of the reform are to (a) continue to reduce the budget's dependence on the border tax, (b) close tax loopholes and make the fiscal playing field less uneven across sectors and types of actors, and (c) generate the resources needed for the massive infrastructure investment effort that awaits national authorities if growth is to continue at the same pace.

In general, revenue goals are achievable with more trade-neutral border taxation. Simulation indicates that removing tariff exemptions would increase revenues by about 7–9 percent (while reducing imports by around 1 percent) and help compensate for the reduction or removal of others taxes while inducing greater economic efficiency. Another simulation capping tariff peaks at 15 percent (international peak) would induce a loss in tariff revenue of 3–7 percent. Tariff revenues would actually decline by about 20–23 percent, but the induced increase in imports (1.7–3.2 percent) would increase the contribution of other taxes.[16] A third simulation that removes the supplementary duty and adopts a uniform rate of 15 percent for customs duties + regulatory duties would increase tax revenues by 0.9 percent, which illustrates the efficiency and revenue potential of simple and uniform taxation. Removing exemptions would increase fiscal revenues significantly. These simulations do not reflect changes in the production structure and consequent changes in value-added tax (VAT) revenues on domestic production. However, timely implementation of the new VAT law will also help increase revenues and modernize the tax regime.

Bangladesh's quality management system could benefit from a more pragmatic approach. Measures include implementing value chain interventions, ensuring the supply of services for quality, and promoting the smooth flow of imports while respecting legitimate needs for import regulation, such as food safety. Potentially fruitful areas for reform of the existing quality infrastructure in Bangladesh include doing the following: (a) consider opportunities to open fishery testing markets for private sector service providers; (b) review the new Plant Protection Act and develop an implementation plan that provides clarity to importers about the prevailing rules and, at the same time, meets the regulatory needs of Bangladesh; (c) review the list of mandatory standards to determine whether they meet legitimate regulatory objectives and can be effectively enforced; and (d) continue ongoing work by the United Nations Industrial Development Organization (UNIDO) and the Indian government to reform or provide technical assistance to the Bangladesh Standards and Testing Institution (BSTI), with the aim of bringing the BSTI structure into closer alignment with international best practice and avoiding conflicts of interest.

Bangladesh stands to benefit from greater openness in the services sector. Significant benefits would accrue to Bangladesh if it positioned itself as a destination for information technology enabled services–business process outsourcing (ITES-BPO). By encouraging this sector, Bangladesh can provide direct and indirect employment to the increasing number of young people entering the job market.[17] Overall, Bangladesh needs to develop an integrated and strategic approach to build capacity and promote exports in selected services where the country has been or is perceived to have potential. An analysis of the services sectors indicates that most of the benefits would accrue from investment in physical and human capital to address physical capacity limitations and supply-side bottlenecks and provide the required skill sets and competencies to leverage the country's potential in labor-intensive services exports (Kathuria and Malouche 2016b, chapters 7 and 8). As part of this strategy, Bangladesh could also initiate negotiations at the multilateral, regional, and bilateral levels to address market access interests.

Openness brings opportunities, but also vulnerability to global shocks. Therefore, appropriate safety nets should be an important part of the globalization process. Globalization allows countries to benefit from the knowledge and technologies that have been developed anywhere in the world, whether embodied in machinery, intermediates, FDI, or people. At the same time, it increases the need for governments to ensure that citizens are able to benefit from these opportunities: workers must be able to acquire the needed skills; firms need to be able to access credit to finance profitable investment opportunities; and farmers need to be connected to markets (Porto and Hoekman 2010). Greater openness also increases the vulnerability of countries to global shocks, with potentially major adverse consequences for the poorest households that do not have the savings needed to survive a period of unemployment or sharp falls in the prices of their outputs (and thus incomes) resulting from global competition. Therefore, it is important that countries have in place mechanisms to assist those adversely affected by trade shocks. These mechanisms should be targeted toward those households that are most vulnerable and have to manage shocks. Governments should more systematically assess, ex ante, the possible trade-related, poverty-distributional outcomes of policy changes. This will help policy makers better design complementary or transitional policies as well as compensation mechanisms and targeted programs to ensure that firms and workers can benefit from the new opportunities generated by trade openness. Policies and actions to achieve these objectives require actions by labor and finance ministries and are not necessarily part of the mandate of trade ministries.

Improving the Environment for Domestic and Foreign Investment

Investment in Bangladesh has stagnated at a relatively low level in recent years, at around 26–27 percent of gross domestic product (GDP). This reflects feeble growth in private investment and declining public investment, to the extent that national savings could not be fully absorbed domestically. Weak incentives for investment appear to be the more binding constraints. Bangladesh has failed to improve its business environment and investment climate. The repetitive political uncertainty during election times, together with frequent general strikes and associated violence, has added to the longstanding energy and infrastructure deficits in dampening the investment climate. Deficiency of infrastructure has been a binding constraint to domestic investment, of which inadequate supply of power and gas is at the top of the list. In 2012, the demand-supply gap of electricity was around 5,000 gigawatt-hours (Ministry of Finance 2013). Bangladesh ranks nearly last among its Asian competitors (only above Nepal) in the prevalence of power outages. It was also ranked 109th in the Global Competitiveness Index 2014–15 of 144 countries and 173 of 189 countries in the Ease of Doing Business 2015 ranking.

Challenges

Although the energy situation is grim, mitigating measures taken by the government have focused on shorter-term solutions, which raise costs and subsidies and add to fiscal vulnerabilities. The government has added 3,594 megawatts (MW) of capacity in the past four years (Ministry of Finance 2013). However, about 2,400 MW of this increase comes from government contracts with rental and quick-rental plants (for terms of three to five years) that run on expensive (and government-subsidized) liquid fuel. Although this strategy has helped to reduce power shortages during the summer and the irrigation season in the past three years, it has further increased the power sector's dependence on the budget for large subsidy payments to these private generators. Thus, the annual budgetary transfer to the power sector was around US$85 million per year during FY2007 to FY2009, US$140 million in FY2010, US$600 million in FY2011, and US$815 million in FY2012. The increases coincided with the introduction of liquid fuel power plants. The annual budgetary transfer was expected to go down to about US$600 million in FY2013 as a result of the tariff adjustments made in phases since February 2011, but the transfer is not expected to reduce further unless short-term rental contracts are terminated and replaced by low-cost, base-load power plants. A number of large, gas-fired and dual-fuel power plants were awarded to the private sector, including one large coal-fired plant (1,320 MW) based on imported coal, but they have yet to reach financial closure.

Land availability is severely limited, as large, unused tracts are not available. What does exist is either owned by state-owned enterprises or the government or used for agriculture, housing, or roads. Smaller firms are cut off more severely from access to land and that access has worsened over time. In 2002, 29.2 percent of firms considered access to land to be a major problem; by 2007, it had risen to 41.7 percent. Unavailability of serviced land is a prominent investment hurdle

(World Bank 2012b). The property registration process is inordinately slow. According to the World Bank's Doing Business Report 2015, Bangladesh ranks 184 of 189 economies, with property registration typically taking 244 days, compared with 47 days in India, 25 days in Indonesia, 57 days in Vietnam, and only 2 days in Thailand. Overall, Bangladesh is not moving fast enough to ease its business regime.

In this unfriendly business environment, FDI has persistently represented a small fraction of GDP and private investment. Bangladesh's FDI inflows reached around US$1.6 billion in 2013, but overall FDI stocks remain below 6 percent of GDP. Average FDI stock as a percentage of GDP was 25.8 percent in LDCs as a whole. It was also higher in comparator countries, such as Vietnam (47.8 percent of GDP) and Pakistan (12.2 percent of GDP, despite difficult conditions there), and it was more than 11 percent in South Asia as a whole and almost 35 percent in Sub-Saharan Africa (figure 3.8).

FDI in Bangladesh has mostly flowed into the services sector. The telecommunications industries and banking sector have attracted the most FDI, followed by the garment, gas, and petroleum sectors. Bangladesh has attracted three totally

Figure 3.8 Foreign Direct Investment Stock as a Share of GDP in Bangladesh and Selected Developing Countries, 2013

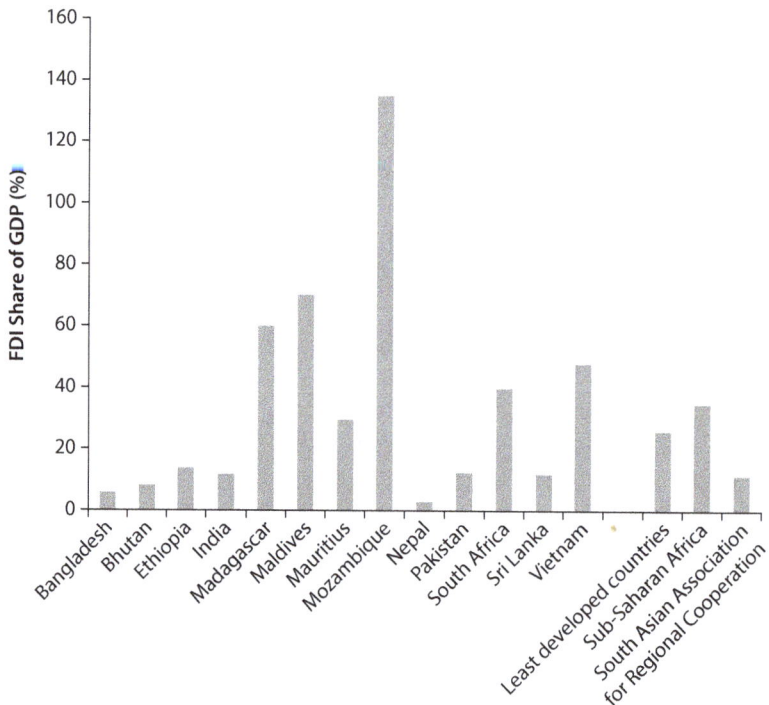

Source: http://unctadstat.unctad.org/ReportFolders/reportFolders.aspx.
Note: GDP = gross domestic product.

foreign-owned mobile telephone providers, as well as a majority-foreign investor in the firm with the largest market share. The banking sector also includes a number of globally renowned banks. The textile and clothing industry has received less FDI, partially because of the obstacles in this sector (UNCTAD 2013). Moreover, Bangladesh has attracted investment from a diverse set of countries. The Arab Republic of Egypt was the largest foreign investor during 2005–11, with investment concentrated in telecommunications. The next largest foreign investors are the United Kingdom, the United States, and Singapore. An important share of FDI in Bangladesh takes place in EPZs. EPZs are export-oriented industrial enclaves that provide the infrastructure, facilities, and administrative and support services for a wide variety of enterprises. Bangladesh's successful EPZs in Dhaka and Chittagong are now complemented by new EPZ developments around the country. As of December 2014, about 405,166 jobs were created in EPZs, mostly the ones in Chittagong and Dhaka, although these cannot be attributed to foreign firms alone, since some domestic firms also locate in EPZs.

To reach East Asian growth rates of 7–8 percent, private investment levels in Bangladesh need to rise to at least 33 percent of GDP (see World Bank 2012b). FDI could help to augment the quality and quantity of investment. Foreign-owned firms are a source of innovation spillovers and perform significantly better than domestic firms in labor productivity and profit margins. They can also help to increase the overall amount of private investment by accessing their own savings as well as international financial markets, thereby easing at least a part of Bangladesh's financial sector limitations.

An unfavorable business environment deprives Bangladesh of the full benefits of FDI as a source for export growth and diversification, technology transfer, and quality upgrading Capacity constraints make access to scarce energy and infrastructure resources a zero-sum game, with the consequence that local incumbents sometimes view FDI (and new entry in general) as game spoilers rather than as sources of technology transfers and overall dynamism. The result is a general lack of competition, diversification, and growth opportunities for smaller firms, as entrenched incumbent positions make entry difficult for local and foreign entrants. Finally, although foreigners can work with corruption, it raises costs and uncertainty.

Although the FDI regime does not seem to be overly restrictive, in practice the regime could be considered unfriendly for foreign investors, in part because of its asymmetric impact on foreign firms. Moreover, the government does not appear to be particularly pursuing an aggressive policy to attract FDI in any sector, to properly value the benefits of FDI for technology transfer, quality upgrading, product and market diversification, integration into regional and global supply chains, or employment generation (the ultimate objective of the government). Thus, opposition to FDI by strong domestic firms, a strong business presence in Parliament, lax enforcement of product standards, and uneven governance standards, in particular, affect foreign firms' incentives to invest. In addition, lack of a proactive FDI promotion campaign, owing to a rather weak BOI with multiple mandates, is another major factor. The asymmetry faced by foreign firms vis-à-vis local firms in Bangladesh is a more serious issue than might appear at first sight. There is a kind of "regulatory arbitrage" that local firms enjoy and it is an obstacle to attracting sustained, quality FDI.

Bangladesh has the potential to attract significantly higher levels of FDI in spite of the challenges it faces, but it has much work to do to turn that potential into reality. It can position itself as a competitive center for labor-intensive manufacturing and attract efficiency-seeking FDI. The country's attractions include an abundant labor supply; a mastery of large-scale, labor-intensive manufacturing in garments and to some extent footwear; a favorable location between two large and dynamic economies, China and India; as well as wide understanding of the English language. Preferential access to key consumer markets in developed countries makes it an attractive platform for export-seeking FDI. Its entrepreneurial private sector is another important asset that could be exploited further with a business-enabling regulatory framework in place. In addition, if Bangladesh is able to stay on its current growth path, its market size could increase quickly and attract a wave of market-seeking FDI. However, to make good of this potential, it would have to address some critical constraints to FDI, including the availability of serviced land and the asymmetry between local and foreign firms, and also adopt a more welcoming and more proactive stance toward FDI.

Sector studies conducted for the DTIS point to the important role FDI can play in export diversification and technology transfer in Bangladesh. Korea has led investment in the garment industry. FDI was critical in the emergence of bicycle exports. Malaysian investors seized an opportunity in the EU market by establishing the first bicycle exporting firm in Bangladesh in 1995. They invested US$2 million in a new plant named Alita in Chittagong. FDI in the shipbuilding sector is close to zero for the moment; however, FDI and joint ventures could help gradually improve Bangladesh's capacity and reputation in shipbuilding. FDI could especially help the linkage of industries through technological advancement and improvement of processes and worker skills. Chinese and Korean investors in particular seek to capture some of the growth in Bangladesh's textiles and services sectors.

Encouraging FDI to Support Jobs, Growth, and Diversification

One of Bangladesh's greatest development challenges is to provide gainful employment to the 21 million new entrants to the job market over the next decade. Both domestic investment and FDI will benefit from unlocking infrastructure constraints, in particular, energy and trade facilitation and access to land. Improvement in the business environment will facilitate investment by reducing the cost of transactions and risk taking, leading to a more dynamic private sector. Properly used, FDI could complement domestic investment and become increasingly important in addressing this challenge, not only to provide more jobs, but also higher quality jobs with regard to pay and benefits, as well as safety and other working conditions.

On energy, it would be critical for Bangladesh to implement sustainable solutions that are able to provide unsubsidized power at competitive prices. This will help all segments of the economy and provide a major boost to investment. Critical actions involve both the public and private sectors, including increasing generation capacity in low-cost, base-load power plants; commissioning of the large gas-fired and dual-fuel combined-cycle power plants awarded to the private sector; converting the Bangladesh Power Development Board's simple-cycle plants to combined-cycle plants; and accelerating moves to import power from Bhutan, Myanmar, Nepal, and India's northeastern states. Measures taken by the government to address this constraint have focused on shorter-term solutions, which raise costs and subsidies and add to fiscal vulnerabilities.

The dispersed administration of public land makes it difficult for Bangladesh to manage its holdings adequately and identify land for industrial zones. Although it is vital for local authorities to be involved in land management, a higher degree of coordination should be achieved at the national level to allocate public land to its most productive and essential use. This could be achieved through a coordination institution or body and the establishment of a public land database that would list all plots available for development by location, size, facilities, and other attributes (UNCTAD 2013). The government could also proactively initiate action to expand existing EPZs and operationalize private zones.

There is a strong need for a major effort to change the perception of Bangladesh through some institutional and regulatory changes. Entry conditions are subject to general regulations as well as sector regulations, which lead to discretionary administrative procedures. BOI plays a rather minimal role in the overall FDI process. A more transparent law on investment should be adopted by Parliament.

Finally, Bangladesh should adopt a more proactive and welcoming stance toward potential foreign investors, with BOI playing a key role to overcome Bangladesh's rather ambiguous attitude toward FDI. Foreign investors should get more administrative support early on when desiring to invest in Bangladesh, thereby reducing the hurdles and uncertainty they may face in a new environment. BOI should arrange more high-level investment promotion missions to large emerging economies, especially in Asia, including to China, India, and Japan. These missions should be preceded by preparatory missions to identify short-term FDI opportunities and requirements.[18] The cost of not seeking out investors may be high, as other competing countries, such as Cambodia and Vietnam, are aggressively pursuing Chinese and other Asian FDI. Bangladesh should also reduce discretion in decision making and more strictly enforce standards so that foreign firms that enforce strict compliance and standards are not penalized. With the persistent global crisis and slow growth, foreign capital will become choosier. This means that attracting FDI will become even more difficult. The domestic private sector, with vested interests, would unlikely support this agenda. Reforms would likely have political costs, since they may affect powerful business groups even if they benefit society. The agenda is daunting and addressing it will require a vision of growth and development that recognizes the major role that FDI can play.

Pillar 3: Improving Worker and Consumer Welfare

Improving Skills and Literacy

As much as 50.7 percent of the labor force has less than secondary education and about one-third has less than primary education. This is the situation despite educational access having increased significantly over the past decade, particularly at the lower levels of education and especially for women. According to the World Bank (2013), just a third of the primary graduates acquire the numeracy and literacy skills they are expected to master by the time they graduate. Moreover, only 0.17 percent of the labor force has a professional degree, such as in engineering or medicine. A World Bank survey of 1,000 garment firms in 2011 found that lack of skills was the major disadvantage for firms located outside Dhaka. High rejection rates in a 2010 UNIDO survey also point to the low average skills of garment workers. In sectors such as ITES, shipbuilding, and pharmaceuticals, part of this DTIS, higher skills are in constant demand (World Bank 2012a, 2012b).

Bangladesh's performance on literacy rates and secondary school enrollment is extremely poor and undermines the development of all sectors (table 3.2). Basic tasks conducted in all sectors, from garments to ITES (see chapter 4), typically need a labor force that comes out of secondary schools and colleges and can then be trained. In this respect, Bangladesh has one of the poorest records among its comparators. The low level of literacy and years of schooling of the labor force make skills acquisition more difficult. In contrast, Sri Lanka has provided a skills environment that allows garment firms to move up the value chain quickly. Bangladeshi firms' choice is mostly restricted to primary school graduates and high school dropouts.

Improving skills and literacy will allow current products, such as garments, to become more competitive, enable a move to higher-quality products, and allow productivity and wage increases. Over the longer term, improvements in product quality may enable Bangladesh to eventually target higher-value

Table 3.2 Benchmarking Literacy and Enrollment Rates, Bangladesh and Comparator Countries, 2011

Percent

Country	Secondary school enrollment	Adult literacy
Sri Lanka	90	91
Philippines	82	95
Egypt, Arab Rep.	81	66
China	76	93
Malaysia	70	92
Vietnam	70	93
India	59	62
Bangladesh	44	56
Pakistan	33	55

Source: Data compiled by Global Development Solutions, LLC, from UNESCO/A.T. Kearney.

apparel segments that require more complex production processes. This agenda will require articulating a comprehensive vision for skills development; reskilling the current labor force through greater access to nonformal training and skill building; and improving the quality of foundational education. Skill building should not be limited to line workers, but should also involve management to develop the talent needed to run effective and efficient international manufacturing enterprises. Realization of this goal is complex and involves many stakeholders, including firms, institutions, and government.

Implementing Labor and Work Safety Guidelines

Minimizing the chances of further tragedies in the garment and other export sectors in Bangladesh has become a precondition for sustained export growth. Workplace safety standards and their implementation, in particular in the garment sector, have become very important in light of the many fatal accidents and deaths among workers. The physical layout of the factory and management practices can contribute to production inefficiencies and hazardous conditions. Ignoring worker safety concerns could result in major damage to Bangladesh's reputation among international apparel firms. Urgent action to address worker safety as well as welfare issues is required so that future tragedies are averted.

A coalition of stakeholders needs to work together to ensure that implementation of promised actions is undertaken. Implementation of standards requires formation of and coordination with worker groups, support of government, and collaboration with the private sector and factory owners. To the extent capital improvements are required, increased access to financing may be needed as well. Many buyers and customers have expressed interest in and pledged funds for enhancing production safety and the sector should leverage this support. Recent decisions taken by EU and U.S. buyers and the amendment of the Labor Act are steps toward this important objective. The International Labour Organization is coordinating some of these efforts. Bangladesh was included in the Better Work Program in October 2013. Seriousness of intent on the part of the government will play a critical role in Bangladesh's trade relations with the European Union and the United States, the major players in post-Rana Plaza events (see CPD 2013) for an update on post-Rana Plaza commitments and the implementation status of these).

Making Safety Nets More Effective in Dealing with Trade Shocks

Making the gains from globalization more inclusive and beneficial to poor households is critical for poverty reduction. The adjustment processes associated with increased global integration contribute to skill- and gender-differentiated inequalities in labor market opportunities and outcomes. Similarly, the benefits from trade are often concentrated in the largest metropolitan areas, further exacerbating interregional inequalities. Promoting internal trade, as well as exports, therefore also matters; it is important to help connect lagging and more remote regions to high-growth areas within countries as well as between them (as discussed in Kathuria and Malouche 2016a, chapter 6, on trade facilitation).

The main priorities in this area should include (a) assisting the most vulnerable to manage trade shocks, (b) doing more to address any gender-differentiated impacts of policy changes, and (c) extending the benefits of trade to lagging regions within countries by ensuring that poor people in these areas can better connect to places where agglomeration occurs.

It is important that countries have in place mechanisms to assist those adversely affected by trade shocks. These mechanisms should be targeted toward those households that are most vulnerable and have to manage shocks. Governments should more systematically assess, ex ante, possible trade-related, poverty-distributional outcomes of policy changes. This will help policy makers better design complementary or transitional policies as well as compensation mechanisms and targeted programs to ensure that firms and workers can benefit from the new opportunities generated by trade openness. Policies and actions to achieve these objectives require actions by labor and finance ministries and are not part of the mandate of trade ministries.

Starting preparation of a safety net and labor strategy that recognizes possible winners and losers in trade liberalization could help reduce opposition to a neutral trade policy. Apart from cash transfers, a key part of this strategy should prioritize finding mechanisms that link poor safety net beneficiaries to more productive employment opportunities with a particular focus on youth. The swelling youth cohorts from the demographic transition offer opportunities and challenges. Investment in appropriate skills development to meet global and domestic demand has the potential to harness substantial gains from globalization, and training and retraining workers will help to ensure their resilience to trade shocks.

Pillar 4: Building a Supportive Environment

Although the DTIS recognizes the importance of sustaining sound macroeconomic fundamentals, this issue has been addressed in several World Bank and IMF reports and is the focus of the ongoing IMF program. However, for the sake of completeness, the macroeconomic issues are summarized below. For in-depth analysis of Pillar 4, the DTIS focuses on the institutional capacity of the Government of Bangladesh to lead and implement successfully an agenda centered on trade competiveness, in line with its 6FYP.

Sustaining Sound Macroeconomic Fundamentals

Despite its stable macroeconomic situation, Bangladesh's near and medium-term outlook is subject to several vulnerabilities—the most important being the prolongation of political instability. No clear end to the instability is in sight. The "on again, off again" political instability and violence has significant economic impacts both in the short and medium term. Without a political settlement acceptable to all significant stakeholders, Bangladesh is likely to pass through phases of instability punctuated by street violence of the kind experienced in the second half of 2013 as well as the first half of 2015.

Unabated political instability is not the only challenge facing Bangladesh in the near and medium term. A protracted slowdown in the European Union could hurt exports, compounding the challenges arising from real exchange rate appreciation of the taka (with the U.S. dollar strengthening against the euro), undermining export competitiveness in Bangladesh's main export markets in Europe. Garment exports are particularly vulnerable. This will be amplified if preferential access to the European Union is withdrawn or truncated for lack of progress in upgrading labor and factory safety standards in the garment industry. There are also concerns about financial weaknesses in state-owned banks and some private banks. These have potential fiscal and financial stability implications. On the flip side, although international financial linkages are growing, Bangladesh's vulnerability to global financial volatility is still small.

Assuming sustained political stability, Bangladesh's strong domestic demand base, gradually improving investment climate, and continued macroeconomic stability are expected to raise GDP growth. Implementing the ongoing IMF program will help anchor the macroeconomic framework.

Building Institutions for Trade Policy Coherence and Implementation

The success of the proposed government export-led development strategy as depicted in the 6FYP would depend on the institutional capacity to lead this agenda. Implementing this policy agenda will require a dedicated, high-level team, strong coordination across various government departments and agencies, and a clear understanding of the objective of promoting trade competitiveness in global markets and in the domestic market. However, trade policy is carried out through a number of institutions in a piecemeal fashion, undermining the effectiveness of the reform agenda. This fragmentation is exacerbated by the absence of a national trade strategy that could otherwise provide an overarching mandate in the formulation of each institution's individual policies. Continuous consultation and consensus building among ministries and agencies involved in trade policy making and negotiations is essential for effectively responding to the opportunities and challenges presented in the international trading environment, and a broad-based consultative process is a prerequisite for good economic governance.

Challenges

The implementation of reforms may be jeopardized by rather weak institutional capacity. The economic growth reform agenda spans several ministries and authorities and would require strong leadership at the very top to succeed. Despite a credible willingness and commitment to the reform agenda, such leadership seems to be missing and rather diluted in several layers of public-private committees and initiatives led by different stakeholders. The trade policy agenda is scattered among a number of authorities and institutions, not necessarily in a coordinated way or with adequate capacity. The reform agenda is further weakened by strong rivalry between the two main political parties. Elections normally bring about political conflict and instability.

In addition, the absence of a formal system for dialogue between the public and private sectors has been felt widely. Another characteristic of Bangladesh's policy space is the role and weight of the private sector. From one side, the private business sector seems powerful and heavily involved in policy making, with influential industry chambers and high representativeness in Parliament. However, on the other side, the private sector also appears as a recipient of policies and information, rather than an equal partner. In fact, the system is characterized by the strong role of certain industry chambers, influencing policy formulation on an ad hoc basis, depending on ruling political parties and connections. However, no system is in place to guarantee a transparent public-private consultation process, with the objective to defend all players in the industry, large and small, urban and rural.

For example, the formulation of selected NTMs is based on a broad consultative process but lacks transparency and analytical rigor. The Ministry of Commerce (MOC) routinely formulates an Import Policy Order to regulate imports by laying out the criteria and conditions under which import controls, bans, permits, licenses and conditions of renewal, standards, and pre-shipment inspection are implemented. MOC scrutiny is basically compliance with the WTO in addition to chairing the Consultative Committee. Coordination in the formulation of import policy is complicated by a lack of transparency; the weak capacity of MOC and key agencies, such as BSTI (under the Ministry of Industries); and lack of analytical rigor in assessing the implications of proposed measures. Moreover, although a range of private sector stakeholders are consulted, the process is, for the most part, captured by the large trade associations, BGMEA and BKMEA, and the Chambers of Commerce and Industry. Other important nongovernmental stakeholders (for example, representatives of consumer interests) are missing from the process. The entire process of formulation of import policy is said to be time-bound, to take almost a year from receiving proposals until the policy reaches the cabinet subcommittee.

Improving Policy Formulation and Coordination to Support Competitiveness

A more cohesive trade policy framework is needed to ensure strategic, consistent, and neutral policies that affect trade and the incentive to export. A more cohesive trade policy framework would recognize that trade policies encompass a much broader agenda, including the direct and indirect ways in which trade and trade-related policies affect welfare. The starting point for creating a more cohesive policy-making process is to reach a consensus on a national vision and strategic direction of trade policy reform that is aligned with Bangladesh's broader economic development objectives as laid out in Vision 2021 and the 6FYP. The objective of such an agenda is to create a unified framework for the development of trade-related policies that balances the interests of all key stakeholders (including the often-forgotten consumer), is linked with Bangladesh's international commitments and helps guide future positions on international negotiations, and has a clear monitoring and implementation plan that clarifies roles and responsibilities. Trade policy formulation is not a one-off event but an iterative process that requires effective interagency coordination and stakeholder consultation and is backed by data and analysis throughout the policy-making lifecycle.

Coordination among the numerous public sector actors and stakeholders engaged in the trade policy lifecycle is critical to ensure that the benefits of Bangladesh's participation in global trade are realized. Effective coordination mechanisms that can adapt to ever-evolving demands from the global trading environment—such as the ongoing fiscal and financial crisis in and rebalancing after the crisis and the expected shifts of global growth toward a more multipolar world—require regular reassessment of the scope and priorities of Bangladesh's trade policies. It is recommended that all trade policies, including tariffs, import taxes, and standards, be vetted through a uniform, standardized process. Moreover, without broader policy consultation with economic and social partners, interagency coordination alone cannot achieve national consensus on trade policy objectives. Interagency coordination and stakeholder consultation processes are complementary and need to be conducted systematically across all stages of the policy-making process.

The new Business Initiative Leading Development (BUILD) will help address the effective contribution of the private sector in policy formulation. This is a joint initiative of the International Finance Corporation–managed and Department for International Development and European Union–funded Bangladesh Investment Climate Fund, Dhaka Chamber of Commerce and Industry, Metropolitan Chamber of Commerce and Industry, and SME Foundation. It has been designed as a sustainable platform for action-oriented business reforms that simplify the process of doing business in Bangladesh, by working closely with the government. BUILD will feature public-private dialogue on four thematic areas—Tax, SMEs, Financial Sector, and Trade and Investment—backed by rigorous analysis and advocacy. The initiative has received commitments from the Bangladesh Bank, National Board of Revenue, and Ministries of Commerce and Industries to co-chair these working committees. BUILD will be supported by a strong, independent secretariat that will undertake much of the analysis and advocacy to support the dialogue process and assist in ensuring that BUILD develops specific, measurable, and results-based recommendations for the government to implement.

Through different working groups co-chaired by a representative from the public sector and one from the private sector, BUILD will focus on issues facing SMEs. It will aim to help create at least two million jobs and generate at least 40,000 new SMEs. However, BUILD's largest impact when this permanent change is made will be in the way the government and the private sector work together to achieve the nation's development goals and ensure a brighter future for Bangladesh.

Strong analytical and research capabilities should underpin the policy formulation process. Coordination and consultation can only be effective if they are built on a sound foundation of economic research and analysis to understand the potential ex ante economic impacts of alternative trade policy reforms and the ex post impacts on the economy. Currently, the knowledge pool and expertise capable of comprehending the demands of the emerging trade agenda are sparse and difficult to attract to the public sector because of the level of compensation and the poor image of public institutes. Eminent economists with competence in Bangladesh are attached to academic institutes, international organizations, or leading think tanks, such as the Centre for Policy Dialogue (CPD), the Policy Research Institute, or the Bangladesh Institute of Development Studies (BIDS). They have often obliged the government with research and advocacy, through the statutory role of BIDS under the Ministry of Planning, CPD's role in the European Union–funded work to develop a comprehensive trade policy, or the various Consultative Committees.

It would be beneficial to mobilize key economists from Bangladesh's existing think tanks and policy institutes more formally to support policy making throughout the lifecycle. They would help bring to bear the analytical and research capacity of these institutes to support policy making; undertake ex ante studies of options, for example, for trade negotiations and regulatory impact assessments (for licensing and standards); and conduct ex post measurement of impacts of trade policy reforms. There is also a need to strengthen the capacity of the lead trade policy institution, the Ministry of Commerce.

The effectiveness of Bangladesh's EPB could be improved by augmenting its in-house expertise and encouraging greater private sector participation. As part of the World Bank's global survey of Economic Partnership Agreements (EPAs), EPB has been compared with other EPAs in several dimensions. EPB has a broad mandate with limited resources, as well as much more narrowly defined strategic objectives than typical EPAs. For EPB's in-house capacity, development partners should consider providing long-term resident experts to augment EPB's skills and capacity development. These experts can be given focused objectives, such as helping exporters to diversify into specific, targeted markets, such as China, India, and Japan. Moreover, image-building and policy advocacy are strong functions of many EPAs worldwide, but not in Bangladesh. Less than 10 percent of EPB's budget is allocated to technical assistance and country image-building. EPB could help to prop up Bangladesh's brand image and position the country to exploit production-sharing opportunities. Finally, EPB could improve its effectiveness by giving the private sector more representation on its board.

BSTI's structure should also be brought into closer alignment with international best practice to avoid conflicts of interest. It is international best practice to separate regulatory powers (such as setting mandatory standards) and conformity assessment (such as testing, inspection, and certification). In contrast, BSTI strongly influences the adoption and formulation of mandatory standards while simultaneously benefiting from the incomes from testing, inspection, and certification against these mandatory standards. In Organisation for Economic Co-operation and Development countries, it is highly unusual to give the National Standards Bureau regulatory functions. In addition, BSTI does not provide information services or undertake any promotional activities on standards for trade and industry. Awareness of the utility and benefits of standards is low,

Figure 3.9 Toward a New Institutional Framework

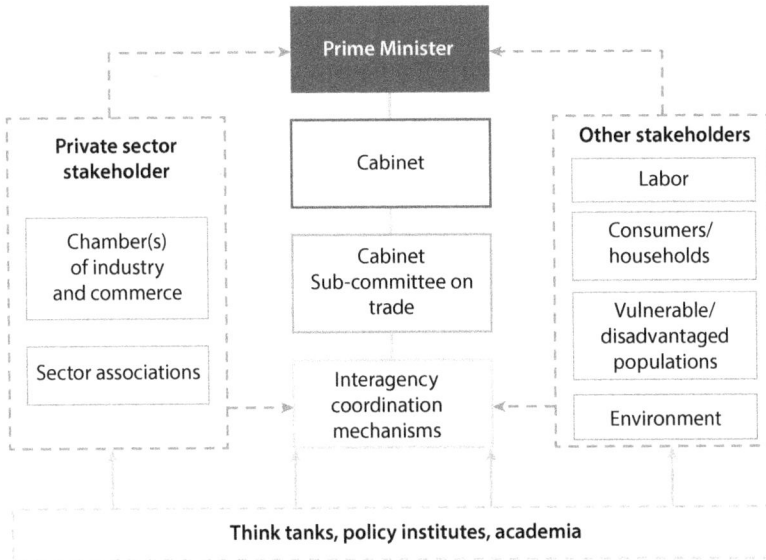

Sources: Kathuria and Malouche 2016a, chapter 4.

with many officials equating standards with technical regulation. BSTI has developed some capacity to participate in international standards through the Bangladesh Quality Support Programme, but participation mostly remains on an observation basis for limited sectors (Sud 2010).

Although there is no one-size-fits-all approach to organizing trade institutions, international experience provides a number of good practices. These could be incorporated into Bangladesh's existing framework to improve the quality of trade policy making, through a systematic approach to make interagency coordination more effective, increase the transparency and scope of stakeholder consultation, and strengthen the quality of research and analysis required to support the policy-making process. Figure 3.9 provides an illustrative approach to organizing Bangladesh's trade-related institutions and stakeholders to initiate, formulate, implement, and monitor trade policy reforms.

Notes

1. Customs allows only 17 types of goods to be cleared in off-dock yards in the Chittagong area (Kathuria and Malouche 2016a, annex 6A). These are mostly bulk commodities that are not containerized.

2. Nationally, road transport is the most important mode of transport, moving more than 80 percent of traffic. Inland waterways handle 16 percent and rail handles 4 percent. The share of traffic moved by road transport has been growing while that by the other modes has been in decline.

3. Dhaka ICD has a storage capacity for only 1,000 TEU at any one time. It was established in 1987 under the joint ownership of Bangladesh Railway and Chittagong

Port Authority. Container handling operations are under the control of Chittagong Port Authority. Since August 1991, dedicated container block trains have operated between Dhaka and Chittagong.

4. About 90 percent of train kilometers are passenger services, nearly all of which are customers traveling second class.

5. See http://www.asycuda.org/.

6. Review of pre-shipment inspection in Bangladesh, Manzur Ahmed, http://www .thefinancialexpress-bd.com/more.php?news_id=17515.

7. The World Customs Organization Safety Advancement for Employees (SAFE) Framework of Standards defines a SAFE AEO as an entity complying with the World Customs Organization or equivalent supply chain security standards and with legal obligations in relation to tariff and nontariff requirements on the import, export, and transit of goods.

8. The Generalized System of Preferences is a trade arrangement that gives preferential tariff treatment (reduced or zero) to imports from developing countries.

9. The trade complementarity index can provide useful information on prospects for intraregional trade. It shows how well the structures of a country's imports and exports match. Furthermore, countries considering the formation of a regional trade agreement can examine the index values of others that have formed or tried to form similar arrangements. The trade complementarity index between countries k and j is defined as: $TC_{ij} = 100 - \text{sum}(|m_{ik} - X_{ij}|/2)$, where x_{ij} is the share of good i in global exports of country j and m_{ik} is the share of good i in all imports of country k. The index is zero when no goods are exported by one country or imported by the other and 100 when the export and import shares exactly match.

10. To capture the improvement in connectivity, a 25 percent drop in the bilateral trade-cost margin between Bangladesh and India is simulated.

11. Border taxation is different from protection, since value-added tax is levied on domestic and import transactions. The data illustrate the size of the tax relative to that of the transaction, rather than the degree of discrimination between imports and domestic production.

12. The ERP is the proportional increase in local firms' value added (or processing margin) resulting from the combined influence of tariff rates on the final good and on intermediate inputs (a pure price effect—a higher ERP does not mean that the protected good has intrinsically higher value added). An escalating tariff structure (higher rates on final goods than on intermediates) raises local value-added and protection levels compared with what would prevail under a zero or uniform tariff structure.

13. This number is a rough approximation and should be taken as indicative. It is obtained by replacing the current total of tariff and para-tariff charges by a flat 10 percent combined border tax in each household's basket and calculating the reduction in expenditure needed to buy the same basket given the new tax rates. Data on household size and sampling weights are then used to extrapolate this reduction (an increase in real income) to the population. The last step consists of calculating the poverty headcount (the number of individuals below the national poverty line) before and after the simulation. Note also that this is a partial equilibrium analysis.

14. NTMs can raise trade costs, divert managerial attention, and penalize small exporters and those located in low-income countries, where access to legal and regulatory information is difficult.

15. The World Bank Services Trade Restrictions Database contains information on policies that affect international trade in services—defined to include the supply of a service through cross-border delivery, establishment of a commercial presence, or the presence of a natural person. The database collects—and makes publicly available—comparable applied services trade policy information across a large range of countries, sectors, and modes of delivery. To date, surveys for 79 developing countries have been collected and comparable information has been obtained for 24 Organisation for Economic Co-operation and Development countries. The five major services sectors covered in the database, namely financial services (banking and insurance), telecommunications, retail distribution, transportation, and professional services, are further disaggregated into subsectors. The choice of sectors was based primarily on the World Bank's assessment of their economic importance from a development perspective, the existence of meaningful restrictions on services trade, and the feasibility of collecting relevant policy data.

16. For technical reasons, taxes had to be combined because of the large number of duties and taxes in Bangladesh. The simulation removes exemptions for the customs duty + regulatory duty but not for other duties and taxes. The 15 percent cap is for the combination of customs duty and regulatory duty (considered as one single duty).

17. According to some estimates, every job created in the ITES-BPO sector creates three to four jobs in supporting sectors.

18. These missions are supported by the Private Sector Development Support Project, financed by the World Bank (UNCTAD 2013).

References

Arnold, J. 2010. "Bangladesh Logistics and Trade Facilitation." Working paper 47781, World Bank, Washington, DC.

CPD (Centre for Policy Dialogue). 2013. "Independent Monitoring Report on 100 Days of Rana Plaza Tragedy: A Report on Commitments and Delivery." Centre for Policy Dialogue, Dhaka.

De, P., S. Raihan, and S. Kathuria. 2012. "Unlocking Bangladesh-India Trade: Emerging Potential and the Way Forward." Policy Research Working Paper 6155, World Bank, Washington, DC.

Francois, Joseph F., Ganeshan Wignaraja, and Pradumna Bickram Rana, eds. 2009. *Pan-Asian Integration: Linking East and South Asia*. Basingstoke, UK: Palgrave Macmillan.

Hoekman, B., and A. Nicita. 2011. "Trade Policy, Trade Costs, and Developing Country Trade." *World Development* 39 (12): 2069–79.

Inklaar, Robert, Marcel P. Timmer, and Bart van Ark. 2008. "Data for Productivity Measurement in Market Services: An International Comparison." *International Productivity Monitor, Centre for the Study of Living Standards* 16: 72–81.

Kathuria, Sanjay, and Mariem Mezghenni Malouche, eds. 2016a. *Strengthening Competitiveness in Bangladesh—Thematic Assessment: A Diagnostic Trade Integration Study*. Washington, DC: World Bank.

———. 2016b. *Strengthening Competitiveness in Bangladesh—Sector Analyses: A Diagnostic Trade Integration Study*. Washington, DC: World Bank.

Kunaka, C. 2010. *Logistics in Lagging Regions—Overcoming Local Barriers to Global Connectivity*. Washington, DC: World Bank.

Mahmud, Tanvir, and Juliet Rossette. 2007. "Problems and Prospects of Chittagong Port: A Follow Up Diagnostic Study." Report, Transparency International Bangladesh, Dhaka.

Ministry of Commerce. 2012. *Import Policy Order 2012–2015*. Dhaka: Government of Bangladesh.

Ministry of Finance. 2013. *Power and Energy Sector Roadmap*. Dhaka: Government of Bangladesh.

Porto, G., and B. M. Hoekman. 2010. *Trade Adjustment Costs in Developing Countries: Impacts, Determinants and Policy Response*. Washington, DC: World Bank.

Sud, Raj. 2010. "Better Work and Standards Programme (BEST)—Better Quality Infrastructure (BQI) Component—Baseline Report." United Nations Industrial Development Organization (UNIDO), Vienna.

Tarr, David G. 2012. "The Impact of Services Liberalization on Industry Productivity, Exports and Development—Six Empirical Studies in the Transition Countries." World Bank Policy Research Working Paper 6023, World Bank, Washington, DC.

Triplett, Jack E., and Barry P. Bosworth. 2004. "Productivity in the U.S. Services Sector." Brookings Institution, Washington, DC.

UNCTAD (United Nations Conference on Trade and Development). 2013. *UNCTAD 2013 Bangladesh Investment Policy Review*. Paris: UNCTAD.

Uzzaman, A., and M. Abu Yusuf. 2011. "The Role of Customs and Other Agencies in Trade Facilitation in Bangladesh: Hindrances and Ways Forward." *World Customs Journal* 5 (1): 29–42.

Van der Marel, E. 2011. "Trade in Services and TFP: The Role of Regulation." Working paper, Groupe d'Economie Mondiale (GEM), Paris.

Wilson, J. S., C. L. Mann, and T. Otsuki. 2003. "Trade Facilitation and Economic Development: Measuring the Impact." Policy Research Working Paper 2988, World Bank, Washington, DC.

World Bank. 2012a. "Consolidating and Accelerating Exports in Bangladesh: A Policy Agenda." Bangladesh Development Series Paper 29, Poverty Reduction and Economic Management Sector, South Asia Region, World Bank, Washington, DC.

———. 2012b. *Bangladesh: Towards Accelerated, Inclusive and Sustainable Growth—Opportunities and Challenges*. Vol. 2 Report 67991, Poverty Reduction and Economic Management Unit, South Asia Region. Washington, DC: World Bank.

———. 2012c. *Connecting to Compete: Trade Logistics in the Global Economy*. Washington, DC: World Bank.

———. 2013. "Bangladesh Poverty Assessment—Assessing a Decade of Progress in Reducing Poverty 2000–2010." Bangladesh Development Series Paper 31, World Bank Office, Dhaka.

———. 2014. *Logistics Performance Index*. http://lpi.worldbank.org/international/global/2014.

CHAPTER 4

Illustrating the Thematic Analysis: Export Constraints and Potential in Selected Sectors

The objective of this part of the Diagnostic Trade Integration Study (DTIS) is to assess the performance of selected manufacturing value chains in Bangladesh, with a view to illustrate the thematic analysis and ground it in sector experiences. It is not intended to be an exhaustive analysis of all potential export sectors. The chapter discusses the export potential of seven products: shipbuilding, jute and jute-based products, non-leather footwear, polo shirts (garments), bicycles as a light engineering product, information technology enabled services (ITES), and pharmaceuticals. The sectors were carefully chosen, in consultation with academia, the government, and other stakeholders, to include light manufacturing, engineering, and services. The study also sought to bring in diverse issues relating to employment intensity and sectors that use both skilled and unskilled labor, the potential for export growth and for diversifying into higher-value products, and the intensity of local inputs and land in the production process. This diversity was expected to be useful in finding common themes and constraints to exports across sectors, as well as policy options. Detailed sector studies can be found in Kathuria and Malouche (2016b).

The discussion begins with some common themes that emerged across the sector analyses. This is then followed by summaries of the current challenges and policy options in each sector. Whenever relevant and possible, competitiveness bottlenecks and key performance indicators in Bangladesh were benchmarked against leading exporters in China and Vietnam.

Some Common Themes across Sectors

Bangladesh's industrial competitiveness is concentrated in a limited number of sectors with the key being the US$24.5 billion textiles and apparel export manufacturing sector. Most manufacturing sectors other than garments, by and large, have not been able to create jobs and generate export revenues of any significant scale.

In Bangladesh, lack of export diversification arises in large measure from distortions related to variations in export facilities across sectors, including special bonded warehouses (SBWs) and cash incentives. SBWs have been mostly provided to ready-made garments (RMGs) and footwear, although they are supposedly open to all exporting sectors. The facility has been selectively offered to other sectors after much red tape, as the authorities believe it is prone to abuse if given generously; hence, SBWs have not become very popular. Based on a firm survey to measure effective rates of protection (ERPs), 31 of 89 exporting firms used SBWs, of which 14 were RMG accessory suppliers (deemed exporters), 11 footwear exporters, one leather products exporter, two jute textiles exporters, two bicycle exporters, and one pharmaceuticals exporter. The cash incentive scheme, originally intended to offset input tariffs, has benefited jute textile exporters significantly, although their imports (less than 5 percent of output) are subject to low raw material duties. Until the end of fiscal year 2012 (FY2012), 19 export sectors were eligible to receive cash incentives (table 4.1). In FY2014, however, the number of export-oriented sectors eligible for incentives was reduced to 14 sectors. The sectors removed from the stimulus package included bicycles, poultry, finished leather, and crust leather. One of the primary reasons for removing bicycle exports was that the sector already enjoys duty-free access to its main market in the European Union.[1] Light engineering products other than bicycles, however, would continue to be eligible for cash incentives of 10 percent.

Table 4.1 Export Promotion Cash Incentives, Bangladesh, FY2012–FY2014
Percent of assessed FOB export value

Sector	FY2012	FY2013	FY2014
Total budget, cash incentives stimulus for exporters (US$, millions)	n.a.	290.0	n.a.
Number of sectors receiving incentives	19.0	15.0	14.0
Agricultural and agro processed goods	20.0	20.0	20.0
Home textiles	5.0	5.0	5.0
All textiles (including home textiles) exploring new markets (excluding Canada, United States, and EU)	2.0	2.0	2.0
Jute goods	10.0	10.0	10.0
Shrimp and other fishery products	10.0	10.0	7.5
Ships	5.0	5.0	5.0
Light engineering products	10.0	10.0	10.0
Leather products	12.5	15.0	15.0
Finished leather	4.0	0.0	0.0
Crust leather	3.0	0.0	0.0
Poultry	15.0	0.0	0.0
Bicycles	15.0	0.0	0.0

Source: Compiled from Bangladesh Bank circulars.
Note: EU = European Union; FOB = free on board; FY = fiscal year; n.a. = not available.

Moreover, the escalating structure of protection results in high ERPs,[2] which bias incentives against exports. As part of the DTIS, the Dhaka-based Policy Research Institute undertook a survey of 118 manufacturing firms located in and around the cities of Dhaka and Chittagong in May–July 2012.[3] The objective was to quantify the size of the distortions for firms producing selected consumer goods with potentially high ERPs. The analysis confirmed especially high ERPs in sectors like footwear (214–342 percent), some agrifood products (381 percent for chira/muri), bicycles (117–386 percent), and ceramics (190–239 percent). Pharmaceuticals fall in a unique category, with ERPs that are only modestly positive. Tariffs on locally produced generic equivalents of brand name drugs are zero or 5 percent, but a highly restrictive drugs policy prohibits imports of all drugs produced domestically, so that local production now meets practically all domestic demand for these drugs (95 percent of local demand according to World Bank [2008]). ERPs on drugs could actually be higher than the actual tariff, but they are restrained by some price controls imposed by the Drug Administration (Drug Control Act of 1982).

With domestic market production protected at high rates, incentives to export are stifled. The bicycle industry, whose initial export drive quickly lost momentum given the asymmetry of incentives, is a case in point. Similarly, in ceramics, exports have virtually stagnated despite the industry's intrinsic strengths in know-how. Given the prevailing tariffs, potential profitability in the domestic market far exceeds that in export markets, although export products are differentiated from what is sold domestically. In the case of footwear, anti-export incentives have been somewhat compensated by a ban on exports of raw leather, which depresses its domestic price and provides an indirect subsidy to footwear exports but also to domestic sales. Notwithstanding the fact that such indirect subsidies are actionable under the World Trade Organization's (WTO's) countervailing duty regulations, they contribute to a maze of regulatory distortions, the net effect of which is unlikely to foster economic efficiency.

The issues of skill inadequacy and poor logistics and Internet connectivity are recurring obstacles to sector growth, according to the detailed industry studies. The low literacy rate is a key reason for low productivity in Bangladeshi plants. These issues have been raised in Kathuria and Malouche (2016b) and recent World Bank reports on education and skills and exports (World Bank 2012a, 2013). Moreover, long lead times make products more expensive and less competitive. To the extent that lead times are reduced, the handicap imposed by lack of local input industries is reduced, but imported inputs can never provide the flexibility and range of options to the exporting sector that a strong local parts industry can.

The cost of trade finance and hindrances in small value payments are other recurring issues for small and large firms. Commercial banks currently lend at 15 percent on average, which is significantly higher than competitors. Moreover, nearly 100 percent of trade finance is bank-intermediated in Bangladesh, while only about 20 percent of total world trade is bank-intermediated, the remaining 80 percent being conducted on an open account or prepayment basis. Bangladesh

Bank export guidelines constrain alternative, cheaper financing, as they require the title document to all exports to be assigned in favor of a local Bangladeshi bank. This effectively prohibits the ability of offshore lenders to enter the market and provide diversified trade finance to exporters. The title documents cannot be released to the overseas buyers without the local bank first receiving payment. In the case of documents being released against acceptance, they must be routed through the importer's bank for release after acceptance. Making current account transactions, such as payments for samples and consultants, etc., hindrance-free would also facilitate exports. The government is preparing a strategy paper to review the Foreign Exchange Regulation Act and, in particular, to lay out a road-map toward exchange control liberalization, assisted by International Monetary Fund technical assistance. The objective of this reform is to facilitate foreign direct and portfolio investment (IMF 2013).

Bangladesh Bank export guidelines could be changed to open up the country's trade finance to a whole range of new financing structures from abroad, increasing liquidity and reducing interest costs. The change would primarily support the garment industry, because it is the largest sector, but would also assist the growing number of other exporters in Bangladesh. It would further help broaden the exporter base and provide finance to small suppliers to the export industry. The International Finance Corporation's (IFC's) Global Trade Supply Finance program could also be introduced. It would, at least in the initial stages, create a controlled environment under which to implement the above proposal. This would ensure close control over the new procedures, including repatriation of funds, and provide a high level of comfort for Bangladesh Bank and the local authorities.

Emerging Sectors: The Case of Shipbuilding

The shipbuilding sector in Bangladesh has recently shown increased activity and has been identified by the Government of Bangladesh as a potential future export growth area. Shipbuilding exports are considered a success story and have significantly improved over the past decade. Nevertheless, the industry is still in its infancy. The story of building seagoing vessels for export in Bangladesh began with Ananda Shipyards and Slipways Ltd. in Dhaka, currently the second largest shipyard in the country. In 2005, after participating in an international tender, the yard was awarded an order for two multipurpose vessels with 2,900 dead weight tonnes (dwt) each, from Danish Stella Shipping. The yard already had some experience with building tugs, pontoons, and ferries under class, that is, vessels adhering to the design, building, and quality requirements of a shipbuilding classification society. After Ananda, Bangladesh's Western Marine Shipyard in Chittagong followed, building on its experience in ship repair and maintenance of classed vessels. Western Marine entered the new building market in 2008 after having attended the Shipbuilding, Machinery and Marine Technology International Trade Fair in Hamburg Germany. The first orders from Stella Shipping were followed by orders for larger multipurpose vehicles from European owners such as Komrowski, Wessels Reederei, and Grona Shipping.

Although several of these orders were canceled, more than 20 vessels have been delivered by these two shipyards to date, with an export value well above US$100 million. Bangladesh has demonstrated the capability to build different types of vessels, but only multipurpose vehicles and ferries have been exported up to now (see figure 1.1 in Kathuria and Malouche 2016b, chapter 1).[4]

The production of the vast majority of Bangladeshi shipyards is still directed toward the domestic market with lower quality requirements. Total output is estimated to be around 250,000 gross tonnes (GT) per year, of which 185,000 GT are for the domestic market (registered production).[5] Production conditions have improved significantly since the mid-2000s. In particular, Western Marine Shipyard has achieved the reputation of a quality player that delivers good ships on time. Because of lower quality requirements, domestic demand for ships is higher than export demand. Local materials and equipment may include steel plates, angles, winches for mooring, anchor windlasses, chain cables of 10–15 millimeters diameter, furniture, upholstery, kitchen utensils, electric cables, switch boards, and power transformers. Against international standards, Bangladesh is also able to produce steelworks and minor items, such as electrical cables, furniture, and welding electrodes. However, engines installed in Bangladesh-built vessels originate exclusively from foreign suppliers. Capabilities in the maintenance sector are sound, but expansion of activities is limited by the lack of dry-dock facilities for larger vessels above 20,000 dwt.

Smaller domestic vessels are often built without application of international (class) or national standards (such as Bangladesh's Domestic Vessel Code[6]), for several reasons. International classification is expensive and legally not required for inland waterway and coastal vessels. Furthermore, most yards do not have the skill to produce under class standards. These vessels must adhere to local standards, which are enacted and enforced by the government. However, local rules and standards are low quality and in many cases they are not even enforced. According to government officials, only three surveyors are taking care of design approvals and supervision tasks for the entire domestic fleet in Bangladesh at present. As a result, domestic non-classed vessels generally have quality levels that are low and vary greatly depending on the executing yard.

Bangladesh has little local supply and is largely dependent on importing raw materials and components. This also holds true for Vietnam, but to a lesser extent. China, by contrast, now has significant own-capacities for steel and marine components, with substantial competition among national and international suppliers. Basic commodities such as iron ore and coal are traded on the world market and are similar for all buyers, but China enjoys abundant availability through its sheer size. Therefore, it will remain difficult for Bangladesh to create a beneficial position for the most important single cost position, materials. In addition, while export shipbuilding is exempt from all tariffs and has been granted full green channel customs support, domestic shipbuilding is subject to import duties for almost all sorts of materials and components. These duties range from 3 percent for sophisticated components and steel to more than 100 percent for components that are easy to manufacture.

Prospects

Stable and growing domestic demand will help the sector improve its quality and productivity. Shipping and shipbuilding markets are in a poor condition at the moment and this will not change significantly over the next few years. Against this background, the question is how Bangladesh can further build up its capabilities, broaden the shipbuilding value chain, and establish its shipbuilding sector as an important part of the economy. In a more positive domestic market situation and with improved competitiveness, Bangladesh could increase the volume and quality of its exports in the long term.

Solid domestic growth rates will provide good opportunities to develop the sector further. Domestic demand has been constantly growing over the past decade, with average growth rates of 25 percent by number of vessels (figure 4.1).[7] Larger vessels are usually more complex and require more capabilities. In addition to the general economic growth forecast of around 6–7 percent (IMF 2014), the Bangladeshi government and private investors have initiated infrastructure projects that create an additional demand for domestic water transport. Several fuel power stations are being built across the country. To transport oil to these plants, 60 tankers of approximately 2,000 dwt have been planned and are under construction. Furthermore, two inland container terminals have already been built so that inland waterways can handle container traffic, which is currently transported overland. The government has assigned 32 licenses for container vessels of 140 20-foot equivalent unit (TEU) containers (2,000 dwt) to various parties to operate on container lines in the country. It is expected that another 32 licenses will be

Figure 4.1 Number of Inland and Coastal Vessels Produced in Bangladesh, 2001–11

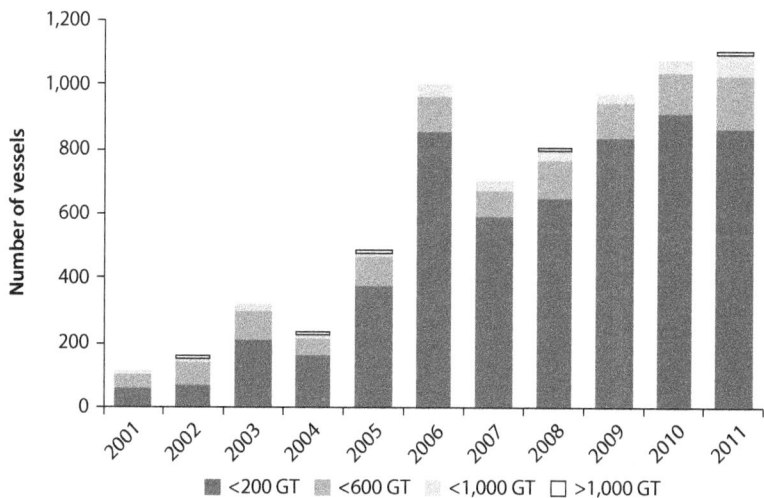

Source: Based on interviews with the Department of Shipping, Bangladesh.
Note: GT = gross tonnes.

granted soon. Both vessel types, tankers and container vessels, need to be built under class, which makes them export quality. However, as the Bangladeshi ship-building industry is not able to deliver sophisticated vessels in sufficient quantities, it is expected that half these vessels need to be built in China. Overall, domestic demand in Bangladesh will likely be detached from international shipping markets. Besides oil tankers and container vessels, demand for inland passenger vessels could increase. Because of high accident rates, safety regulations for these vessels could change. Experts predict there will be demand for 300–400 smaller ships over the next 10 years.

A general shortage of suitable land in Bangladesh makes it difficult for shipyards to expand. Infrastructure around shipyards has been rated rather problematic by many stakeholders. Reliable road and rail connections do not exist for many shipyards, making transportation of goods difficult. Furthermore, the supply of power, gas, and water is not reliable. Existing sites are sufficient to maintain levels of production for small vessels, but growth and scaling up is hardly possible. The Ministry of Industry estimates that about 2,000 acres of land need to be declared as shipbuilding zones to attain significant growth of the sector. Furthermore, the depth of waterways and clearance of bridges puts a natural cap on ship size.

Another big challenge to the industry at the moment is intermediate financing. It is a key enabler and is related to other factors such as cost, quality, and growth. Shipyards finance themselves at very high interest rates of 15 percent on average. In addition, they bear the cost for import letters of credit (L/Cs) and bank guarantees. The administrative effort for these L/Cs is significant for both suppliers and yards, which affects export and domestic shipbuilding. For export vessels, it drives up cost significantly and diminishes the competitive advantage that can be generated from low labor costs. For domestic vessels, it has another important implication. Local materials and components are more extensively used in domestic vessels, since the regulations for building these are less strict than for export vessels and local materials are cheaper and do not bear the cost and administrative burdens associated with L/Cs. However, this lack of regulation has a negative effect on quality and does not allow firms to build experience in the production of quality components.

Foreign direct investment (FDI) in the shipbuilding sector is close to zero at present. The reasons for this that are often mentioned are the poor infrastructure, absence of proper management structures, lack of critical mass for shipbuilding products in the domestic market, lack of a skilled workforce, and widespread corruption (Transparency International 2011). Bureaucratic and non-transparent decision making, including allegations of corruption at the top, has also turned away foreign investors. In past years, Bangladesh has conducted efforts to attract more FDI with the help of the IFC and in partnership with the U.K. Department for International Development and the European Union.

Lack of adequate management and technical staff for yards is another constraint to the growth of the shipbuilding sector. Limited capabilities in work organization and planning by senior staff are a problem often mentioned by industry stakeholders. This affects the productivity and the time taken to produce a vessel. With regard to senior staff, high-quality shipbuilding has relied to a significant extent on foreigners or Bangladeshi staff educated and trained abroad. Universities and marine academies have recognized the demand for qualified graduates and have increased enrollment and made the curricula more relevant, which will influence the situation positively in the long term.

The expansion of maintenance and repair services could create new opportunities. Maintenance and repair services for fleets in service are more stable and labor-intensive businesses than building new ships. Since larger and smaller vessels ply Bangladeshi waters, there is a general opportunity to benefit from this traffic and expand maintenance and repair facilities for larger vessels as well. This would require establishing more appropriate sites and dry docks beyond the existing Chittagong dry dock with its maximum capacity of 20,000 dwt.

Reform Agenda

An important area where the government can play a critical role is quality upgrading. Whereas quality is rated "good" for export vessels, only a small number of export vessels have been built by only two yards in Bangladesh. Most yards are building vessels under lower quality standards as classification is not legally required and would mean higher cost. Quality for local sales is not enforced, although measures such as the domestic vessel code exist in theory. The code is not applied for several reasons, mainly lack of resources. The supervisory body (the government) does not have enough qualified staff and employees at the yards do not have sufficient training to put the rules into practice. To build up quality, the following actions are considered essential: (a) implement enforcement of the current rules by appropriately educated surveyors employed by the government, (b) update and improve the domestic vessel code with stricter technical rules and standards, and (c) increase the share of classified vessels among domestic vessels. Most countries delegate the quality control and enforcement of their local standards to so-called recognized organizations for cost reasons. The government could also improve the quality of materials and components and make shipbuilding more attractive and cheaper for the domestic market by reducing import taxes for critical materials and components.

FDI and joint ventures could help bridge the capability gap with more advanced shipbuilding nations and increase reputation. FDI could bring shipbuilding in Bangladesh forward, especially in linkage industries, as it fosters technological advancement, improves processes, and enhances the capabilities of people in the industry. It is difficult to build up the industry to provide more complex marine components without technological know-how from foreign manufacturers. Improvement of the local market and the infrastructure situation would help attract more FDI, especially for those product families that have applicability in other sectors, such as generators. FDI could also provide an important source of financing, as shipbuilding is a capital-intensive industry and investment in large yard facilities is associated with significant risk.

An investment of approximately US$50 million is needed for setting up a shipyard with an annual capacity of ten 40,000 dwt vessels.

Proper training is the most urgent need, as formal training for workers is rare. The training at Western Marine Shipyards is a good model to follow. The situation at the management and engineering level is more challenging than at the shop floor level, where productivity gains are leveraged more easily.

Revival of Jute and Jute-Based Products

Bangladesh is the second largest producer of jute in the world, after India, and the leading exporter of jute and jute products.[8] Bangladesh is considered to produce higher-quality jute than that of India and is a bigger player than India in the export market. While Bangladesh exports more than 60 percent of its jute products, India exports only 10–12 percent.[9] Jute and jute products constituted only 2.7 percent of Bangladesh's exports in FY2014, down from about 15 percent in FY1993 (figure 4.2), and even higher in earlier years. Within the overall jute sector, low-value-added and traditional products account for more than 99 percent of exports; thus, diversified jute products currently represent less than 1 percent of jute sector exports. Production capacity for all jute, raw and processed, is higher than demand, indicating an opportunity to add value and manufacture products in demand in domestic and international markets.

Bangladesh has public and private sector jute mills, all operating below capacity.[10] The private sector accounted for 80 percent of the total export of jute goods during FY2012. Combined earnings of the public and private sectors

Figure 4.2 Share of Jute and Jute Goods Declined over Time, Overtaken by Garments, FY1993–FY2014

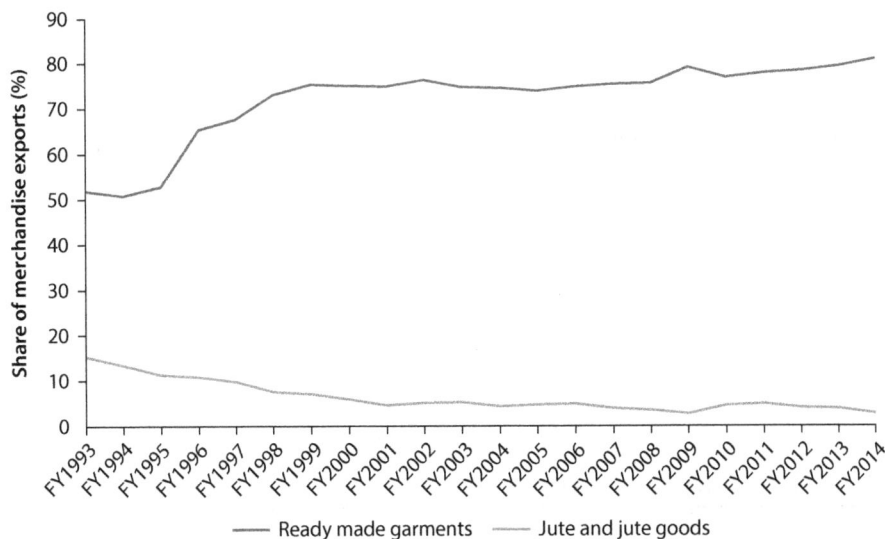

Source: Authors with data from the Export Promotion Bureau of Bangladesh.

totaled Tk 50 billion (US$610 million) from the export of jute goods. Bangladesh Jute Mills Corporation is the largest public enterprise and operates 27 mills. There are also private jute mills and spinning facilities in the country. In addition, within Bangladesh, there are 177,315 installed spindles in jute spinning mills, of which 85 percent are operating. All firms operate below capacity. For example, in mills under the Bangladesh Jute Mills Corporation (public sector), the overall capacity utilization of looms is 63 percent, while at the Bangladesh Jute Mills Association (private sector), capacity utilization is only 38 percent of installed capacity (table 4.2).

Much of the milling machinery in Bangladesh is 50–60 years old. China, India, Japan, Turkey, and other countries purchase raw jute from Bangladesh and process it with modern, more cost-effective equipment than is available in Bangladesh. Compounding the age of the machinery in Bangladesh is the fact that the company that manufactured the machines, Dundee (Scotland), went out of business decades ago and spare parts are not available. Spare parts must be custom made in local machine shops, making it difficult to match the original parts. Replacement parts are increasingly less reliable. More modern equipment is used in India, and the newer machines are more efficient and able to weave four times faster than the machines in Bangladesh. All these factors add up to India producing fabric for 30 percent lower cost than Bangladesh. Part of this challenge is caused by the lack of information and awareness regarding available technology and equipment in the market. New entrants to jute milling are purchasing new machines, but these mills (private sector) are typically small enterprises.

Raw jute and jute goods for mills and spinners are granted a subsidy (10 percent of free on board export value). This applies to traditional products, raw jute, and yarn. If a manufacturer who does not operate a jute mill of any type exports a jute-based product that is not considered a handicraft, there is no subsidy. An example would be a jute goods producer with no backward integration into the jute processing segment (that is, milling or spinning) that produces machine

Table 4.2 Selected Public and Private Sector Jute Milling Operations in Bangladesh, 2012

Organization	Status	Number of mills	Number of employees (est)	Average production of jute goods (tons)	Average internal consumption of jute goods		Average export of jute goods		
					Tons	Type	Tons	BDT × 10⁶	US$ × 10⁶
BJSA	Private	81	62,000	422,000	27,000	Yarn/twine	387,362	2,972	36.2
BJMA	Private	106	45,000	160,000	35,000	Sacking/hessian	97,891	713	8.7
BJMC	Public	27	64,000	207,000	31,500	Sacking/hessian	123,025	932	11.4
Total		221	171,000	789,000	93,500		608,278	4,617	56.3

Source: Bangladesh Jute Spinners Association.
Note: est = estimate; BDT = Bangladeshi taka; BJMA = Bangladesh Jute Mills Association; BJMC = Bangladesh Jute Mills Corporation; BJSA = Bangladesh Jute Spinners Association.

made nursery pots (not considered handicrafts[11]). This is a jute product, but the producer does not qualify for the 10 percent jute export subsidy. In addition, the industry benefits from duty drawback; 100 percent value-added tax (VAT) exemption for exports; and 15 percent income tax rate (as opposed to the standard 37.5 percent). For those who are 100 percent exporters of jute, the VAT exemption on gas and energy used in the factory can be applied as a drawback (which takes three to six months) or the factory can be approved and VAT is not charged (an exemption), and duty on imported capital equipment is 1 percent (as opposed to the standard 3 percent).

Although a relatively simple product, jute bags in Bangladesh have high potential for several reasons highlighted in the value chain analysis conducted as part of the DTIS. First, jute bags are simple products, do not require large capital investment, and are made by Fair Trade artisans as well as commercial factories. Second, shopping bag demand is growing and expected to continue based on external market forces.[12] Substitute materials other than jute (such as cotton, linen, synthetics such as nylon, woven poly, and non-woven plastic) are available, but buyers continue to increase orders for jute shopping bags. One large producer of jute shopping bags in Bangladesh states that orders over a two-year period went from 300,000 pieces to 2,000,000 pieces. Third, examining the production process (shown below), shopping bags require better quality fabric, which is typically laminated; require some type of printed design (logo, pattern, or otherwise); and may also be dyed. Therefore, several different production processes and supply chain dynamics must be considered, which captures the types of analysis required for other diversified products. Finally, value addition of the shopping bag returns a minimum of threefold higher profits over raw jute. For example, one ton of jute can produce 1,500 yards of fabric, which in turn can produce 2,300 shopping bags at a profit of approximately Tk 27,600. This profit is 3.9 times greater than the profit from the sales of raw jute, which is approximately between Tk 5,000 and Tk 7,000 (US$61–US$85) per ton. The advantage of jute products is that these earnings stay in the country, since the jute is locally sourced and labor is a significant component along much of the jute and jute products value chain. As such, shopping bags cover several issues that can arise in the diversified sector.

Depending on the buyer's requirements, the production process for a jute shopping bag may rely on outsourcing certain processes. The jute fabric is acquired and, if dyeing is necessary, the fabric must be dyed externally at a dyeing facility. This is not done at the jute mills but in some cases the fabric producer will provide the service of getting the fabric dyed; this is more typical of a small miller developing a clientele. If lamination is required, then this necessarily is outsourced to a laminating facility; there are 17 such facilities throughout Dhaka. The fabric is returned to the shopping bag producer, cut to size, and, if silk screening is required by the buyer, then this too is usually outsourced. Virtually all export-bound shopping bags require some form of screen printing. Although in-house printing is possible to do for some producers, most prefer to send the panels out for printing. While the panels are out, the handles are readied. The panels are returned and then the bag construction (stitching) takes place (photo 4.1).

In Bangladesh, the two leading cost drivers, fabric and laminating, are particularly noted as uncompetitive when compared with counterpart pricing in India. Fabric preparation dominates the value chain, as it accounts for 62.4 percent of the overall cost of producing the bag. And, as is the general case with diversified jute products, the jute fabric itself is the highest cost driver. Moreover, stakeholders agree that Indian lamination is far superior in durability and lamination material. Lamination in Bangladesh is either polypropylene or high-density polyethylene, with the one noted exception of cellulose, whereas bag producers claim that low-density polyethylene is preferable. Indian equipment accommodates low-density polyethylene, which adheres better and for a much longer period (multiple years as opposed to approximately a year for lamination applied with machines in Bangladesh). The equipment that is generally used in India can cost as much as US$150,000; this cost is not only prohibitive for most manufacturers in Bangladesh, but the volume of production in the country is sufficiently small that it would warrant only two facilities operating such equipment.

The spot market price for raw jute is set in Bangladesh. The price of raw jute has risen dramatically in the past 10 years, more than doubling (107 percent) between 2001 and 2011, from US$331 per ton to US$688 per ton (figure 4.3). Most of the price rise has occurred during 2006–11 when prices rose 79 percent, in response to increased demand for jute as a substitute for other fibers as well as mandatory packaging laws that require (in the case of India, sacks) or encourage (in the case of plastic shopping bag bans) the use of jute. Rising prices in 2010 led to expanded jute cropping in 2011, which resulted in oversupply and depressed prices. However, the overall trend is still positive given the many and

Photo 4.1 Design Features of Two Styles of Jute Shopping Bags

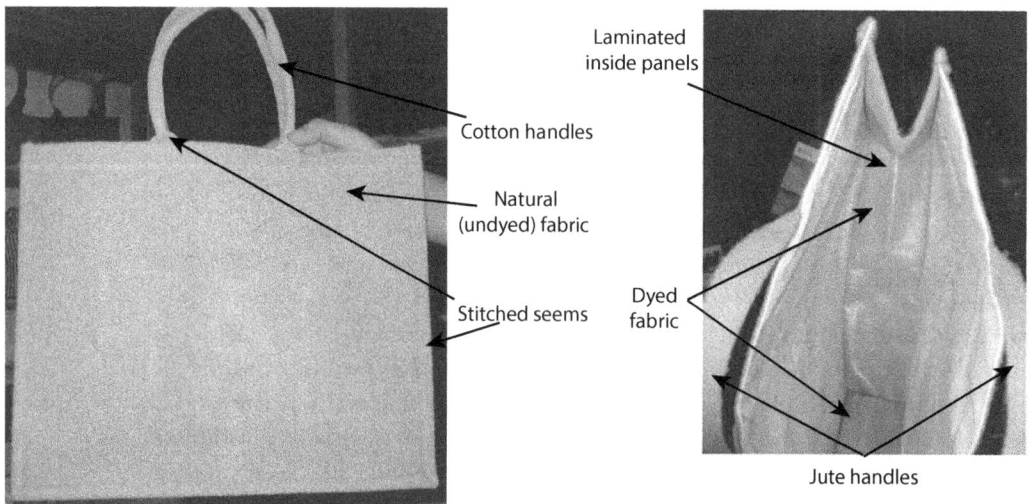

Source: Global Development Solutions LLC.

Figure 4.3 Historical Jute Prices, 2001–11

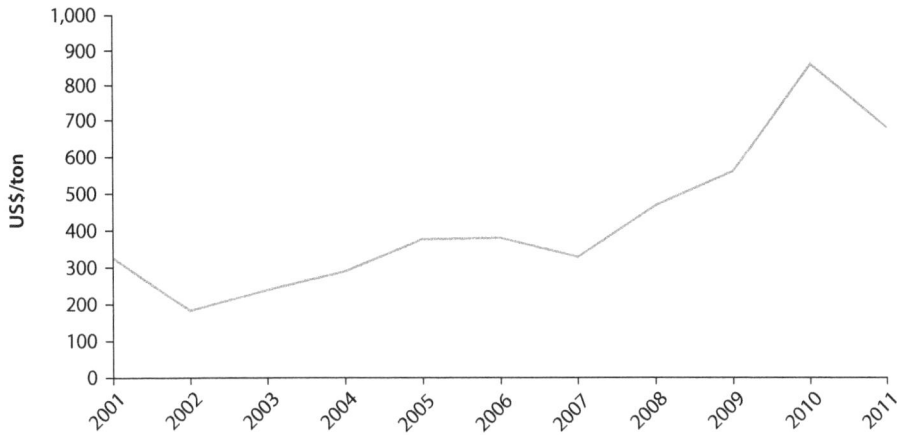

Source: Bangladesh Jute Mills Corporation, The Public Ledger, as quoted on FAOSTAT.
Note: Annual averages, Jute-bwd (free-on-board Mongla, at sight, Friday closing price).

expanding uses of jute in various products and applications. Among major jute-producing countries, while Bangladesh enjoyed the lowest producer prices in 2005, by 2009 that advantage had eroded. Bangladesh, China, and India had similar producer prices. Thailand now has a cost advantage, and Nepal is expensive relative to other major jute producers.

Prospects

Jute was declared a priority sector according to the government's Industrial Policy Order 2010, implying a number of incentives for the sector. Furthermore, the government adopted a jute policy pursuing the following major objectives in 2011: (a) ensuring production of jute and jute goods according to the consistent demand of local and foreign markets, (b) developing land use planning for jute cultivation, (c) producing quality jute seed and supplying it to farmers, (d) preserving and expanding jute and jute goods markets to assist in developing a favorable trade balance for the country, (e) innovating various diversified jute products and increasing production activity of diversified jute products, (f) ensuring effective networking of all stakeholders related to the jute sector, and (g) developing and maintaining a jute-related information management system. Moreover, the government has passed a mandatory jute packaging law (Law 53 in 2010), but it has yet to be enforced. A diversified jute products manufacturing industry is also in the process of being set up in the Mongla Export Processing Zone at a cost of US$36.94 million. The handicraft subsector by itself offers a wide variety of possibilities, ranging from various rugs and carpets (flat weave, braided, plush), to bags of all fashion levels, to toys and Christmas ornaments.

In Bangladesh, diversified products have come to light only over the past five or so years and, as such, it is a sector in its infancy. By contrast, India has been developing a diversified jute sector for at least 15 years. Bangladesh has much to do to catch up from the perspective of public policy in the form of government support programs, availability of formal support institutions, and support for market linkage and development, as well as product diversification.

Bangladesh has the potential to further broaden its scope within jute and realize higher value added from its rich jute resources. Despite the small share of diversified jute products relative to the jute sector as a whole, there is a wide range of products within the subsector. Manufacturers and exporters of jute products often are involved in both traditional and diversified products. For example, one firm interviewed exported hessian cloth, hessian bags and sacks, mesh soil savers, twine, yarn, carpet backing cloth, webbing, shopping bags, wine bottle bags, women's handbags, gift bags, children's bags, and food bags, all made of jute. Looking at the jute goods product mix on a metric ton basis, Bangladesh's predominant categories are other goods, specifically yarn and twine (55.4 percent), followed by jute sacks (30.5 percent), whereas India's jute products consist primarily of jute sacks (64.9 percent) and hessian cloth (19.0 percent). With regard to its ability to produce high volumes of yarn, Bangladesh is better positioned than India in the area of nontraditional jute goods. However, as India makes many of its diversified jute goods from fibers and cloth from Bangladesh, Bangladesh is not fully realizing its value-added potential in the subsector.

Demand for jute shopping bags has increased, as has demand for other alternatives to plastic bags. As a consequence, orders for Bangladeshi shopping bags reportedly increased from 300,000 units in FY2011 to nearly 2,000,000 units in FY2012. Among the buyers are prominent international corporations, such as Walmart, The Body Shop, Home Depot, and Tesco. Jute bags are favored because they are perceived to be less harmful to the environment while retaining the durability and convenience of plastic. Despite the recent success, jute shopping bags represent a negligible portion of the total annual world demand for shopping bags of approximately 500 billion pieces. In selecting reusable shopping bags, shoppers seek bags that are affordable, durable, washable, and sometimes fashionable. Those who are more environmentally conscious may also want to buy a more "natural" bag, that is, one made from natural textiles, biodegradable, or recyclable. In this respect, while the "bring your own bag" movement represents an opportunity for jute shopping bags, in reality there are many materials from which such bags can be made, including cotton, canvas, linen, or recycled polyester. Many bags are marketed as eco-friendly simply because they are durable enough to be reused, even if the underlying material is not of natural fiber. Thus, the jute sector needs to make a strong case for its product, perhaps in cooperation with India and the Jute Study Group.

The first challenge for diversified jute producers has been competitive sourcing of the original fabric. For small producers, this had been a problem in the past. Many small jute goods producers are located in and around Dhaka, while the closest mill to Dhaka is an hour and a half from the city, making it difficult for small-scale producers to source fabric effectively. In response to this challenge, the Jute Diversification Promotion Centre established a consolidation program in 2011 so that fabric is available in Dhaka at the Jute Diversification Promotion Centre warehouse. Small producers can now purchase quantities according to their needs from the warehouse rather than having to meet prohibitive minimum orders. Fabric still requires dyeing and the jute goods producers must bring their fabrics to the dyeing mills or mills can deliver fabric to dyeing facilities at a small charge. In general, the time lapse between procuring the fabric and having the material dyed and laminated is approximately a week.

Availability of fabric types is another advantage that Bangladesh concedes to India. For example, in Bangladesh, only a half-dozen or so fabric varieties are readily available on the market, whereas in India the selection covers 50–55 different fabrics. The mindset of the Bangladeshi jute sector, particularly the public sector, is still largely set on the traditional uses for jute. Specifically, jute continues to be viewed as a basic packing material that does not require a variety of colors, uniform weave, or fabric variety (different thicknesses). Recently established private mills, however, are more apt to pursue better equipment and produce diversified fabric. A recent entrant, albeit very small, to the market expressed that his reason for investing in a mill was his inability to find jute-cotton fabric blends. As a result, at a cost of Tk 2,000,000 (US$25,000), this entrepreneur self-financed the establishment of a mill that employs secondhand Chinese machinery capable of weaving 1,000 meters of jute-cotton blend fabric per day.

Only a few mills are experimenting with new fabrics, all in the private sector. For example, there is only one mill that experiments extensively with developing new fabrics and can produce very soft fabrics for fashion items, such as handbags, and very thin fabrics for garments. However, it does not manufacture the fabrics for inventory, so the fabrics are only produced upon a buyer's request. Being specialty fabrics, delivery can take up to one month, minimum purchase orders are required (10,000 yards or greater, depending on the type of fabric, which is well in excess of what many small and medium diversified jute product manufacturers require for most consignments), and the mill requires payment in advance. Although high-quality jute fabrics are considered specialty products in Bangladesh, similar products are readily available in India, where there are multiple suppliers of blended and fine jute fabric. In Bangladesh, the prospective buyers may not be able or willing to purchase that much in one order, so the fabrics remain difficult to access.

Bangladeshi firms will also continue to face the threat of new entrants in markets and products. While Bangladesh and India control more than 96 percent of world jute production, other countries, including China, Nepal, Uzbekistan, and Vietnam, have had success on a limited scale (40,000 metric tons or less). Given the right growing conditions, there is no reason why these countries could not grow their indigenous jute rather than importing it. Moreover, although Bangladesh is a leading exporter of jute and jute products, the country has not exploited this position and made Bangladesh as synonymous with jute as, say, France is with cheese or Thailand with rice. Despite the versatility of jute, many other materials perform similar functions in common with jute products. For example, while the jute shopping bag is a niche product for Bangladesh, reusable shopping bags of various materials are popular in the global market, including other natural fibers such as cotton or kenaf as well as synthetic materials such as nylon or recycled/laminated plastic. In jute footwear components—espadrille soles exported to be made into finished shoes elsewhere—while the traditional base (sole and midsole wrap) of espadrille soles is jute, substitute materials have been introduced globally to the footwear components market, including hemp rope, synthetic jute, and cork footbeds, threatening Bangladesh's footwear components niche. Substitutes for jute twine include cotton, polycotton, staple fiber polyester, high tenacity multifilament polyester, tobacco, and sisal.[13]

However, while a tiered supply chain is an essential element for the effective and efficient growth of a sector, the current supply chain system in Bangladesh revolves mostly around informal structures and relationships between a number of small-size players, particularly with respect to dyeing, laminating, and printing. In this context, even if a high volume of high-quality, fine jute fabrics becomes available in the market today, the subcontracting supply chain, as illustrated above, is unlikely to be able to handle the volume and quality of product needed to be competitive with Indian manufacturers.

Reform Agenda

The jute packing law needs to be enforced. Enforcement will result in increased domestic demand for raw jute and should provide a possibly more stable source of demand for the jute industry. This could affect exports, but the primary concern of policy makers should be total employment and output, including that which owes to export demand.

The incentives to public jute mills may hurt the long-term strength of the sector. Subsidies in general are not sustainable. They also hurt the private mills, which are arguably more efficient (since they compete without subsidies), and prevent the stronger ones from becoming larger players. If such subsidies were no longer provided, private mills would expand and could be encouraged to hire from the public sector. This could help keep overall jute mill employment intact. The money saved by the government could be used for other support programs, such as more effective research and outreach to farmers and more effective marketing and branding support.

The high cost of borrowing and difficulties accessing finance present significant obstacles to stronger sector performance and new entrants. Restricted access to finance pushes firms to internally finance growth, which contributes to slow growth and slow product diversification. Even with a letter of credit as a guarantee, a local bank will usually provide only 35 percent of the working capital requirement. Entrepreneurs generally must rely on 100 percent internal financing to grow their companies from micro enterprises to small enterprises. One such entrepreneur who was interviewed was able to diversify into weaving with the purchase of an internally funded power loom, although his development has taken two decades to attain this level.

Development partner financing for reducing costs and increasing fabric variety could be considered. Development partner financing to stimulate further research and development (R&D) in the sector for the development of additional diversified fabrics and to decrease the cost of the currently available high-end fabrics could be useful. The Jute Research Institute, for example, has a pilot project regarding diversified jute fabrics and is exploring collaboration with some garment and textile units for large-scale runs. Fabrics further developed can also be provided in the fabric bank for diversified jute product producers.

Lack of production and trade data and poor access to market information make strategic benchmarking and planning difficult for companies. Interviews with stakeholders along the diversified jute sector indicate continued lack of and access to market information, particularly in regard to available production technology, and sources of equipment and technology for upgrading production of basic and complex fabrics. Moreover, there is little to no current, readily available information regarding diversified jute products over the range of products within diversified jute, inconsistent application and lack of product-specific codes, and lack of an internal census carried out with regularity that does not overlook nontraditional jute products. As a consequence, Bangladesh, as well as jute products, are off the radar of many international databases, limiting the country's marketing reach.

Some of the issues, such as marketing, research, and branding, could be addressed together with India and Nepal. If the numbers are correct, there is potentially a huge demand for natural fibers like jute, which could be more effectively realized with a joint approach to marketing and branding. If South Asian countries get together and share marketing and branding costs under a regional approach, this can help all parties. Another approach is to restrict this to the two largest production countries and brand "Bengali" jute from Bangladesh and India. Either of these initiatives could be undertaken under the Jute Study Group's mandate. Joint R&D to complement domestic research efforts offers another possibility.

Diversified Jute: Non-Leather Footwear

Bangladesh is highly competitive in the espadrille market and this could be another major niche area in the future. Bangladesh is among the top Asian producers of footwear, with production in 2011 of 276 million pairs and a 1.3 percent world market share. Bangladesh exports mostly leather footwear, although non-leather footwear is growing. Footwear exports totaled US$335 million for FY2012, consisting mostly of leather footwear (US$240 million or 71.5 percent); others included non-leather footwear (US$76.5 million or 22.8 percent) and footwear components (such as soles).[14] All of Bangladesh's espadrille production is exported. Of the leading non-leather footwear categories, Bangladesh's largest export markets are Spain, the Republic of Korea, and Japan (HS640419 under the Harmonized System of trade classification); Germany, France, and Spain (HS640220); and France, Italy, and Germany (HS640520). Bangladesh's non-leather footwear is currently in the non-luxury niche. Therefore, changing consumer attitudes bode well for demand for Bangladeshi shoes.

Photo 4.2 Sample Espadrille Styles

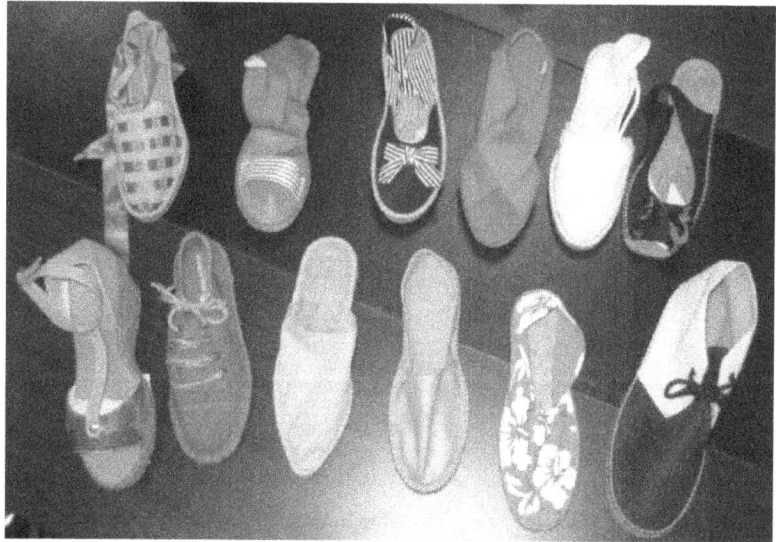

Source: Global Development Solutions, LLC.

As a producer of high-quality jute, Bangladesh has become a manufacturing center for premium quality jute soles and complete espadrilles (photo 4.2). The shoe design originated in the Pyrenees (Spain and France), but today espadrilles are made in full or in part in a number of countries. It is possible that much or most of the world's total production of complete espadrilles is manufactured in Bangladesh,[15] while manufacturers in France, Italy, and Spain import jute soles from Bangladesh to finish espadrilles in those countries. Complete espadrilles are also manufactured in Argentina, Bolivia, Colombia, Paraguay, and República Boliviariana de Venezuela.

The Bangladeshi non-leather footwear industry is dominated by four companies and includes a multitude of small entities. According to the Leather Goods and Footwear Manufacturers and Exporters Association of Bangladesh, there are four companies (recently down from five) in Bangladesh that export non-leather shoes.[16] Of these four, three can be classified as large firms (more than 250 permanent employees, assets of at least US$122,000), with the fourth company on the cusp between medium and large. All four companies boast strong annual sales growth of more than 20 percent for the past several years. A fifth manufacturer, the most recent entrant, exited the espadrille market in 2011 but continues to operate in the footwear sector.[17] The sector also includes a multitude of small and micro companies that are available to the larger firms during peak season. These smaller entities may be an individual working from home or a group of individual producers coordinated by a contractor (acting either as a subcontractor to the large companies to handle peak season overflow or directly filling local orders for simple shoes such as PVC/PU [polyvinyl chloride/polyurethane] shoes and sandals).

By the nature of its organization, it is not possible to quantify the number of entities in the subsector, although estimates of the overall number of workers in the non-leather footwear sector were quoted at upward of 30,000 people.[18]

Large firms rely on local subcontractors to meet demand during the high season. They produce as much as 1.5 million pairs of basic espadrilles and 150,000 pairs of various high-fashion espadrilles throughout the year. Since most of these orders are received during the peak season, a short period of time, producers must regularly rely on local subcontractors. Examples of this are sewing uppers onto the completed sole subassembly (performed manually) or sewing elaborate decorations (such as sequins and beads) onto uppers. While the current subcontracting structure with individuals and micro enterprises creates employment opportunities for local workers, the informal nature of the relationship and the lack of a structured subcontracting supply chain inhibit producers from responding effectively to large production orders.

Footwear manufacturers must compete for access to fabric from domestic producers in a very competitive and tight market. As a major exporter of ready-to-wear garments, demand for textile fabric in Bangladesh is high, not only from domestic garment producers, but also from foreign markets, which account for more than three times the demand compared with domestic demand for knit and woven fabric. For example, the projected demand for fabric in 2014–15 is estimated to be about 15,712 million meters, of which 4,123 million meters are expected to be absorbed by the domestic market. Moreover, as of 2009, there were 363 spinning mills and 1,131 weaving mills operating in Bangladesh, producing fabrics to meet the growing domestic and export demand.[19] As a consequence, footwear manufacturers are required to have a minimum order size of 5,000 meters of fabric. This amount of fabric can produce as many as 35,000 pairs of basic espadrilles. But the average order size received by large producers ranges from 15,000 to 20,000 pairs per consignment, thereby creating a challenge for producers to figure out what to do with the remaining material.

The value chain analysis suggests that raw material is the primary cost driver for the production of espadrilles in Bangladesh. Subassembly accounts for nearly 60 percent of the total value chain for the production of an espadrille. Further breakdown of the value chain for subassembly shows that jute preparation and the mid-sole and outer sole account for more than 97 percent of subassembly costs. Raw material inputs, namely jute and rubber, account for more than three-quarters of the total subassembly cost. The second highest cost associated with espadrille production is the preparation of uppers, which accounts for nearly 25 percent of the total production cost. Similar to the subassembly, breakdown of the upper preparation costs also points to input material as the highest cost driver in the value chain.

There is no current FDI in the espadrille sector, but export processing zones (EPZs), particularly Chittagong, have received FDI in non-leather footwear (not espadrilles). Some foreign assistance has been provided to local espadrille manufacturers in the past. For example, a private French company assisted one of the manufacturers in setting up its espadrille manufacturing operations.

The espadrille producer purchased machinery in France and the French company aided in the set-up and training of the processes. While there is also no EPZ specifically for footwear, there are footwear companies (not specifically non-leather) in the three EPZs. Nonetheless, industries tend to form informal clusters in geographic areas where labor with relevant skills and know-how is concentrated. For example, the Comilla EPZ is in close proximity to a large concentration of espadrille producers.

Footwear (leather and non-leather) was designated a priority sector by the Government of Bangladesh in 2009. As such, the sector is entitled to the following benefits: (a) bonded warehouse facilities, (b) 100 percent duty drawback for re-exported inputs, (c) 1.5 percent income tax (compared with 15 percent for non-priority sectors), and (d) tax-free import of capital equipment. In addition, leather footwear exports receive a 12.5 percent export subsidy targeted toward the export of finished leather goods. In reality, the duty drawback is not much for espadrilles, considering the high local content of the shoes (greater than 75 percent).

Small companies face entry barriers, mostly because incentive policies are extended to jute products but not espadrilles. Jute-based products receive an export subsidy of 10 percent, but espadrilles cannot collect this subsidy as long as they are classified along with the general footwear sector. Two of the four major espadrille producers have backward linkages into the jute processing sector. This allows these companies to take advantage of the 10 percent jute export subsidy, thus providing them with a built-in advantage over new entrants that do not have an integrated operation in the jute sector. Specifically, unless new market entrants also operate jute mills (either spinning or weaving), they face a 10 percent cost disadvantage against existing market players. Moreover, duty drawback or subsidy payments can take up to a year, contributing to cash flow pressures for new entrants. However, in the case of espadrilles, considering that local content is greater than 75 percent, espadrille producers often do not make the effort to claim the duty drawback. Manufacturers claim that the delay is so long that the amount is not significant enough to expend the effort in applying for the drawback. In addition, financing is not easy for potential entrants. It seems to be generally available to those with a pre-established banking relationship and relationships initially are established through personal or political connections and are not dependent on viable business plans or creditworthiness.

Prospects

Once considered peasant footwear, designer espadrilles are now widely available in many modern interpretations. Leather's share of the global footwear market is on the decline, for environmental and other reasons. As the health and environmental repercussions of tanning become known worldwide, there may be a backlash against use of leather in all products, including footwear, which would benefit the non-leather footwear segment. Although the popularity of espadrilles has ebbed and flowed (boosted notably by Hollywood stars sporting espadrilles in numerous movies and TV shows), today espadrilles are considered a summer staple whose natural material has become synonymous with warm-weather fashion. Espadrille footwear designs include slingback, peeptoe, wedge, and platform styles, sold by value-priced as well as luxury global design houses. Espadrilles sold by Burberry, Ferragamo, Marc Jacobs, and Missoni may retail for more than US$400 per pair, albeit these higher-end espadrilles have leather components. The common denominator in all is the jute (or jute rope-like) sole or wrapped midsole. Currently, none of these extremely high-end espadrilles is fully assembled in Bangladesh, although they may be manufactured with components from Bangladesh in countries such as Brazil, France, Italy, or Spain. One espadrille company in Bangladesh reported to have exported more than a million pairs of completed espadrille subassemblies (jute midsole with vulcanized rubber outsole) to France in the past year, with orders increasing yearly.

With the Generalized System of Preferences (GSP), Bangladesh espadrille manufacturers have an advantage over the Chinese in European markets, but not in the United States. Given its status as a least developed country, Bangladesh benefits from GSP privileges in most major markets (including Australia, Canada, the European Union, Japan, Korea, and New Zealand) and as such has zero import duty. However, non-leather footwear exports to the United States are subject to an import duty of 36 percent[20]—the leading country in footwear import quantity and value (APICCAPS 2012). Currently, 99 percent of all footwear sold in the United States is imported, of which more than 80 percent is imported from China, a country that also has no GSP privileges in the United States.[21] Bangladesh manufacturers report strong competition from China when vying for U.S. market share, with the long-established Chinese offering a greater variety of styles and materials (amounting to one-stop shopping) and faster delivery.[22]

The labor cost advantage over China—combined with locally available jute, fabric, and rubber—creates a substantial competitive advantage for manufacturers in Bangladesh over its biggest market rival, China. However, espadrille producers in Bangladesh have been confined to selling basic espadrilles at the low end of the market, given the challenges associated with timely access to special-order dyed fabrics. But high-fashion designs fetch 3–12 times the value of a basic espadrille. China, by contrast, is more prevalent in fashion because there are many fabric producers and dyed material fabric is readily available in virtually any quantity desired. Interviews with manufacturers suggest that even if a particularly unique color is not available, it can be produced within one week in China. It is this fact that lends China a competitive advantage over Bangladesh in the U.S. market.

Espadrille manufacturing is not a utility-intensive process, but the industry suffers from erratic electricity supply. Thus, many firms rely on generators, leading to increased production costs. When the generators are running heavily, which was reported to be every other hour during the summer months in 2012, the cost of electricity increases by two to three times and the total electricity bill per pair was approximately US$0.054 per pair. While the operating cost of a generator is generally manageable for most producers, the initial investment cost and access to finance to purchase a generator are generally prohibitive for small producers.

There are also frequent retroactive electricity rate hikes. Four rate hikes took place in the six months from April to September 2012. The latest rate hike was on March 2014, in when the average retail tariff for small industries and commercial users increased by 8.14 percent and 6.49 percent, respectively. According to the Bangladesh Power Development Board, these increases are still not enough to cover the cost of power generation, so enterprises expect the rates to continue to rise. Given the gap between the cost and prices of electricity, such hikes can be expected. However, the lack of predictability of rate hikes makes cash flow and financial planning difficult for producers.

Footwear manufacturers point to further challenges related to lack of coordination and market information. First, there is no forum in which footwear and fabric manufacturers can discuss upcoming trends and fabric needs. As a consequence, no systematic approach to supply and stock management exists in the fabric-to-footwear supply chain. Second, in the absence of up-to-date intelligence on market demand and trends in key markets, particularly in the EU market, nearly all of the orders received by footwear manufacturers in Bangladesh occur during trade shows. With a 90-day order-to-delivery window from EU footwear buyers, this leaves little advance notice for fabric manufactures to plan their production once they receive an order from footwear manufacturers. As a result, delivery of fabric takes as much as 60 days, resulting in footwear manufacturers often subcontracting production rather than optimizing their own production facility.

Reform Agenda

To enhance competitiveness, Bangladesh could reduce and eliminate its own policy distortions, including removing entry barriers, and capitalize on the trend toward non-leather footwear. It can also encourage further local value added and move into higher-quality and higher-value product markets. Policy actions in this context should be seen together with those for diversified jute products. Bangladesh should move toward a more neutral policy regime that does not discriminate between types of raw material or by extent of vertical integration. The government provides subsidies to leather footwear exporters and for exports of jute mills. However, espadrille manufacturers that are not integrated into jute weaving or spinning do not get this subsidy. The government should conduct a review of all cash and other fiscal incentives, with a view to providing a more coherent, transparent, and predictable set of incentives. The incentives should also incorporate a firm sunset clause, so that industry, while enjoying the certainty of the regime, can also plan to work without the incentives.

Bangladesh is currently absent from membership in the International Footwear Conference (Lan 2012). At the global level, institutions such as the World Footwear Congress and the International Footwear Conference meet periodically (in this case, every three years and every year, respectively) to discuss industry issues. The International Footwear Conference meets annually in an Asian country (the last meeting was in March 2012). All members of the Conference currently are Asian (China; Hong Kong SAR, China; India; Indonesia; Japan; Korea; Malaysia; the Philippines; Taiwan, China; Thailand; and Vietnam).

Garments: Moving Up the Value Chain—The Case of Polo Shirts

This section presents the value chain analysis of polo-style shirts, which are a value-added apparel product with more complex production than simpler products such as T-shirts. The basic polo shirt model is somewhat standardized globally, thus facilitating comparison of Bangladeshi productivity with the other apparel-producing countries for which data are available: China, Ethiopia, and Vietnam. The choice was endorsed by the domestic private sector, the polo shirt being a good proxy to represent the sector for value chain analysis. In Bangladesh, most polo shirts are destined for export.[23]

The RMG industry is a strategic sector for Bangladesh. In FY2013, it was the largest employer, with more than 5,600 factories; provided four million direct jobs (figure 4.4); and contributed to more than 75 percent of foreign exchange earnings.[24] About 80 percent of employees in the Bangladesh Garment Manufacturers and Exporters Association (BGMEA) member factories are women. The scale and size of RMG factory operations has also grown, with RMG factory employment averaging 300 workers per factory in FY1984 and growing to approximately 714 garment workers per factory in FY2013. The industry has been credited with empowering women and economically disadvantaged populations in general. For example, BGMEA provides scholarships to the children of garment workers, vocational training, distribution of food at a subsidized price during Ramadan, and medical centers. Medical services include HIV/AIDS awareness instruction and reproductive health services.[25]

Bangladesh, similar to China, Ethiopia, and Vietnam, maintains various input and output subsidies or rebates to encourage industrial production and exports. In Bangladesh, support includes subsidies, mainly to mills for costs they incur

Figure 4.4 Bangladesh Garment Industry Factories and Employment, FY1984 to FY2013

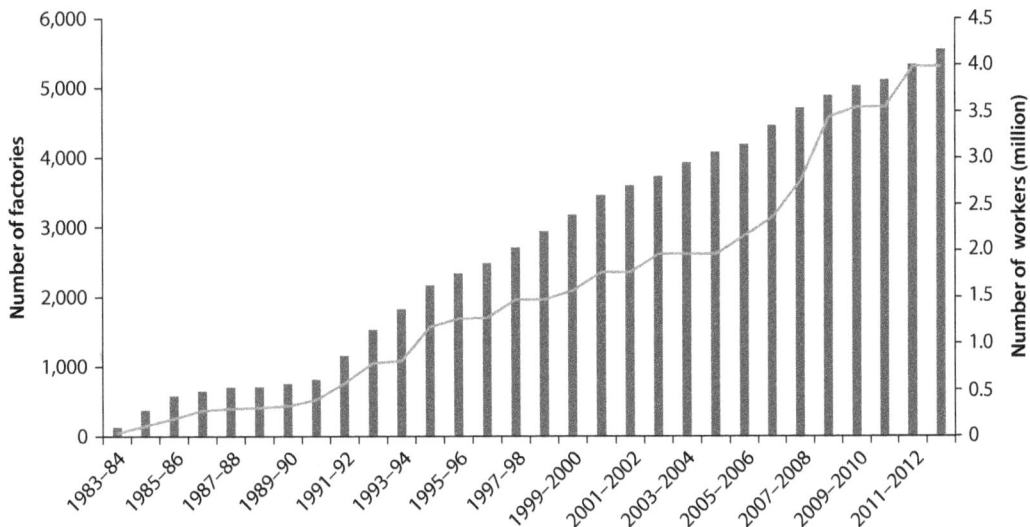

Source: Bangladesh Garment Manufacturers and Exports Association (http://www.BGMEA.com.bd).

from cotton import price volatility, coupled with tax reductions on imports of chemicals, machinery, and equipment and spare parts for effluent treatment plants. In addition, enterprises in EPZs receive tax holidays, duty-free import of machinery and equipment, and duty-free import and export of raw materials and finished goods, among other benefits. In China, apparel exporters are given a 16 percent rebate on the exported price of apparel, to compensate for the VAT that manufacturers pay on inputs.[26]

Bangladesh's apparel exports have benefited from duty-free access to the European Union via the GSP privileges accorded to least developed countries (LDCs). In addition, Australia, Canada, Japan, and Norway provide duty-free, quota-free market access for Bangladesh's exports. However, the European Union adopted a new GSP on October 31, 2012, effective January 1, 2014, and prospective beneficiary countries must apply for new GSP+ benefits. Furthermore, Bangladesh benefits from the European Union's Everything But Arms initiative, which provides LDCs with duty-free, quota-free access to the European market for all products except arms and ammunition. Like Bangladesh, China, Ethiopia, and Vietnam are current GSP beneficiaries, but their future status has yet to be determined. Bangladesh's apparel is considered "sensitive" by the United States and as such is not covered under the U.S. GSP program (this was the case even before the post-Rana Plaza suspension of Bangladesh's GSP privileges; see Kathuria and Malouche 2016a, chapter 3, for a broader discussion of GSP). As a result, exported apparel from Bangladesh, like other exporting countries, such as China, faces tariffs in the United States, ranging from 0 to 32 percent.[27] By contrast, the majority of Ethiopian apparel exports to the United States are duty free under the African Growth and Opportunity Act. Despite lack of preferences in the U.S. market, Bangladesh is the fourth largest apparel exporter to the United States after China, Vietnam, and Indonesia.

Bangladesh has built a strong reputation centered on price advantage via low-cost labor and investment incentives; production capacity, particularly in EPZs; and satisfactory quality levels, especially in value and mid-market price point segments. According to the Bangladesh Export Processing Zone Authority, in 2010, wage rates in Vietnam were nearly twice as high and in China nearly 10 times as high as those in Bangladesh (figure 4.5).

Worker safety and welfare remains a critical issue, as evidenced by numerous fires since 2007 that resulted in the deaths of hundreds of garment workers (chapter 1, box 1.1). Most factory buildings in Bangladesh lack fire escapes, sprinklers, and other modern safety equipment. Fires and other incidents have prompted companies to cancel orders. In response, international apparel brands have pledged major improvements to safety. The collapse of the eight-story Rana Plaza multipurpose building in Savar, Dhaka, on April 24, 2013, has had domestic and international repercussions. A mostly European consortium of more than 190 apparel brands, retailers, and importers has agreed on a legally binding plan (the Accord) to inspect Bangladeshi garment factories that supply the companies. As of November 2014, 1,103 factories have been inspected and 500 corrective action plans have been published. In addition, 26 American

Figure 4.5 Monthly Minimum Wages in Selected Countries, 2014

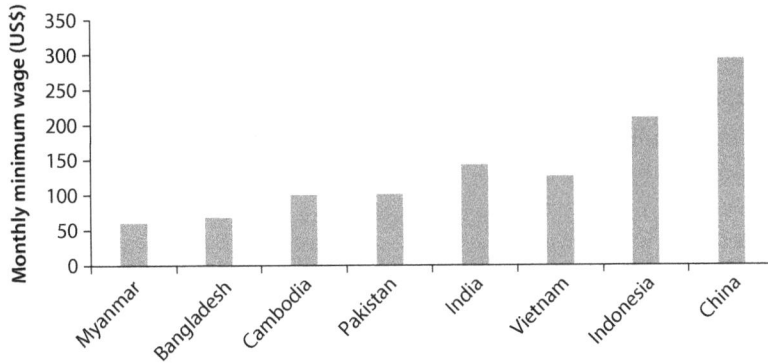

Source: World Bank: Bangladesh Development Update October 2014, using data from www.wageindicator.org.

retailers (the Alliance) completed inspections of 100 percent (580 factories) of alliance member factories and finalized almost 300 corrective action plans. Domestically, the government adopted a new Labor Law on July 15, 2013; rules and regulations necessary for implementation of the new law are being prepared, although progress is slow. More needs to be done to fulfill the commitment of improving workplace compliance with international standards.

Prospects

For Bangladesh, opportunities for growth in the apparel manufacturing sector lie in enhancing productivity within existing production value chains without adversely impacting social welfare in the sector. Multiple problems persist in Bangladesh's cotton-to-garment processing chain. These include the relatively low-skilled labor force that reduces productivity, the raw cotton imports that take many days to clear customs, and the inadequate energy and power supply that leads to higher production cost and lower capacity utilization.

The unit cost of producing a basic polo-style shirt in Bangladesh compares favorably with the unit cost in China. The value chain analysis reveals that the unit cost in Bangladesh is approximately US$3.46 (Tk 283.72) per shirt, excluding margins and the cost of transportation to port, against US$3.93 per shirt in China and US$3.06 per shirt in Ethiopia.[28] Although a polo shirt costs only US$0.39 to manufacture in Vietnam (see figure 5.8 in Kathuria and Malouche 2016b, chapter 5), the value chain analysis for Vietnam is not directly comparable to that of Bangladesh, China, or Ethiopia. Apparel production in Vietnam is dominated by the cut, make, and trim process and as such Vietnamese manufacturers do not incur the cost of raw materials, including fabric, which is the most expensive component of making polo shirts.

However, the Bangladeshi labor productivity rate of 13–27 polo shirts per person per day is substantially lower than the 18–35 pieces per person per day achieved by similar factories in China.[29] Bangladesh's minimum wage rates are set by the government, not the employing companies, and minimum wages are higher in the EPZ than outside the EPZ. Wage rates vary by skill level; currently wages range from US$39 per month for an apprentice, to US$48 per month for a helper, US$61 per month for an operator worker, and US$109 per month for a high-skilled worker. Work weeks reportedly are 48 hours per week, six days per week. Unions are permitted under the new labor law; however, its implementation has been slow. Turnover is high, with few workers staying longer than a few years.

Relative to Asian competitors, there is clear room for improvement for Bangladesh in rejects, wastage, and labor absenteeism. In examining polo shirts as a proxy for the apparel sector, capacity utilization in Bangladesh was slightly lower than that of Vietnam and China and significantly higher than that of Ethiopia. However, Bangladesh's in-factory average product rejection rates (4–8 percent) were higher—the result of lower-skilled labor. Relative to Bangladesh, both Chinese and Vietnamese enterprises had lower labor absenteeism rates, although absenteeism is a significant issue in Ethiopia. Bangladesh's labor inefficiency (including lower skill levels, lower motivation, absenteeism, and high turnover) and production inefficiency (for example, waste and reject rates) have been documented in the value chain study by Global Development Solutions. Technical efficiency can be measured by wastage, reject rates, labor absenteeism, and capacity utilization (table 4.3).

Bangladesh also fares unfavorably when it comes to fabric, the highest cost component in polo shirt production in Bangladesh, China, and Ethiopia, where fabric represents 77.5, 62.2, and 54.6 percent of total costs, respectively. The Bangladeshi textile sector, which supplies fabric to the garment subsector, relies mainly on imports of raw cotton. China and Ethiopia produce cotton domestically. Ethiopian garment makers import the fabric for polo production, since the locally sourced fabric is of inferior quality and not competitively priced. There is no cost of fabric for manufacturers in Vietnam, since they use the cut, make, and trim process.

The time it takes to import inputs is another major complaint of textile manufacturers. They believe that the delay erodes general textile and garment competitiveness, since it affects the entire supply chain. On average, based on the requisite steps, procedures, and logistics, it takes 68.2 days (with a range of 61.5–75 days) to import inputs from the date of obtaining a valid trade license.

Table 4.3 Efficiencies in Capacity Utilization, Waste, Rejects, and Absenteeism, 2012

Percent

Polo shirt manufacturing	Bangladesh	China	Ethiopia	Vietnam
In-factory product rejection	4–8	2–3	2–5	1–3
Product rejection by client	0–3	0	1–3	0–1
Production waste or scrap	5–12	5–10	10–11	1–7
Capacity utilization	73–80	60–85	55–70	80–95
Labor absenteeism rate	0.3–3	1	6.0–12	0.3–2

Source: Global Development Solutions, LLC.

Because some activities can be performed concurrently, there is room for major improvements, provided the various parties involved (freight forwarders, customs brokers, customs authorities, transports, shipping lines, and others) can work more closely together.[30] Similarly, there are delays for exporting finished goods to buyers; and given the nature of fashion trends, buyers can thus only rely on Bangladesh to supply low-value, basic garments.

The World Bank Garment Firm Survey in 2011 (World Bank 2012b) noted that the lead time for surveyed firms (number of days from order receipt to delivery) in Bangladesh is much longer than that in China or India, with an average of 88 days in Bangladesh but only 40–60 days in China and 50–70 days in India. The difference was attributed chiefly to inefficiency at the Port of Chittagong, where it reportedly takes 4.5 days to turn around a shipment of 800 TEU containers compared with 8–12 hours in Singapore.[31] In addition, the narrow Dhaka-Chittagong highway slows apparel shipments (Haroon 2012). Long lead times for imported inputs and exported products are impediments to sector growth. (For import and export transport costs, see tables 5G.3 and 5G.4 in Kathuria and Malouche 2016b, annex 5G.)

Bangladesh currently ranks last in electricity availability in relation to its competitors in the value chain analysis. While the cost of on-grid electricity is comparable to that in competing polo manufacturing countries, the percentage of time off grid is three times higher and the cost of off-grid power is substantially higher.

Reform Agenda

Although Bangladesh's competitive position for low-cost labor may eventually erode, other factors may drive its RMG growth. In any case, the country needs to go beyond low-cost labor as a source of competitiveness.

The Government of Bangladesh recently adopted a new textile policy, the Textile Policy of 2011, applicable only to textile mills, to replace the textile policy enacted in 1995. The main objective of the new policy is to adapt and reshape the textile sector in light of changes in the global textile industry. The policy emphasizes R&D of technologies, production of value-added multiple items, domestic production of cotton, human resources development, technical support, and fiscal incentives to sustain growth of the textile sector. The policy also indicates that export-oriented textile mills will be licensed to utilize bonded warehouse facilities to import raw materials, chemicals, and accessories at zero tariffs. Moreover, the Bangladesh Textile Mills Association has been empowered to recommend the renewal of bonded warehouse licenses for its member mills. With regard to cotton waste, the minimum export price has been raised to US$4.50 per kilogram from US$1.60 per kilogram (BTMA 2011). Ten percent of the production of EPZ industrial units and 20 percent of the production of outside units would be cleared for sale in the local market, subject to payment of government taxes and duties as applicable.

An important recommendation is to upgrade worker skills to increase efficiency, decrease wastage, realize cost savings, and use resources more efficiently. Over the longer term, improvements in product quality may enable Bangladesh eventually to target higher-value apparel segments that require more complex production processes. Skill-building should not be limited to line workers, but should also involve management to develop the talent needed to run effective and efficient international garment manufacturing enterprises.

Increasing competitiveness would require reengineering import and export logistics. Significant reductions in import and export times will help Bangladesh participate in fast fashion cycles and better meet customer inventory management needs. Without this improvement, Bangladesh will be stuck in the low-value, basic garment segment and have little ability to utilize its existing production capacity for higher-value garments. The bottlenecks for import and export affect the textile and garment sectors and are for the most part beyond the control of the manufacturers. The operations of logistics providers, such as customs authorities, transporters, shipping lines, maritime service providers, and insurance providers, also need to be streamlined.

Bangladesh garment manufacturing would benefit highly from better supply of energy and power. Improved power reliability would reduce manufacturing costs, increase productivity, increase capacity utilization, better utilize human resources and capital assets, and increase overall competitiveness by speeding production and attracting greater sector investment. These improvements require direct government intervention and significant public and private investment.

The sector must create and implement workplace safety standards. Inadequate standards and implementation can generate major reputational risk for Bangladesh's overall garment exports and will need to be carefully managed. Concerns have been heightened recently following a series of fatal incidents and the government has been pressured to take a number of measures to improve workers' safety. International buyers and governments have also reacted strongly to these events (chapter 1, box 1.1). On June 27, 2013, the United States suspended GSP trade privileges for Bangladesh over concerns about safety problems and labor rights violations in the garment industry. Minimizing the chances of further tragedies in the garment sector and other export sectors in Bangladesh has become a precondition for sustained export growth. Whatever measures the government will implement under domestic and international pressure, the important issue will be enforcement and commitment to ensure better and safer practices. The government needs to demonstrate its seriousness by providing leadership on this front, partly to convince the European Union and the United States, the major players post-Rana Plaza. In doing this, it will need to partner with the domestic and international private sectors. To the extent capital improvements are required for workplace improvements, increased access to financing may be needed as well. Numerous buyers and customers have expressed interest in and pledged funds for enhancing production safety. The sector should leverage this support.

Bangladesh will gain from becoming recognized as a socially responsible producer. International apparel companies are increasingly focusing on social and environmental responsibility in their supply chain, to appease customer and investor demands and to ensure operational sustainability. Particularly for publically traded companies, disclosure is no longer limited to financial statements. Rather, disclosure now involves integrated reporting that reflects the commercial, social, and environmental context within which the entity operates and demonstrates organizational stewardship under corporate social responsibility parameters (Pawlicki 2012). Moreover, vendors are increasingly subject to supply chain vendor code of conduct requirements, under which companies must disclose environmental, social, and governance information. In some cases, companies must have this information verified by a third party to supply to large retail organizations. Consumer demand is another significant driver of sustainability reporting, as customers are showing a preference for socially and environmentally responsible products and companies that offer these products can command a price premium.

The Challenge of Moving to More Capital-Intensive Light Engineering: The Case of Bicycles

Bicycles are the single largest export product of Bangladesh's engineering sector, contributing about 7.5 percent of engineering exports. Bicycle exports began around 1995 and have been growing gradually since then. Bangladesh's bicycle exports are highly concentrated in three key markets: the United Kingdom (64 percent), Germany (14 percent), and Belgium (9 percent). The bicycle and bicycle parts export industry has emerged relatively recently in the industrial landscape of Bangladesh. Investment opportunities emerged for capturing shares in the EU market after the imposition of antidumping duties on Chinese exporters. The first antidumping measures were imposed in 1993: after continuous lobbying from the European Bicycle Manufacturers Association, the European Union imposed antidumping duties of 30.8 percent on bicycles made in China.[32] This duty provided an opportunity for existing producers and new investors in other countries to enter the lucrative bicycle market of the European Union (estimated at US$7 billion in 2011). Potential linkages with the rest of the economy are substantial in this sector, given the nature of the product as an assembly of a large number of parts. And production is not very energy intensive. As such, it was felt that a case study of bicycles could help provide insights regarding the potential of not only bicycles, but also much of the engineering industry.

The bicycle manufacturing sector in Bangladesh is split into two distinct supply chains: (a) modern, export-oriented, original equipment manufacturers (OEMs) and (b) the small-scale, cottage bicycle and bicycle parts industry, which caters exclusively to the local market. The two supply chains operate independently with extremely limited interactions or linkages between the two (figure 4.6), owing to differences in market demands.[33] No suppliers in Bangladesh occupy the middle part of the supply chain, which consists of specialized parts and component manufacturers. Local suppliers cannot produce parts and components of the quality required for export-oriented OEMs. Suppliers of bicycle parts and components in Bangladesh historically have been exclusively oriented toward the local market, where quality requirements and standards have been low.

Figure 4.6 Bicycle Manufacturing Sector Supply Chain, Bangladesh

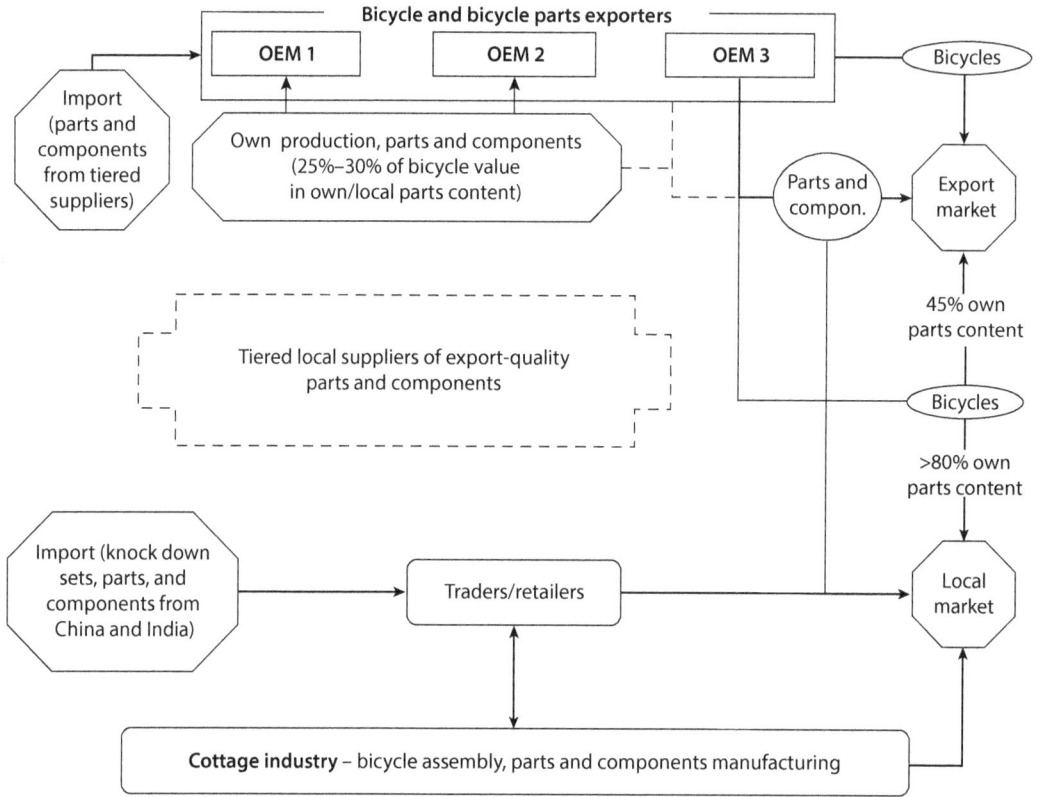

Source: Global Development Solutions, LLC.
Note: OEM = original equipment manufacturer; dashed lines indicate missing links in the supply chain.

Local producers of parts and components have few incentives to make significant quality improvements to their products geared solely to export market demands.

There are strong incentives for small firms to be exclusively oriented toward the local market. Bangladesh has a cottage industry of small-scale bicycle assemblers, parts manufacturers, and retailers, with beginnings dating to the 1970s. This cottage industry remains understudied and statistical information on it is extremely limited. Nevertheless, based on interviews with the Business Owners Association of the Bongshal Market in Dhaka, an estimated 1,500–2,000 people work in the Bongshal market in businesses directly related to bicycle assembly, component manufacturing, and retailing.[34] Firms are small (usually up to 10 employees), have extremely old machinery (in many cases over 30 years old), and are limited in their ability to graduate out of the low-quality segment of the market. Many small firms combine parts manufacturing with bicycle assembly and retailing of "complete knockdown" or "semi knockdown" kits imported from China and India. The strong incentive for firms to focus on the domestic market comes from low tariffs on inputs and high tariffs on output (56 percent), creating effective protection rates that average 219 percent for the domestic market.

Since domestic quality requirements and standards have been low, local producers of parts and components have few incentives to make significant quality improvements to their products geared solely to export market demand.

Alongside the local cottage bicycle industry, FDI was critical to the emergence of the bicycle export sector. Malaysian investors were the first to seize the EU market opportunity by establishing the first bicycle exporting firm in Bangladesh in 1995. A domestic trading group, Meghna, was the next firm to enter the bicycle export manufacturing industry. Meghna's founders had been involved in bicycle and parts trading in the 1960s, manufacturing bicycle spokes in the 1970s, and doing bicycle assembly for the local market in the 1980s. After diversifying and becoming a highly successful trading conglomerate, the Meghna Group grew to become the largest bicycle and bicycle parts manufacturer in the country. It now has two factories dedicated to the export market, two factories dedicated to bicycle manufacturing for the local market, and five bicycle components factories. The third and last market entrant in the bicycle exporting industry is German Bangla Bicycles, established in 2009 as a joint venture between a German bicycle manufacturing firm (Panther) and a Bangladeshi company (Powertrade Engineering) whose major business interests are in heavy manufacturing (telecom towers, electrical grid infrastructure, and so forth). Like the other two firms, German Bangla is an original equipment manufacturer, but by and large only for European brands.

Imported parts and components dominate the exportable bicycle value chain in Bangladesh. The final assembly stage dominates the cost structure of bicycle manufacturing, with a little over 51 percent share, consisting essentially (98 percent) of costs of parts and components. Bangladeshi OEMs import the bulk of the bicycle parts and components from China; Hong Kong SAR, China; Malaysia; Singapore; Taiwan, China; and Thailand. The cost of assembly is followed by frame assembly (21 percent) and wheel and tire assembly (10 percent). Frame and wheel manufacturing and assembly are also dominated by input material and parts costs.

The share of labor costs in the production of a bicycle is quite low across all manufacturing stages in Bangladesh. The share of labor costs is about 10 percent at the frame assembly stage, 13 percent at the wheel assembly stage, and 2 percent at the final bicycle assembly stage. When all stages of production are included, the direct labor costs associated with producing a bicycle in Bangladesh range from US$3 to US$5 per bicycle, depending on capacity utilization at any given time and on production location.[35] Bicycle manufacturing across all stages, including frame and wheel manufacturing and assembly, is relatively capital intensive. As a consequence, bicycle manufacturing can be and is successful in countries with relatively higher labor costs than Bangladesh. In China, for example, the average monthly payroll per employee in the transport equipment industry (including bicycles) is US$500. In Taiwan, China, the average monthly payroll in the industry is US$1,300.[36] Notwithstanding these comparatively high labor costs, producers in these countries are market leaders in the bicycle industry: China is the world leader in bicycle exports in general and Taiwan, China, is among the leaders in medium- to high-end bicycles.

Prospects

The lack of a local base of suppliers of quality parts and components has significant implications. First, OEMs that do not have deep enough pockets for investing in additional parts and components manufacturing must source parts in foreign markets. Currently, two of the three Bangladeshi OEMs import parts worth 60–75 percent of their bicycles' export value. Interviews suggest that these producers will likely increase the foreign content of parts and components in the future to the maximum allowed by EU rules of origin.[37] Second, OEMs that are strong financially, like Meghna, have made significant investments in parts and components manufacturing. For bicycles sold locally, Meghna's share of own parts and components is estimated at 80 percent and for exported bicycles, up to 45 percent. This, and the issue of scale economies in the manufacture of parts, probably limit opportunities for independent suppliers of export-quality parts and component suppliers to emerge. In modern bicycle production, scale economies and precision engineering are clearly important. These aspects have allowed China and even higher-wage countries to remain competitive in segments of the bicycle market. In Bangladesh, modern export firms have vertically integrated to overcome partially the lack of a modern parts supplying industry, but the firms rely on imports for the bulk of their needs for parts. This approach has meant that their export prices are 10–20 percent higher than China's export prices.

The third implication stemming from foreign sourcing of export-quality parts is a negative impact on lead times. For example, Bangladeshi exporters' lead times to the U.K. market are estimated to be 30–50 percent longer compared with those of Chinese exporters (see table 4.4). It is estimated that the bulk of the lead time gap arises from the Bangladeshi firms' need to source a large part of parts and components from abroad, which can take up to a month after all the required paperwork and shipping. Chinese exporters can rely on a vast local supplier base that enables them to source parts and components within a few days. Furthermore, shipping transit times to and from Chittagong are uncompetitive.[38] For example, it takes approximately the same number of days (27) to ship a container from Chittagong to the United Kingdom and to ship a container from

Table 4.4 Comparative Lead Times, Bicycle Exports, Bangladesh vs. China, 2011
Days

Lead time category	Bangladesh	China
Preprocessing (parts ordering), Lead Time A (L/C & other paperwork)	8–15	1
Preprocessing (parts ordering and delivery), Lead Time B (shipping/transportation)	15–20	2–7
Processing lead time (bicycle manufacturing/assembly)[a]	25	25
Post-processing lead time (shipping to United Kingdom)	27–30	27
Total lead time	75–90	55–60
Lead time difference (Bangladesh/China)	+35% to +50%	

Source: Global Development Solutions, LLC.
Note: L/C = letters of credit.
a. For illustration, assumes identical order size, processing time, and destination market for both countries. This comparison is for illustration purposes only; lead times vary significantly depending on bicycle complexity.

much further east in Shanghai to the United Kingdom; it takes half as many days to ship a container from Sri Lanka (two weeks).

Another concern is that the quality of electricity is extremely poor and creates major problems for small and medium enterprises (SMEs) that cannot afford generators. Although SMEs consider the price of electricity to be high (US$0.09 per kilowatt hour), it is generally the quality of electricity in relation to price that generates this perception.[39] Daily brownouts are a frequent occurrence in Dhaka. The duration of brownouts is reported to range from a fraction of an hour to three to four hours at least once a week. Frequent brownouts create major production problems. In an example highlighted in the value chain analysis of the steering column producer, all the processes come to a halt and all the cutting, extrusion, and lathing machines have to be retooled. This generates losses in time, materials, and quality of product. Poor electricity combined with other production bottlenecks leads to major losses in this particular SME that amount to as much as 8.3 percent of production.

Furthermore, OEMs report difficulties in finding qualified workers in a number of areas. The level of workforce education is very poor. Most of the workers producing parts and components in the interviewed SMEs are young and have little to no education. Typically, SMEs have at least one experienced technician, equally uneducated, to pass on process and other knowledge to less experienced workers; "learning by doing" is the mode of operation in all SMEs. For some SME business owners, the uneducated workforce is an advantage, since it is not complicated to make the product, and allows for lower wages. Most owners, however, recognize that any future technological and process upgrading in their operations will be extremely difficult to accomplish with the current level of know-how and education of the workforce. Finding qualified welders for the frame assembly stages of production is reported to be particularly difficult. Welders are among the highest-paid members of the workforce in assembly plants, earning up to US$150 per month in Dhaka. This is a relatively high manufacturing wage in Bangladesh. Yet despite the significant premium over standard assembly line wages (up to 50 percent), finding and attracting a sufficient number of qualified welders is a challenge. Finding and attracting qualified middle managers is also reported to be difficult, as management and business graduates are reported to prefer working in the telecom and other service sectors.

Lack of access to finance prevents the modernization of machinery for SMEs. Old machinery contributes to production inefficiencies and losses among SMEs, in large part owing to lack of access to finance. The value chain of the steering column producer suggests that the SME has three pipe-cutting machines, two lathing machines, and four impact extrusion machines, all of which are at least 25 years old and some of which are 40 years old. The owner would like to replace some of the machines, but was not able to obtain a loan from a local bank three years ago. In fact, none of the SMEs interviewed had received any loans from local banks. The few producers that had recently purchased relatively new machinery did so with their own funds. Technological upgrading of SMEs will be highly dependent on access to finance that is currently not forthcoming.

Finally, the competitiveness of Bangladeshi OEMs across all stages of bicycle production also suffers from unnecessary bureaucratic practices.[40] For example, OEMs need to obtain two permits to import welding gases (argon-based and other specialized welding gases) that are not available locally: a "prior permission" to import and then a "final permission" to import. Both permits are issued by the Explosives Department of the Ministry of Energy, which regulates the trade in these generally dangerous materials. According to OEMs, this two-stage process is a typical example of an approval process designed for rent-seeking. The so-called prior permission is almost identical to the final permission: most information sought in the prior permission (gas content and cylinder specifications) is also provided to the authorities at the final permission stage (via packing lists, invoices, and specifications). Current regulations (the Explosives Act or the Gas Cylinder Rules amendments) are not sufficiently clear about the necessity of a prior permission as a procedure.

Reform Agenda

How can Bangladesh reduce the costs of its bicycles to become more competitive in a more contested market setting? How can it diversify its markets and break into markets such as Japan and the United States and regional urban clusters in South Asia? Fortunately, most of the answers to these questions involve support at a broader policy level, rather than support that is specific to bicycles. For example, trade facilitation reforms and business facilitation measures will be critical to improve lead time and reduce the cost of doing business, strengthening the competitiveness of the industry.

The parts industry will need to invest in modern tools and equipment, such as semi-automated and, where necessary, automated precision equipment. A modern parts and components industry that progressively produces more and more in-country would help the overall competitiveness of bicycle exports. Producing this kind of programmable equipment locally will allow different kinds of parts to be produced on the same assembly line with low downtimes and high precision. Additional scale economies can be reaped by focusing on standardized parts that are common to different types and makes of bicycles.

Reducing output tariffs and thereby domestic ERPs and increasing competition for the domestic market could help provide consumers with a choice of high-quality bicycles and, in time, potentially narrow the gap between the two markets. Bicycle production for the domestic market is highly protected and helps to perpetuate keeping the domestic and export markets separate. As in other industrial sectors, a growing domestic base of export-quality products could help existing and potential manufacturers to export. Of course, lower domestic ERPs would also help reduce the anti-export bias.

Better access to finance will help those producers whose desire to invest in equipment has been hampered by financial access. One way is for the large OEMs to support such investment by guaranteeing bank loans for the suppliers on the basis of their (OEM) orders. This could be complemented by improved financial access for the SME sector as a whole.

Bangladesh could court FDI and also seek to become part of the international and regional supply chains in bicycles and parts. Development and exports of particular components can help achieve scale economies and create positive externalities for the sector as a whole. Large firms in China and India could potentially invest in Bangladesh or be encouraged to make Bangladeshi firms part of those countries' supply chains.

Expanding Services: The Case of Information Technology Enabled Services

The information technology (IT) industry is a service sector that is considered by the public and private sectors to have high growth potential. The industry employs an estimated 70,000 people, generating an estimated US$400 million in annual revenues. Although the majority of firms in the industry report software development and maintenance to be their core business, information technology enabled services–business process outsourcing (ITES-BPO) generates more revenues in the industry than software development. The value of exports from the formal software and ITES-BPO sector in FY2013 was US$101.63 million, a relatively low amount compared with other countries in the region. Despite high expectations, the sector remains a marginal contributor to Bangladeshi exports. Nevertheless, a number of recent developments have raised the hopes for the sector in the near future: exports are on the rise and multinational corporations are investing in R&D centers in the country. In light of these developments, ITES-BPO was selected as a service sector for value chain analysis in this study.

In Bangladesh, more than 1,000 software and ITES companies are registered, employing about 70,000 people and generating an estimated US$400 million in annual revenues.[41] About two-thirds of the firms are small, employing 10–30 people. In addition, there are an estimated few hundred unregistered small companies doing software and ITES-BPO business for the local and international markets. Another 5,000 people are estimated to be working as freelancers. Many firms provide a range of software and ITES-BPO services at the same time. (For more details, see Kathuria and Malouche 2016b, chapter 7, on ITES.) Approximately half of the officially registered companies provide a range of ITES-BPO services: data and form processing, graphic and web design, content management, and other services.

The industry has generated limited exports in the past, but a number of recent developments have raised hopes for the sector. Officially reported exports have grown from US$26 million in FY2006 to US$101.63 million in FY2013. These export figures do not include an estimated US$20 million to US$30 million in annual exports generated by the freelancers as well as by informal companies that are not captured by the official records. Bangladesh Association of Software and Information Services (BASIS) estimates that 160 IT and ITES-BPO companies are involved in exports. The industry has also recently gained new multinational members: Samsung opened its R&D center in 2010, employing more than

200 engineers, and more than 30 joint ventures have been established in Dhaka to provide offshore services to clients in international markets.

In Bangladesh, the majority of ITES-BPO service providers operate in the lower end of the business process outsourcing (BPO) pyramid, from data capturing or transcription to some level of problem-solving or basic voice services. Until 2011, Bangladesh did not export any basic voice services, but according to a recent study, some revenues (US$2 million) were generated in this area in 2011.[42] The bulk of revenue and exports, however, remains in the areas of basic data capturing and rule-based processing. This report provides value chain analyses for the typical data-capturing and rule-based processing BPO services provided in Bangladesh: (a) vectorization data processing (image processing) and (b) accounting rule-based processing of data (invoices and similar data). In addition, a third, higher-value-added value chain of industrial engineering BPO services will be provided.

In this context, the industry depends heavily on the government's effective implementation of its long-standing plans for improvement of domestic and international connectivity. According to the Digital Bangladesh strategic plan, the government plans to expedite the process of having a second and even third submarine cable connection, to ensure minimal redundancy and reliability in nationwide Internet connectivity, and take initiatives to reduce the price of bandwidth.[43] It is anticipated that a rapid and robust implementation of these policy initiatives is needed to bring the country's Internet connectivity infrastructure at par with other countries competing in the international BPO market. Sri Lanka, for example, has four international submarine cables; fairly developed broadband, leased-line, satellite connectivity; as well as developed 3G and 4G technologies. India has an even more advanced connectivity network. By comparison, Bangladesh has the least developed network compared with countries with developed ITES-BPO service industries (see table 4.5).

The IT and ITES sector benefits from a number of preferential policies. IT and ITES-BPO firms are exempted from income taxes. This relief is set to

Table 4.5 Benchmarking the Information and Communications Technology Network and Overall Infrastructure, 2012

Country	Network readiness	Overall infrastructure
Ireland	5.0	5.3
Malaysia	4.8	5.1
China	4.1	4.5
India	4.0	3.6
Sri Lanka	3.9	4.1
Egypt, Arab Rep.	3.8	3.6
Philippines	3.6	3.2
Bangladesh	3.2	2.2

Source: Compiled by Global Development Solutions, LLC, from World Economic Forum Global Competitiveness/Information Technology Reports, 2011–12.
Note: Network readiness is defined as "the degree to which economies across the world leverage information and communications technology for enhanced competitiveness." Scale: 1 = underdeveloped, 7 = efficient by international standards.

expire in 2015, although the industry has called for an extension until 2018. The industry also enjoys various VAT exemptions for some imported hardware, software, and related service purchases. Moreover, an estimated 20 IT and ITES firms have been provided access to grade-A office space at preferential prices at the government-owned Janata Tower premises in central Dhaka. The industry can also use the Equity Entrepreneurship Fund (EEF), a venture capital fund offering equity support and managed by Bangladesh Bank, in place since 2001. An estimated 40–50 IT and ITES companies have made use of roughly US$10 million in the past 10 years, but according to the industry, bureaucratic procedures have made access to this fund difficult.

Prospects

Worldwide spending for IT and BPO exceeded US$1.7 trillion in 2011, a growth of 5.4 percent over 2010. Software products, IT, and BPO services continued to lead, accounting for more than US$1 trillion (63 percent) of the total market. With regard to the maturity of different segments of the BPO industry, services such as document management, customer services, and application development and maintenance are reaching maturity, whereas banking, insurance, and procurement BPOs are at the phase of rapid growth. Life sciences, health care, and utilities BPOs are in the early, emerging stage of growth (see figure 4.7).

The current state of infrastructure is a key component in the supply chain of ITES-BPO service exporters. From the perspective of BPO clients, outsourcing a business process to a BPO service provider only makes sense if it delivers services in a timely and reliable manner. Bangladeshi BPO service providers report major difficulties in building quality and reliability reputations with foreign clients because their delivery of services is interrupted by the poor supply of Internet connectivity and electricity. Without major improvements

Figure 4.7 Outsourcing Maturity Curve, 2011

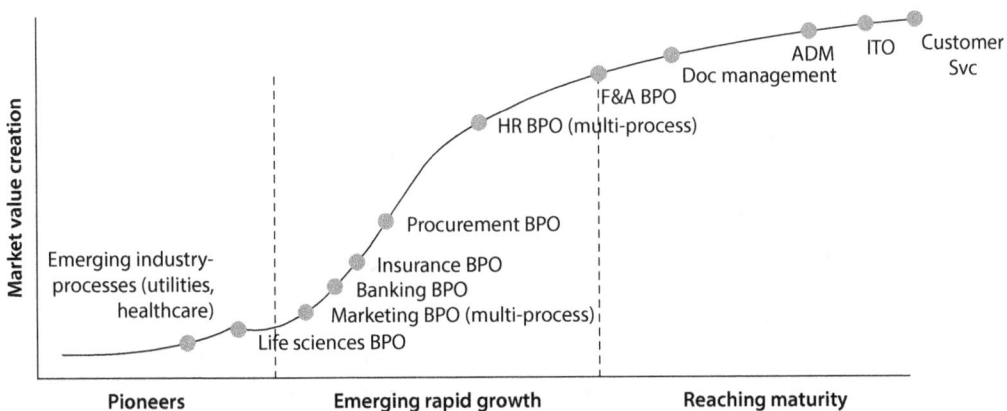

Source: Horses for Sources, State of Outsourcing in 2011 as quoted in www.softec.sk.
Note: ADM = administration; BPO = business process outsourcing; DOC = document; F&A = finance and accounting; ITO = information technology outsourcing; HR = human resources; Svc = service.

in the quality of basic infrastructure, labor or other cost arbitrage will not be enough to make the Bangladeshi ITES-BPO industry attractive internationally. Bangladesh would only be attractive for the most basic data entry and similar low-risk business processes.

Internet costs are a heavy burden on the cash flows of ITES-BPO SMEs and can result in delivery costs that resemble those of manufacturing value chains. The cost of purchasing Internet services contributes approximately 50 percent of the total cost of delivering services to clients. Since Internet connectivity is needed for both data reception and data delivery, when the two stages are included, Internet costs contribute 11 percent to the total cost structure of an image-processing SME. Although data reception and delivery are by and large automated and done electronically, the value chain structure of ITES-BPO service providers more closely resembles manufacturing value chain structures that involve costly transportation and delivery of physical goods. This is because Internet access in Bangladesh is costly. Notwithstanding the fact that Internet service prices are decreasing, BPO SMEs spend between US$10,000 and US$14,000 per year to secure a relatively modest Internet connection bandwidth.

In addition to and despite its high price, the quality of Internet services is poor. First, Internet network failures are common. At least once and up to three times a month, the Internet connection is not available for six to eight hours. Shorter duration failures of a few hours are more frequent. One of the key reasons for Internet network failures owes to the existence of only one international submarine cable. For image-processing BPOs, Internet network failures present a challenge, but only to a limited degree: data (images) that could not be received or sent in any given day can generally be received or sent the following day. By contrast, other ITES-BPOs that operate in segments that need real-time and continuous business process support are highly impacted by the poor quality of Internet services. Moreover, the limited bandwidth effectively caps the amount of throughput to 7,000–8,000 images per month that can be uploaded to client-dedicated servers. Second, the maximum available bandwidth is five megabits per second. For invoice-processing and other BPOs, limited bandwidth reduces their ability to offer complementary voice and other helpdesk services to their clients. The current network infrastructure, therefore, is not conducive to ITES-BPO growth.

Bangladeshi ITES-BPO service providers operate in a supply chain without any captive BPO centers (figure 4.8). BPO service providers need to have domain-specific knowledge of business processes to provide BPO services in finance, human resources, insurance, procurement, or any other outsourcing field. Lessons from successful ITES-BPO supply chains in countries like India and the Philippines suggest that local BPO service providers obtain vital business process knowledge through business relationships with captive BPO centers. Bangladesh has a distinct competitive disadvantage because it is not able to acquire business process knowledge and expertise directly from captive BPO centers. This leaves Bangladeshi ITES-BPO service providers with two choices: acquire business process expertise from local clients in the banking, insurance, telecom, and similar service sectors or

Figure 4.8 ITES-BPO Sector Supply Chain, Bangladesh

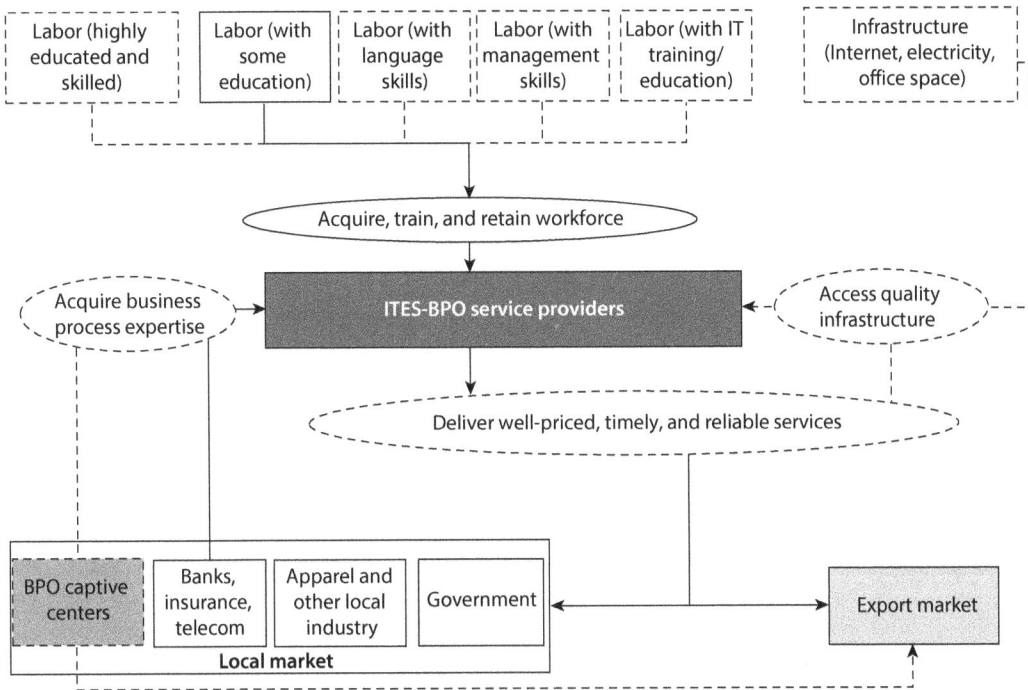

Source: Global Development Solutions, LLC.
Note: Dashed lines indicate underdeveloped parts of the supply chain. ITES-BPO = information technology enabled services–business process outsourcing; IT = information technology.

directly from international clients abroad. Acquiring expertise and specialization through these two channels is slow and arduous, as Bangladeshi ITES-BPO firms have discovered.

Captive BPO centers are a critical source of business process information for local BPO service providers. Captive BPO centers are BPO centers set up and owned by multinational corporations. American Express, General Electric, British Airways, Citibank, and hundreds of other multinational corporations own BPO centers in India, the Philippines, and other countries. Moreover, depending on where they are in the trajectory of the build-operate-transfer business model, foreign-owned captives become deeply embedded in local BPO supply chains: numerous linkages along cross-ownership, subcontracting, vertical industry specialization, and other lines emerge between captives and local BPO centers. This way, local BPOs not only gain deep understanding of business processes in a range of industries, but also grow together with captive centers through third-party business relationships.

In the absence of captive centers, Bangladeshi BPOs must create market demand on their own, which is extremely difficult. In India, for example, captive units dominate the ITES-BPO industry—in 2005, they accounted for over 65 percent of the value of the work offshored to India.[44] Captive centers are generally involved in developing local managerial and other talent; this option generates considerable cost-savings compared to the parent firms sending over their expatriate managers. Furthermore, with the current technologies, parent companies adopt virtual training methods that generate additional savings and at the same time accelerate manpower development in the countries where they operate their captive centers. Deep familiarity with the parent company's business process is a major advantage in outsourcing, and Bangladesh suffers in this respect.

Bangladesh's performance on literacy rates and secondary school enrollment is extremely poor and undermines the development of the sector. Basic data processing BPOs typically need a labor force that comes out of secondary schools and colleges and can then be trained. In this respect, Bangladesh has one of the poorest records of any country competing in the BPO market and major improvements are needed to improve the access of ITES-BPOs to an educated workforce. With regard to information and communications technology (ICT) literacy, the national ICT Policy 2009 goals stipulate, among others, the following objectives in the area of education: (a) boost ICT tools at all levels of education; (b) extend the reach of ICT literacy throughout the country by incorporating ICT courses in secondary, technical, and vocational education; (c) encourage closer collaboration between academia and industry; and (d) ensure that all universities provide education with global ICT standards.

Reform Agenda

When it introduced its "Digital Bangladesh by 2021" vision in 2009, the Government of Bangladesh gave new impetus to the ICT industry. Digital Bangladesh is an ambitious policy agenda that envisions utilization of information and communication technologies as pro-poor tools, "to eradicate poverty, establish good governance, ensure social equity through quality education, health care and law enforcement for all and prepare the country for climate change."[45] The government also updated the ICT Policy 2009 and ICT Act 2009, which represent the current strategic and policy framework for the ICT sector in the country. ICT Policy 2009 has a comprehensive list of objectives across a wide range of areas, from social equity, health care, and environment to employment generation, export growth, and support to the ICT sector. It includes a specific policy objective related to improving access to finance for software and ITES companies. In late 2011, the Ministry of Information and Communication Technology was established to spearhead ICT policy implementation. Giving the ICT industry priority is a powerful message given by the government and can lead to positive returns if implemented in a strategic manner.

The problem is that the ICT policy is wide-ranging, lacks prioritization, and has been poorly implemented. The policy has guidelines for budgetary allocation, which have not been implemented.[46] The general perception in the industry is that government ICT policy each year recycles the same initiatives without major action and financial commitment to back them up. Annual budgets have for many years emphasized establishment of high-tech parks, setting up a second submarine telecommunication cable, and many related initiatives that by and large are considered by the industry as paper-based policies only. According to the industry, there are 306 action items in ICT Policy 2009 for which various agencies have been designated as key or supporting implementing agencies. Although some agencies, most notably Bangladesh Bank, have already implemented or started to implement some action items during the past three years (including e-commerce, national payment gateway, etc.), many other initiatives, such as special education loans for ICT graduates, technology parks, etc., remain unaddressed. Recently, the Cabinet approved the National ICT Policy 2015, but this is yet to be approved by Parliament.

A priority area for the government would be to provide quality Internet services at affordable rates. Uninterrupted connectivity with latency and high bandwidth are basic necessities to compete in the global market, particularly at the higher-value-added end of ITES-BPO service provision. As is stated in the Digital Bangladesh strategic plan, two additional international submarine cables should be installed to ensure minimal redundancy in case of failure of one of the three cables. Tax exemptions do not seem to apply for items that are purchased more frequently by ITES-BPO companies. Most notably, the Internet connections sourced from local service providers are taxed at 15 percent. Import tariffs on ICT-related products and accessories are also considered too high by the private sector. Microphones, headphones, and related accessories used by BPO providers of voice-related services have a tariff of 25 percent. (Optical fiber cable imports face tariffs of 12 percent; Uninterruptible Power Supply/Instant Power Supply (UPS/IPS) backup devices have a tariff of 5 percent; and modems, routers, and similar networking equipment have a tariff of 3 percent.) If duties protect a particular sector and hurt a sector that is potentially large and promising, then such duties need to be looked at carefully. It appears that the protection for the domestic optical cable manufacturer, for example, may be hurting the rest of the sector.

Addressing the skills gap is another priority for the sector, including high school students, dropouts, as well as graduate students. The BASIS Institute of Technology and Management could develop a combination of training programs, coaching, workshops, and certification for individuals as well as organizations. International experts can be instrumental in developing curricula and leading courses that will be relevant for multinationals requiring ITES-BPO services. The donor community can help in sourcing appropriate international experts. In addition, with donor support, curriculums in the traditional school system should be adapted to international trends. Building on students' basic computer skills acquired from primary school, vocational secondary schools could offer courses appropriate to ICT and also focus on the soft skills lacking in the market. Training would also cover management practices, marketing techniques, and English language courses.

The industry also particularly suffers from stringent foreign exchange (forex) regulations and an inflexible payment regime. According to Foreign Exchange Circular No. 15, foreign exchange intermediaries can remit on behalf of IT and ITES firms only up to US$10,000 in a calendar year for fees related to software registration, domain registration and hosting, server maintenance, and similar fees. Increasing this limit to at least US$50,000 per year and expanding the list of eligible expenditures to include technical training fees, web advisement, listing fees, and conference and event registration fees would help. And the maximum allowable forex outward remittances for technical services is 6 percent of the previous year's sales and permission from the Board of Investment is required for each transaction. These rules restrict the scope of business. Finally, IT and ITES companies cannot purchase or renew soft-copy, downloadable software licenses through a letter of credit. As a result, IT and ITES companies face problems when they want to import software through the Internet in legal ways. Allowing payment by letter of credit for nonphysical software purchases would facilitate doing business through ease of transactions and would also help reduce the use of illegal software and licenses.

Access to SME loans is one of the largest challenges for the ICT sector. ITES-BPOs, with the exception of large ones, are generally unable to access credit easily. Most of them have limited physical collateral, which prevents them from accessing credit. In this context, policy support that improves access to specialized credit facilities, such as an EEF or other government- or donor-based SME financing facility, is anticipated to improve access for finance for ITES-BPOs in Bangladesh. Policy support can help improve access to existing funds (EEF and the Japan International Cooperation Agency-funded SME loan facility). Analysis should be made to determine what intervention is necessary to the EEF program to improve the valuation tools, fund repayment policies, proposal evaluation, fund disbursement, supervision, and monitoring and evaluation.

Finally, a focused and sustained promotion campaign—country branding and sector branding—and high profile networking events aimed at proactively addressing the main concerns of industry players in target markets would help better position Bangladesh. This should be carefully thought out, in partnership with the private sector and international consultants. Among the goals here could be to bring in an anchor investor in the captive BPO segment, which could have major positive spillovers for the sector as a whole. Demonstrable and long-run commitment by the government is also essential to boost investor confidence. For example, an IT and ITES business portal for the country could help develop a positive reputation for Bangladesh's ITES sector. Presenting the sector as a whole has advantages beyond individual companies attempting to place their URL at the top of the search list. This can also be done in partnership with the industry.

Pharmaceuticals

Although the pharmaceuticals industry has been able to meet the bulk of domestic needs, it has not done well on the export front, despite long being held up as a major export prospect. Under the Trade Related Aspects of Intellectual Property Rights (TRIPS) agreement, signed by all members of the WTO in 1995, developing countries agreed to honor product patents for drug manufacturing after 2005.

LDCs like Bangladesh were exempted from TRIPS obligations until 2016. This gave Bangladesh an edge over other countries, such as India and Brazil, between 2005 and 2015, wherein Bangladesh could legally reverse-engineer patented pharmaceutical products and sell them in its domestic market as well as export to other countries (mostly LDCs) where the product patents were not recognized.

The import regime consists mainly of banned items, restricted items, and freely importable items, while tariffs on inputs and outputs are low. Importation of final medicine and vaccine products is based on a list of importable items published in the government gazette by the Directorate General of Drug Administration (DGDA). The procedures for importation are facilitated by creating a "block list" of imports for each recognized pharmaceutical company approved by the director of the DGDA. The block list describes the raw material, packaging material, value, and quantity according to the annual production plans of the pharmaceutical companies. The list is usually prepared as part of product registration. Companies importing raw materials have to present an import invoice and an analysis report of the quality, value, and quantity for each import. The analysis report of the raw materials must be certified by DGDA or be prepared by a government-approved pre-shipment inspection agent (Ministry of Commerce 2012).

The pharmaceutical sector has been among the highest priority sectors of Bangladesh's export policy since 2006. Highest priority sectors are entitled to income tax exemption for export earnings, export credit at reduced rates, assistance in marketing in overseas markets through participating in export fairs, and so on. In addition, the government reduced or exempted duties on some capital machinery and raw materials imported for use in pharmaceutical production.[47] The sector also enjoys a tax holiday and duty drawback scheme. The export policy of 2012–15 doubled the value of samples allowed to be sent by the pharmaceuticals industry to overseas buyers to US$60,000 a year. Empirical field-work conducted for this report estimates the ERP for the drugs that are exported to be mildly negative (0 to 0.5 percent).

Exports have been low and stagnant, while other countries, such as India, have emerged as major players in the generics market. By the late 1980s, Bangladesh had become a drug exporting country, but exports have stagnated and are a small share of production. Bangladeshi pharmaceutical exports totaled US$69.2 million in FY2014, only 0.2 percent of total export earnings. The bulk of export earnings owe to Novartis-Sandoz. Exports comprise only around 8 percent of the total production of the local pharmaceutical companies that are exporting. Currently, the world generic market is around US$130 billion, with India holding roughly a one-fifth share. As of 2014, Bangladesh was exporting pharmaceuticals to more than 80 countries, but mostly to the less regulated markets. Bhutan, Kenya, Myanmar, Nepal, and Vietnam are examples of such markets. Bangladeshi pharmaceuticals are also exported to two other types of markets, but to a much lesser extent. One is the semi-regulated or moderately regulated market, for example, Malaysia, the Russian Federation, and Tanzania. However, the largest market in generics is the United States, which is strictly regulated. Australia and the United Kingdom are also strictly regulated markets in which Bangladeshi exports are minimal. Only a select few firms have the proper accreditation and they export only a few products. The largest barriers for Bangladesh's entry into regulated markets are lack of manufacturing facilities, which cost at least US$50 million each, and lack of know-how (World Bank 2008).

Bangladesh is almost self-sufficient in manufacturing pharmaceuticals. In 2011, 97 percent of the country's needs were met by domestic manufacturers (including locally-based multinational companies) and the rest was imported (Beximco Pharmaceuticals 2011). The imported drugs are mostly specialized pharmaceutical products, including vaccines, anti-cancer drugs, and essential lifesaving drugs. Industry insiders believe that this ratio might shift further in favor of local producers, as some of the large, domestic firms are preparing to manufacture these drugs in house. The sector emerged in the early post-independence period of Bangladesh when multinational companies dominated the pharmaceutical sector. Eight leading multinational companies enjoyed 75 percent of the total domestic market (Bangladesh Tariff Commission 2010), producing vitamins, enzymes, and cough syrups locally, and imported other essential drugs from their sister units located abroad. Then, the National Drug Policies of 1982 and 2005 helped the formation and growth of a domestic pharmaceutical sector. Under the National Drug Policies, multinational companies could no longer produce vitamins, enzymes, and cough syrups. Only local companies were allowed to produce them. Multinational companies were also restricted to producing injectable vitamins for local supply. Furthermore, contract manufacturing by Bangladeshi companies for multinationals was prohibited.[48] The policy also restricted importation of a pharmaceutical product or a close substitute as long as the pharmaceutical product was being produced in the country. As a result of these restrictions, several multinational corporations sold out their companies to local entrepreneurs. This led to the formation of local pharmaceuticals companies and an increase in domestic production. Bangladesh, which was once a drug-importing country, became a drug-exporting country by the late 1980s.

The domestic pharmaceutical market is highly concentrated and has been growing steadily. According to DGDA, there are currently 274 pharmaceutical companies in Bangladesh. Among these firms, 67 are termed "nonfunctional" or "suspended." The companies include medium-to-large Bangladeshi companies with international links, specialized subsidiaries of multinational companies, and a number of small companies. However, the top 10 firms (all of which are locally owned) hold 67.6 percent of market share while the top multinational companies hold only 9.1 percent of the total market (IDLC 2011). In the past five years, the domestic pharmaceutical market has experienced robust growth and has almost doubled in value to more than US$1 billion. This owes to the growth in the market and rising health care spending, improved access to health care, and an increase in new types of illnesses.

Pharmaceutical companies employ the highest number of white collar workers in Bangladesh (Bhuiyan, Maniruzzaman, and Sultana 2011). Pharmaceutical manufacturing is a capital-intensive and technically challenging industry where skilled labor is essential. Around 115,000 workers are employed in this sector, of which 58.6 percent work in management and 41.4 percent work in production. Only 2.1 percent of the total workforce in this industry is female (Bangladesh Tariff Commission 2010).

Prospects

Bangladesh's pharmaceuticals industry does not have any significant capability for research or sophisticated production. Pharmaceutical manufacturing generally consists of two steps (World Bank 2008). Manufacturing of active pharmaceutical ingredients (APIs), the first step, is a highly sophisticated, technically demanding chemical and biochemical fermentation and synthesis process. Firms can either manufacture their own APIs or purchase them on the open market. Commodity API manufacturing tends to be a high-volume, low-margin business based extensively on scale economies and large dedicated manufacturing lines. Smaller manufacturers therefore have limited opportunities to compete globally. The second step is the drug's final formulation. Unlike the chemical business of API production, final formulation belongs to the manufacturing sector. During this process, firms mix APIs and excipients (other non-active ingredients); press the mixture into pills, tablets, or solutions; and then package the product for the consumer market. Final formulations are equally as complex as API manufacturing but require different skills. Because firms can produce 50 or more products in a single plant with adaptable equipment, economies of scale are less important for final formulations than for API manufacturing.

Exporting pharmaceutical products is challenging. Each country has its own product regulations, registration requirements, language requirements, cultural preferences, national packaging requirements, and industry protection mechanisms. Sales on the global market are quite competitive, with firms from around the world vying for business. Furthermore, initiating exports requires a significant investment in money, time, and paperwork to register the product in the target country. Because generic products are branded in less regulated markets, pharmaceutical firms also need to make significant investments in sales and marketing. Testing and certification investments are also critical. All these investments are made without a guarantee of future sales.

Several factors within the industry have prevented Bangladesh's pharmaceutical exports from growing as hoped. Also field interviews indicate that perhaps the expectations for the industry were too high. The industry is inherently a capital-intensive one, where quality of production and highly sanitized conditions are at a premium. The share of labor in total production cost is low, especially when the cost of APIs is included in the overall cost of production. Moreover, the incentives created by policy (as opposed to exhortations by policy makers) have led to a private sector focus on import substitution. Thus, the industry has not focused on the capacity to reverse engineer to take advantage of the TRIPS waiver.

Other critical export constraints include weak enforcement of quality regulations and strict foreign exchange controls. The lax enforcement of regulations has allowed local companies to fall below the standards necessary for the more strictly regulated export markets. Strict foreign exchange controls deter firms from undertaking critical activities to increase exports. These include receiving certification from foreign regulatory authorities, using consulting services to advise on best practices in manufacturing, and having drug samples tested. Obtaining permission to transfer large amounts of foreign currency is a lengthy and cumbersome process that is creating a nontax barrier for exports. Lack of an API production facility means that Bangladesh has to rely on imported APIs for formulation and, although this is not insurmountable, it could create a handicap vis-à-vis companies in countries that have in-house or in-country API production.

Despite extensive rules, the pharmaceutical market remains under-regulated because of the lack of capacity of the regulatory authority. The primary responsibility for drug quality control lies with the manufacturers and the top firms have their own quality control mechanisms. However, DGDA has to ensure the quality, efficacy, and safety of pharmaceutical products through the implementation of relevant legislation, via its monitoring and supervision functions. Although DGDA was upgraded from "department" to "directorate general" status after the adoption of the revised National Drug Policy in 2005, DGDA continues to suffer from funding, staffing, and technical competence constraints. It is severely understaffed, given the rapidly growing pharmaceutical market, large number of registered products, and large population size,[49] and the enforcement of standards suffers. As of September 2014, there were 370 personnel vacancies at different levels, against which 226 had been filled. With limited human resources and staff not sufficiently trained in recent developments in quality control, compliance is difficult to test and enforce. Local inspectors have been found to be less stringent compared with international inspectors and DGDA has issued some questionable certifications. To overcome this issue, some pharmaceuticals firms are adhering to different manufacturing quality standards, such as those of the Therapeutic Goods Administration of Australia and the United Kingdom's Medicines and Healthcare Products Regulatory Agency; other firms are operating below WHO standards. This is preventing the use of a harmonized global standard in drug regulation.

The drug-testing laboratories also have insufficient capacity. Testing of drugs is required for evaluating preregistration and the quality of post-marketed drugs and medicines. The two laboratories under DGDA have extremely limited capacity with inadequate staffing and equipment. According to an UNCTAD (2011) study, there are three technical staff members in the Chittagong Laboratory and eight in the Dhaka Laboratory. There is neither a central reference laboratory nor any independent contract research organizations in the country. Companies that export to international markets have their products tested and certified in established laboratories in other countries.[50]

Reform Agenda

Improvement in Bangladesh's regulatory functioning is of extreme importance for increasing exports. Strict regulatory environments are associated with higher-quality drugs. Initiatives should focus on building DGDA into an effective regulatory body by providing the agency with the necessary facilities, a full staff, and authority. Institutional measures should be investigated to increase transparency and provide inspectors with incentives to find, report, and fine low-quality manufacturing. Many governments have satisfactorily appointed a semi-autonomous regulatory authority. The authority's independence promotes a professional discharge of responsibilities. Capacity-building of the regulatory body will help harmonize quality standards.

To ensure quality standards for the export market, Bangladesh needs to modernize its drug testing laboratories and establish bioequivalent testing facilities.[51] There is a need to develop accredited laboratories and clinical setups to conduct bioequivalent tests to ensure that drugs meet globally accepted standards. Domestic bioequivalence testing facilities could help reduce costs and time delays and potentially help open up regulated markets, even for manufacturers of medium size. As for testing labs, government-approved and internationally accredited independent private testing laboratories could provide drug monitoring and quality services. These private labs could have industry representatives from associations, academics, civil society, and a government representative as their board members.

Deregulation in foreign exchange controls and capital investment is also critical for the growth of Bangladesh's pharmaceutical exports. Deregulating the foreign exchange regime would reduce the costs of complying with global standards, receiving certification from regulatory authorities of other countries, hiring consulting services to create best-practice manufacturing, and making pharmaceuticals more competitive. In addition, entering regulated or semi-regulated markets through registering products and acquiring certifications is a lengthy process. Current regulations do not allow domestic companies to invest abroad except on a lengthy, case-by-case basis. This can be changed.

Gradual introduction of competition may improve the quality of products. Bangladesh should consider opening up its domestic pharmaceutical market to global competition, allowing FDI through joint ventures to begin. Similarly, import restrictions also need to be gradually lifted, to benefit the consumer with greater choice of drugs and induce domestic firms to compete not only on price, but also in quality terms. This could reduce the market share of spurious drugs that are clearly a major problem in Bangladesh, provided that it is accompanied by a major initiative to improve the drug testing and certification infrastructure. FDI-based tie-ups with Indian and Chinese firms that manufacture API competitively could help the government's plans to establish an API park. To produce API, ensuring the quality of education and human resources and a supply of skilled labor in the chemistry and engineering fields would need particular attention.

Notes

1. For a broader discussion on the sector, see Kathuria and Malouche (2016b, chapter 2, on bicycles).

2. The ERP is the proportional increase in local firms' value added (or processing margin) resulting from the combined influence of tariff rates on the final good and intermediate inputs (a pure price effect—a higher ERP does not mean that the protected good has intrinsically higher value added). An escalating tariff structure (higher rates on final goods than on intermediates) raises local value added and protection levels compared with what would prevail under a zero or uniform tariff structure.

3. With financial support from the World Bank and in partnership with the local survey firm Data International.

4. The actual number of people employed in the shipbuilding industry in Bangladesh could be less than 100,000. The number for semi-skilled and skilled employees of Bangladeshi shipyards often quoted in publications is 150,000–200,000. However, this results in a high average figure of 750 staff at each of the 200 yards with a total production volume of 250,000 GT. The largest yards—Western Marine Shipyards and Ananda Shipyards—employ around 3,000 and 2,000 people, respectively, whereas smaller yards employ fewer than 100 people. As a comparison, in 2008 China employed 400,000 people in 2,000 shipyards and related industries, with a production volume of 14 million GT; in 2010 Vietnam employed 110,000 workers for a production volume of 600,000 GT.

5. Data collected from the Department of Shipping, as of 2011.

6. Published in 2001, in accordance with the Inland Shipping Ordinance, 1976.

7. Although this is the officially reported number and shipbuilding at unregistered yards (of the approximately 200 shipyards in Bangladesh, only 124 are registered) might have a significant share, it can be expected that the number for large vessels above 200 GT is fairly exact.

8. The jute sector can be viewed in three major categories: (a) raw jute; (b) traditional products (hessian [burlap] cloth, gunny sacks, and carpet backing cloth); and (c) diversified (also known as nontraditional) jute products, including specialty yarns and fabrics.

9. Jayajit Dash, "India Declines to Import Jute Bags from Bangladesh and Nepal," *Business Standard*, September 7, 2012.

10. Sector stakeholders for raw material include farmers, intermediaries, processors, and exporters; for finished products, stakeholders include spinners, millers, and manufacturers of traditional and diversified jute products.

11. Handicrafts can receive a subsidy of 15–20 percent, but this is not specific to jute; it covers all handicrafts, so it is not considered to be support specific to the sector.

12. Although a few large international firms have been purchasing jute shopping bags for the past several years as part of their efforts to position themselves as environmentally friendly, foreign governments have recently been banning disposable plastic shopping bags. Italy and Uganda have already banned plastic bags. The United Arab Emirates declared a ban on plastic bags starting in 2014. The United States and Canada are slowly phasing out the use of plastic bags as some major cities, including Chicago and Toronto, have banned the use of plastic bags. The European Union as a whole is set to cut usage of plastic bags by 50 percent by 2019 and 80 percent by 2025.

13. Abingoni Packaging Equipment Suppliers, Africa, www.abingoni.com/twine.htm.

14. Volume data are unavailable in comparable terms with the rest of the world.

15. Wikipedia article on espadrille (http://en.wikipedia.org/wiki/Espadrille).

16. This does not include companies located in export processing zones, since those companies are not represented by the Leather Goods and Footwear Manufacturers and Exporters Association of Bangladesh. The only EPZ with non-leather shoe manufacturers is located in Chittagong.

17. From 2008 to 2011, three new market entrants were unable to compete and have since left the market.

18. Bangladesh institutes a census of manufacturing industries, which is supposed to be collected monthly and yearly and classified by manufacturing sector activities following the Bangladesh Standard Industrial Classification at the four-digit level. The most recent information on the Bangladesh Bureau of Statistics website is for November 2010 and is incomplete, having only tracked leather footwear manufacturers.

19. In the absence of further investment, given the current installed capacity, the country could face a shortfall of more than 6,455 million meters by 2014–15.

20. If the textile content is less than 50 percent of the sole that comes in contact with the ground, then the U.S. duty is 36 percent. If the textile content is greater than or equal to 50 percent, then the U.S. duty is reduced to 8 percent. For what is termed the basic espadrille shoe (the proxy non-leather shoe style used in the value chain analysis), manufacturers have large cut-outs in the sole when selling to the United States. This generally is not possible with fashion espadrilles, however.

21. American Apparel and Footwear Association, https://www.wewear.org/aafa-on-the-issues/category/?CategoryId=96.

22. With GSP prospects for its footwear uncertain, Bangladesh's exports to the United States may possibly be helped by the Affordable Footwear Act, legislation moving through the U.S. Congress that seeks to end import tariffs on footwear (American Apparel and Footwear Association, https://www.wewear.org/aafa-on-the-issues/category/?CategoryId=96). If this occurs, it will also benefit China and other exporting countries.

23. Polo shirts are exported at a free on board price of Tk 388 (US$4.80) per polo. Only about 3 percent of total production is sold in the local market, at Tk 340 (US$4.20) per polo at the factory gate and Tk 500 (US$6.17) retail. The selling prices are based on the market and are therefore similar among producers. However, the cost of production varies greatly among garment manufacturers and depends on variables including age and quality of machinery and factory-specific wages.

24. Values refer to BGMEA member factories.

25. "Leading Bangladesh to Prosperity," http://www.BGMEA.com.bd.

26. The rebate rates and the list of items that qualify for export rebates change frequently depending on policy makers' assessments of various trends, such as the global price outlook, local market developments, etc.

27. Product-wise customs duties for the United States can be found at http://hts.usitc.gov.

28. This is based on factory-level cost collected in all four countries by the consultancy firm Global Development Solutions.

29. However, given the competitive labor rates, the unit production cost per polo shirt produced in Bangladesh (US$3.46 per piece) has the potential to be competitive (with respect to quantity and quality) with similar operations in China (US$3.93–4.33 per piece).

30. Details of importing inputs are summarized in Kathuria and Malouche (2016b, table 5G.2 in annex 5G).

31. More than 90 percent of import and export activity in Bangladesh is done through the Port of Chittagong.

32. Regulation Number 2474/1993 was initially extended by regulation number 71/97 and subsequently maintained and gradually increased. The current antidumping duty is 48.5 percent until October 2016.

33. The only exception is Meghna's supply of some components to the local market (mostly steel frame tubes, frame joints, wheels and spokes, and tires and inner tubes).

34. Nevertheless, based on interviews with the Business Owners Association of the Bongshal Market in Dhaka—the hub of the cottage bicycle industry of Bangladesh—general features of the market can be discerned.

35. Wages in Dhaka are reported to be at least 20 percent higher than in Chittagong.

36. Global Development Solutions, LLC, from industry sources.

37. In January 2011, EU rules of origin were relaxed significantly. First, an exporter from an LDC, including Bangladesh, could import up to 70 percent of the ex-works price of a bicycle in components from the European Union. Second, regional cumulation allowed component sourcing between different groups of countries, including between East Asia (Brunei, Cambodia, Indonesia, the Lao People's Democratic Republic, Malaysia, the Philippines, Singapore, Thailand, and Vietnam) and South Asia (Bangladesh, Bhutan, India, the Maldives, Nepal, Pakistan, and Sri Lanka).

38. Most mother vessels do not call at Chittagong port because of poor navigability. As a result, transshipment through major regional ports increases transit times.

39. Electricity prices below US$0.10 per kWh are generally considered competitive at the international level.

40. For example, interviews with OEMs suggest that "speed money" is quite prevalent as a means to expedite customs procedures. Reported aggregate amounts of unofficial payments, at different stages of interaction with customs officials, range from 0.30 percent to 0.75 percent of the value of a finished product (bicycle).

41. Source: Bangladesh Association of Software and Information Services (BASIS).

42. ITC and KPMG, "Bangladesh Beckons: An Emerging Destination for IT/ITES Outsourcing," white paper, KPMG, Amsterdam, January 2012. Information on how much was exported from the US$2 million voice-based BPO revenues is not available.

43. *Strategic Priorities of Digital Bangladesh*, draft, October 2010. Prime Minister's Office.

44. PriceWaterhousCoopers India, 2005.

45. *Strategic Priorities of Digital Bangladesh*, draft, October 2010, Prime Minister's Office.

46. The ICT 2009 policy guidelines stipulate that 5 percent of the annual development budget and 2 percent of the revenue budget are to be allocated to the IT sector. These guidelines generally are not followed in budget allocations and fund distribution and utilization.

47. The FY2013 budget reduced the total tax burden for 46 essential items of pharmaceutical manufacture from 38–59 percent to 3 percent. In the FY2013 and FY2012 budgets, duties were withdrawn or reduced on machinery such as air handling units, heating ventilation, cartridge filters, sandwich panels, and leukocyte filters.

48. In 2005, the National Drug Policy was revised and the ban on Bangladeshi companies manufacturing under contract and license for multinationals was lifted.

49. System for Improved Access to Pharmaceuticals and Services, assessment funded by the U.S. Agency for International Development and U.S. Food and Drug Administration,

http://siapsprogram.org/2013/02/11/strengthening-the-pharmacovigilance-system
-in-bangladesh/.

50. Source: Interviews with local firms.

51. Under the US$350 million Health Sector Development Program, the World Bank, along with the World Health Organization, is supporting the modernization of the National Drug Testing Laboratory in Dhaka. The drug testing laboratory has been modernized and is functioning. More details are available in the Project Appraisal Document, Health Sector Development Program, May 3, 2011, p. 39–40 and the Progress Report by the Ministry of Health, September 2014.

References

APICCAPS (Portuguese Association of Manufacturers of Footwear, Components, and Leather Goods). 2012. *World Footwear 2012 Yearbook*. http://www.apiccaps.pt/c /document_library/get_file?uuid=7d10300e-b8e0-40ae-b9be-246e4327714c &groupId=10136 or http://www.worldfootwear.com/docs/2012/2012WorldFootwear Yearbook.pdf.

Bangladesh Tariff Commission. 2010. "An Analysis of Assistance to the Pharmaceutical Industry." Bangladesh Tariff Commission, Dhaka.

Beximco Pharmaceuticals. 2011. "Annual Report, 2011." Beximco, Bangladesh.

Bhuiyan, Md. Arafater Rahman, Maniruzzaman, and Sharmin Sultana. 2011. "Analysis of Pharmaceutical Industry of Bangladesh." *Bangladesh Research Publications Journal* 5: 142–56.

BTMA (Bangladesh Textile Mills Association). 2011. *Report of the Board of Directors of BTMA for 2011*. Dhaka: BTMA.

Haroon, Jasim Uddin. 2012. "WB Survey Finds BD Lead Time Higher." *The Financial Express*, November 17.

IDLC (Industrial Development Leasing Company). 2011. "Pharmaceutical Industry of Bangladesh." Report, IDLC, Dhaka.

IMF (International Monetary Fund). 2013. "Bangladesh: Second Review under the Three-Year Arrangement under the Extended Credit Facility and Request for Modification of Performance Criteria." International Monetary Fund, Washington, DC.

———. 2014. *World Economic Outlook: Legacies, Clouds, Uncertainties*. Washington, DC: IMF.

Kathuria, Sanjay, and Mariem Mezghenni Malouche, eds. 2016a. *Strengthening Competitiveness in Bangladesh—Thematic Assessment: A Diagnostic Trade Integration Study*. Washington, DC: World Bank.

———. 2016b. *Strengthening Competitiveness in Bangladesh—Sector Analyses: A Diagnostic Trade Integration Study*. Washington, DC: World Bank.

Lan, Percy. 2012. "Report on the 31st International Footwear Conference." *Peditimes*, March 12. http://www.peditimes.com/specialreport/2012-06-19/1.html.

Ministry of Commerce. 2012. *Import Policy Order 2012–2015*. Dhaka: Government of Bangladesh.

Pawlicki, Amy. 2012. "Emergence of Social Stock Exchanges and Other Market Drivers of Sustainability." *AICPA Insights*, November 19.

Transparency International. 2011. "CPI Index." http://cpi.transparency.org/cpi2011/.

UNCTAD (United Nations Conference on Trade and Development). 2011. *Local Production of Pharmaceuticals and Related Technology Transfer: A Series of Case Studies by the UNCTAD Secretariat*, 57–88. Geneva: United Nations. http://www.who.int /phi/publications/ Local_Production_Case_Studies.pdf.

World Bank. 2008. "Public and Private Sector Approaches to Improving Pharmaceutical Quality in Bangladesh." Bangladesh Development Series Paper 23, World Bank, Washington, DC.

———. 2012a. "Consolidating and Accelerating Exports in Bangladesh: A Policy Agenda." Bangladesh Development Series Paper 29, Poverty Reduction and Economic Management Sector, South Asia Region, World Bank, Washington, DC.

———. 2012b. *Bangladesh: Towards Accelerated, Inclusive and Sustainable Growth— Opportunities and Challenges*. Vol. 2 Report 67991, Poverty Reduction and Economic Management Unit, South Asia Region. Washington, DC: World Bank.

———. 2013. *Seeding Fertile Grounds: Education That Works for Bangladesh*. Dhaka: World Bank.

CHAPTER 5

Conclusions

Bangladesh has a solid development record. The country has posted robust and resilient growth over the past decade and reduced the number of poor from 63 million to 47 million over 2000–10. Growth in labor incomes and favorable demographics have been key factors behind poverty reduction. Bangladesh now faces one of its greatest development challenges: to provide 21 million jobs to new entrants to the labor force over the next decade. Moreover, only 58.1 million of the country's 103.3 million working-age people are employed, reflecting low female participation in the labor force.

Fortunately, outward orientation can provide the answer, as recognized in the Sixth Five-Year Plan. Bangladesh's experience is a testimony to the power of the global market. In gaining 5 percent of the global garment market, Bangladesh has provided jobs to four million people and indirect jobs to about 10 million. Only a fraction of this employment would have been possible in catering to the domestic market.

The example of Vietnam shows that accelerated, export-oriented development is possible, even in the context of the current global environment. Vietnam moved from being one of the poorest countries in the world to a lower-middle-income one in the space of 25 years, with foreign direct investment (FDI) and trade playing a dominant role in the economy: exports and imports are each 90 percent of gross domestic product (GDP) and, with 88 million people compared with Bangladesh's 150 million, Vietnam exports four times as much as Bangladesh today.

For Bangladesh to sustain and accelerate export growth will require actions centered on four pillars:

1. *Breaking into new markets* through (a) better trade logistics to reduce delivery lags as world markets become more competitive and newer products demand shorter lead times to generate new sources of competitiveness and thereby enable market diversification and (b) better exploitation of regional trading opportunities in nearby growing and dynamic markets, especially East Asia and South Asia.

2. *Breaking into new products* through (a) more neutral and rational trade policy and taxation and bonded warehouse schemes; (b) concerted efforts to spur domestic investment and attract FDI and to contribute to export promotion and diversification, including by easing energy and land constraints; and (c) strategic development and promotion of services trade.
3. *Improving worker and consumer welfare* by (a) improving skills and literacy, (b) implementing labor and work safety guidelines, and (c) making safety nets more effective in dealing with trade shocks.
4. *Building a supportive environment*, including (a) sustaining sound macroeconomic fundamentals and (b) strengthening the institutional capacity for strategic policy making aimed at the objective of international competitiveness to help bring focus and coherence to the government's reform efforts.

With the implementation of the four-pillar agenda, a virtuous circle of export-led growth can be put in place, with multiple sources of strength. In combination with skill improvement, this will help improve the overall competitiveness of the economy and provide sources of strength other than low wages.

A neutral trade policy needs not only to correct the anti-export bias but also to take due account of consumer interests, which are linked to welfare. Distortions affect critical areas that affect consumer welfare, such as medicines and consumer products, and producer interests have tended to dominate over consumer interests.

The ultimate goal of export-led growth is poverty reduction and the enhanced welfare of Bangladesh's citizens. Accordingly, skill development and worker safety need to be part of the goals. Rapidly growing exports and the millions of new jobs accompanying them, along with skill upgrading, will increase productivity and wages, which over the long term is the only sustainable way to improve living standards; it will also begin a discourse to move beyond wage-based competitiveness. Improving skills will also allow people to participate effectively in growth. Improving labor standards and worker safety is part of this agenda, and, in the wake of recent tragic incidents in the garment sector, has become part of the preconditions for garment exports.

With a coherent vision centered on international competitiveness and strong leadership to ensure implementation of that vision, Bangladesh can see itself as a larger, more efficient economy that uses more labor and yet pays higher wages to its workers. As the share of trade rises from the current 55 percent of GDP toward 100 percent of GDP, the economy will become more efficient and will also use its abundant resource, labor, more intensively. Rising skill levels, complemented by other sources of competitiveness, will help ensure that productivity and wages also increase, enabling higher living standards among the citizens of Bangladesh.

Bangladesh is well placed to take on some of its strongest development challenges, with the right leadership. Its track record on growth and employment is strong. To grow faster, absorb more labor, and continue its pace of poverty reduction, it will need to build on that record and improve on it. The good news is that a number of reforms are relatively low-hanging fruits, may be implemented in the short-to-medium term, and can bring large payoffs.

Bangladesh will need strong leadership to support its multisector competitiveness agenda. In many cases, it will require taking on strong domestic interests that may not welcome competition, either through imports or FDI. In other cases, it will require cohesion and coordination between different ministries and departments, such as the National Board of Revenue; the Ministries of Commerce, Finance, and Industry, and the Roads Division. If the Sixth Plan and Vision 2021 goals are to be achieved, this leadership has to be exercised.

Proposed Action Matrix

Table A.1 Proposed Action Matrix

Phase 1: 12–24 months; Phase 2: 24–48 months; Phase 3: 48 months and beyond

Issue to be addressed	Proposed policy measure/ project/ technical assistance/ capacity building	Responsible government unit	Potential implementation challenges	Expected results	Progress as of August 31, 2015
PILLAR 1: BREAKING INTO NEW MARKETS					
A. Improving trade facilitation					
Coordination of trade, transport, and logistics strategies across different sectors and modes of transport	Establish an Inter-Ministerial Trade and Transport Facilitation Committee	Ministries of Commerce (Chair), Shipping, Road Transport and Bridges, Planning Commission, and NBR	Agencies may still prefer to design and implement their programs without consulting other agencies and the private sector	Better coordination and prioritization of interventions to improve performance of national logistics system	Cabinet approval being sought for the Inter-Ministerial Committee.
Containers being unloaded in the port or immediate vicinity of the port	Adopt a coordinated strategy to improve performance of Dhaka-Chittagong corridor (including infrastructure, transport services, Customs)	Inter-Ministerial Trade and Transport Facilitation Committee, Ministry of Railways, Ministry of Shipping, Ministry of Road Transport and Bridges, NBR	Potential resistance from private sector and workers who are heavily vested in current systems	Reduced logistics costs for containerized shipments	Follow-up measures are being undertaken. Studies are being conducted on the railway reforms necessary to support container transport, and reforms needed at Chittagong Port. New inland container depot on PPP basis proposed, near Dhirasram Railway Station. Ministry of Railways has taken the decision to establish a container company. To increase the modal share of container transport by railway along Dhaka-Chittagong Corridor, 220 flat wagons have been procured. Khulna-Mongla rail line is under construction. Master plan of Pangaon Port is approved.

table continues next page

Table A.1 Proposed Action Matrix *(continued)*

Issue to be addressed	Proposed policy measure/ project/ technical assistance/ capacity building	Responsible government unit	Potential implementation challenges	Expected results	Progress as of August 31, 2015
Declining proportion of container movement by rail on Dhaka-Chittagong Corridor	Dual-track the main line between Dhaka and Chittagong	Bangladesh Railways	Insufficient financing to complete the dual tracking	Increased movement of containerized cargo	Construction of double-line track from Tongi to Bhairab Bazar scheduled to be completed by June 2016. Construction of 2nd Titas and 2nd Bhairab Bridges is in progress. Dhaka-Chittagong four-lane road in progress. Track between Laksam and Chinki-Astana has been doubled and opened for traffic.
Limited capacity of port to sustain increasing traffic volume	Build new terminal (Karnaphuli) and deep-sea port	Ministry of Shipping, Chittagong Port Authority	Limited financing from public funds	Increased port capacity given increasing trade volumes	Government plans to establish deep-sea ports in Payra and Sonadia. Payra Port Authority act has been enacted.
Limited use of inland water transport system for container movement	Dredge sections of inland waterway network and modernize the vessel fleet and invest in handling equipment and dredging	Ministry of Shipping, MOF	Potentially slow additions to container vessel fleet, as seen in vessels serving newly opened Pangaon Inland Container Terminal	Reduced transport costs for containerized shipments moved by inland waterways transport	
Air shipments and samples being subjected to the same clearance formalities as all other cargo	Raise limit for operation of simplified procedures and adopt and implement new procedures for expedited clearance of small shipments	NBR	Possible reluctance to apply policy to all shipments up to a revised maximum value/quantity	Expedited clearance of small air shipments up to new upper limit	New Customs Act 2015 has been formulated incorporating provisions of the Revised Kyoto Convention and some provisions of WTO TFA.
Limited capacity and less than efficient ground handling at airport	Introduce competition in ground handling, especially of cargo	Ministry of Civil Aviation and Tourism	Potential decline in revenue for Biman	Increased efficiency of ground handling operations, especially for garment industry	Ministry of Civil Aviation and Tourism and Biman looking into joint venture possibilities for cargo handling.

table continues next page

Table A.1 Proposed Action Matrix (continued)

Issue to be addressed	Proposed policy measure/ project/ technical assistance/ capacity building	Responsible government unit	Potential implementation challenges	Expected results	Progress as of August 31, 2015
High customs clearance times	Implement recommendations from time-release studies conducted at key border posts, introduce risk management practices, roll out authorized economic operator program following World Customs Organization/WTO TFA guidelines, and implement National Single Window	NBR, Port Authorities, BSTI, Plant and Fish Quarantine, Drug Administration, Atomic Energy Commission, BB, Sonali Bank, CCI&E	Development of a clear plan for phased modernization of customs and reduction in clearance times	Faster clearance for compliant traders, enabling greater focus on risk-based coordinated border management	Ongoing programs are addressing Customs processes, border management, risk management, valuation practices, authorized economic operator, and implementation of the National Single Window. Rolling out of ASYCUDA World to five priority LCS has been completed and others are ongoing. Simplification of the business process of ASYCUDA world is ongoing.
Long clearance times for goods shipped overland	Automate all land customs stations by rolling out ASYCUDA World software for customs back-office automation Allow pre-arrival clearance of goods	NBR, Port Authorities, BSTI, Plant and Fish Quarantine, Drug Administration, BB, Sonali Bank, CCI&E	Improved reliability of information technology connections to all major LCS	Faster clearance of goods, easier collection of statistics	Proposed New Customs Act 2015 has incorporated pre-arrival clearance of goods. ASYCUDA World is interfaced with BB for submission of e-LCS.
Costly trade finance hurting competitiveness of exporters and producers	Review Foreign Exchange Regulation Act	BB	Overall control system	More modern foreign exchange regime	Foreign Exchange Regulation (Amendment) Act 2015 has been approved by the Cabinet.
	Leave title documents "open" and not assigned to a local bank, to open up Bangladesh to new trade financing structures from abroad, improve liquidity, and significantly lower financing costs	BB	Need to ensure controls so that export proceeds are correctly repatriated	Significant increase in foreign financing of exports; lower interest rate costs	BB is working on the possibility of introducing export factoring services, which will allow export on open account. This would allow phasing out the requirement of title documents.

table continues next page

Table A.1 Proposed Action Matrix *(continued)*

Issue to be addressed	Proposed policy measure/ project/ technical assistance/ capacity building	Responsible government unit	Potential implementation challenges	Expected results	Progress as of August 31, 2015
	Permit all exporters whose suppliers import inputs (not just for those exporters who have bonded warehouses) to use back-to-back letters of credit	BB/NBR	Ensure proper controls in place to avoid leakage	More exporters able to pass the benefits to their suppliers	

B. Promoting Economic Integration with Asia

Issue to be addressed	Proposed policy measure/ project/ technical assistance/ capacity building	Responsible government unit	Potential implementation challenges	Expected results	Progress as of August 31, 2015
Transloading of trucks across international borders inhibits movement and creates long, avoidable delays	Negotiate either regional or bilateral instruments with neighboring countries to allow the cross-border movement of trucks	Ministry of Road Transport and Bridges, Ministry of Shipping, NBR	Possible resistance from labor employed at border posts to transload cargo	Faster movement of cargo through border posts; increased vehicle utilization	Motor Vehicle Agreement signed between Bangladesh, Bhutan, India, and Nepal in June 2015.
Limited transit trade	Grant transit rights and conclude road transport agreements with Bhutan, China, India, Myanmar, and Nepal	MOC, Ministry of Road Transport and Bridges, NBR	Possible objections from security establishments, likely protracted discussions on cost sharing and internal opposition in some countries	Increased regional trade going through Bangladesh and potential spillover effects on Bangladesh's own trade	Motor Vehicle Agreement is a first step in this regard.
Design of new border infrastructure in India is not always in sync with existing facilities in Bangladesh	Establish formal mechanisms for consultations at policy and operational levels on border management	Ministry of Shipping, NBR, security agencies, Ministry of Foreign Affairs	Redefinition of long-standing mechanisms to include technical agencies and experts	Synchronized and more efficient traffic flow patterns through border posts	Ongoing technical assistance is helping to improve coordination of synergies in border infrastructure.

table continues next page

Table A.1 Proposed Action Matrix *(continued)*

Issue to be addressed	Proposed policy measure/project/technical assistance/capacity building	Responsible government unit	Potential implementation challenges	Expected results	Progress as of August 31, 2015
Space requirement for LCS delaying improvement in border infrastructure	Customize design of border infrastructure depending on predominant flow, import or export, and volume	NBR	Dynamic trade setting renders infrastructure planning difficult	Greater efficiency in use of resources	There are three joint working groups (between Bangladesh and India) on Trade, Customs, and Inland Water Protocol. These meet periodically to discuss bilateral issues.
Limited border haats (border trade market) geographical area and unit value	Redefine border trade regime extending 5 miles to 10 mile radius and increase product coverage (Korgas model)	MOC, NBR	Border security more difficult	Increased cross-border trade, which can have a positive impact, especially on the poor	Bangladesh and India jointly working on establishing border haats. Four border haats already established. New border haats are being established, with increases in geographical area and the value of goods.
Road map of mutual recognition of food-related border procedures between India and Bangladesh	Technical assistance to examine legislation, assess border procedures, promote mutual understanding, identify critical elements, hold technical discussions, and support necessary reform	BSTI/MOI	May necessitate deep reform of Bangladesh regulation and conformity assessment	Fewer delays for food traded between India and Bangladesh	A Bilateral Cooperation Agreement was signed between BSTI and Bureau of Indian Standards in June 2015. The purpose of this agreement is recognition of food-related and other test certificates by Indian Customs and vice versa. BSTI certificates have already been accepted by India for 25 products.

PILLAR 2: BREAKING INTO NEW PRODUCTS

A. Rationalizing Trade Policy to Level the Playing Field

Removing anti-export bias of trade taxes and the trade policy regime to encourage diversification	Merge para-tariffs with import tariffs to boost transparency; reduce dispersion of import tariffs	NBR, MOC, MOI, BTC	Perception of revenue loss and protectionist claims from industry lobby	Lower consumer and intermediate goods prices	The proposed new Value-Added Tax and Income Tax Ordinance/Act will promote compliant traders, close tax loopholes, and ensure better collection of legitimate revenue. The BTC Act 1992 needs to be reviewed.

table continues next page

Table A.1 Proposed Action Matrix *(continued)*

Issue to be addressed	Proposed policy measure/ project/ technical assistance/ capacity building	Responsible government unit	Potential implementation challenges	Expected results	Progress as of August 31, 2015
	Reduce overall nominal protection rates	NBR; MOC, MOI, BTC	Perception of revenue loss and protectionist claims from industry lobby	Lower consumer and intermediate goods prices	The proposed New Customs Act incorporates new provisions for warehousing, which would allow extending the bond facility to a wider range of exporters and their supply chain members.
	Close tax loopholes	NBR	Perception of revenue loss and protectionist claims from industry lobby	Higher tax revenue	
	Extend access to bonded warehouse facilities to reputable companies and trusted traders under authorized economic operators	NBR	Possible leakages of imports and consequent arguments about maintaining status quo	More exporters will be able to access inputs efficiently at world prices	
	Reduce delays for duty-drawback refunds	Duty Exemption and Drawback Office	Rent-seekers who gain from the status quo	Reduced import costs for exporters	
Several fiscal incentives and tax holidays offered without clarity about their effectiveness, coherence, and sustainability	Review existing programs and adopt more coherent, transparent, predictable, and time-bound (incorporating sunset clauses) policies	MOF, MOC, NBR		More cost-effective provision of support to private sector	MOC has reviewed the existing programs.
Absence of data and strategy on trade in services	Formulate and adopt a strategy for services trade	MOC		Identify potential for trade in services and increase in trade in services	A study can be conducted on trade in services and a database established. To make this happen, MOC needs to consult and coordinate with the many ministries/divisions involved in services.

table continues next page

Table A.1 Proposed Action Matrix *(continued)*

Issue to be addressed	Proposed policy measure/ project/ technical assistance/ capacity building	Responsible government unit	Potential implementation challenges	Expected results	Progress as of August 31, 2015
	Establish a database on trade in services	MOC		Better knowledge on services trade in terms of specific services, trends, and markets	
Streamlining quality standards	Review mandatory standards with a view to introduce more flexible standards in compliance with international best practice according to the Technical Barriers to Trade agreement	BSTI, MOI	Resistance can be expected as BSTI depends on testing and certification revenues	An import regime and government certification system closer to international best practice	National Quality Policy has been drafted, now awaiting cabinet approval. The policy includes 12 ministries. According to the Import Policy Order, 55 products require mandatory certification from BSTI. BSTI has rolled out implementation of the e-Certification Mark program to facilitate trade.
Clarity in the Plant Quarantine Act 2011	Develop and implement new rules that provide clarity to importers about the prevailing rules for sanitary and phytosanitary standards	Ministry of Agriculture, Department of Agricultural Extension, Plan Quarantine Wing	Awareness of other border clearance agencies and traders		Plant Quarantine Wing of the Department of Agricultural Extension has drafted Plant Quarantine Rules 2015. It is awaiting stakeholder validation and approval.

B. Improving the Environment for Domestic and Foreign Investment

FDI is managed by a complex set of laws and regulations under various authorities, and subject to discretionary administrative procedures	Consolidate and make transparent and clear laws on investment More transparent and clear administrative guidelines to reduce scope for rent-seeking	PMO, BOI	Lack of adequate understanding about the positive role of FDI, and lack of empowerment of officials in BOI	Technology transfer facilitated and new markets created in various sectors	

table continues next page

Table A.1 Proposed Action Matrix *(continued)*

Issue to be addressed	Proposed policy measure/ project/ technical assistance/ capacity building	Responsible government unit	Potential implementation challenges	Expected results	Progress as of August 31, 2015
Serviceable land for domestic and foreign investment	Pro-actively initiate action to expand existing economic zones, develop infrastructure, operationalize private zones, and identify land for industrial zones	PMO, BEZA	Bureaucratic inertia and leadership capacity relating to private sector development	Expansion in private investment	BEZA is endeavoring to address this issue. Four private companies have been given a prequalification certificate to establish a free economic zone.
Energy shortages and reliance on short-term, high-cost solutions that have put strains on the budget	Increase generation capacity in low-cost base load power plants; make commissioning of the large gas-fired/dual fuel combined cycle power plants awarded to the private sector the top priority	Ministry of Power, Energy, and Mineral Resources, Power Division	Continued challenges of procurement and an adequate PPP framework	Increase in power generation and closing of gap between demand and supply of electricity	
	Convert BPDB's simple cycle plants to combined cycle plants	BPDB		More efficient use of natural gas	
	Accelerate moves to import power from Bhutan, Myanmar, Nepal, and India's northeastern states	Ministry of Power, Energy, and Mineral Resources, Power Division; PMO	Insulating the power import process from political changes and opposition	Potentially cheaper power as evidenced in the price of imported Indian electricity	Power is being imported from India since 2013, and power cooperation between the two countries is rapidly expanding.
Limited enforcement of standards	Enforcement of standards so that compliant firms are not penalized and disadvantaged	MOI, BSTI, Directorate General of Drug Administration, etc.	Lobbying by local firms to continue to benefit from favored treatment	More interest from potential foreign investors; higher investment by existing foreign investors	

table continues next page

Table A.1 Proposed Action Matrix *(continued)*

Issue to be addressed	Proposed policy measure/ project/ technical assistance/ capacity building	Responsible government unit	Potential implementation challenges	Expected results	Progress as of August 31, 2015
Lack of a concerted and coordinated effort to attract FDI	BOI should provide up-front administrative support to potential investors and set up a one-stop shop for all procedures	PMO, Cabinet, BOI	Industry lobbies that are ambivalent toward FDI		
	BOI should pro-actively seek FDI through more high-level investment promotion missions to selected emerging economies (such as China, India, and Japan) and seek investment in higher-technology sectors such as shipbuilding and bicycles	PMO, Cabinet, BOI	Industry lobbies that are ambivalent toward FDI		

PILLAR 3: IMPROVING WORKER AND CONSUMER WELFARE[a]

A. Improving Skills and Literacy

Issue to be addressed	Proposed policy measure/ project/ technical assistance/ capacity building	Responsible government unit	Potential implementation challenges	Expected results	Progress as of August 31, 2015
Despite reported shortages of skilled labor, few incentives for the private sector to impart training	Enhance linkages between publicly funded technical and vocational education and training and the private sector	Ministry of Education, Ministry of Labour and Employment in partnership with private sector		Training more relevant to the private sector	
Low level of literacy and years of schooling of the labor force make skill acquisition more difficult	Pursue quality early child development	Ministry of Education, Ministry of Health and Family Welfare, Ministry of Women and Children Affairs		Development of skilled labor force meeting local demand-supply gap and increasing employment potential at home and abroad	

table continues next page

Table A.1 Proposed Action Matrix *(continued)*

Issue to be addressed	Proposed policy measure/ project/ technical assistance/ capacity building	Responsible government unit	Potential implementation challenges	Expected results	Progress as of August 31, 2015
Market supplies inadequate training because of job-hopping and training externalities	Introduce trainee-targeted and employer-targeted financing of training			More effectively trained labor coming out of the programs	
B. Implementing Labor and Work Safety Guidelines					
Workplace safety standards not uniformly enforced	Government to provide coordination and leadership for implementation of agreements signed among EU and U.S. buyers	Ministry of Labour and Employment		Better worker safety and improved perception of Bangladesh as a source country	Inspections of most factories have been completed under the agreements with European and American retailers. These factories need regular monitoring, and the government has taken initiatives to strengthen its monitoring capacity by recruiting staff.
	Implement International Labour Organization activities, including the Better Work Program	Ministry of Labour and Employment			
C. Making Safety Nets More Effective in Dealing with Trade Shocks					
Inadequate safety net programs to mitigate the impact of trade-related adjustments	Start preparation of a safety net and labor strategy that acknowledges possible winners and losers in trade liberalization, and recognizes the role of cash transfers and gives primacy to youth employment and training and re-training of workers	Ministry of Labour and Employment, MOF	Lack of widespread recognition that there will be winners and losers in the process of globalization, which relates to a willingness to prepare an appropriate safety net strategy	Greater confidence in pursuing the globalization process	

table continues next page

Table A.1 Proposed Action Matrix *(continued)*

Issue to be addressed	Proposed policy measure/ project/ technical assistance/ capacity building	Responsible government unit	Potential implementation challenges	Expected results	Progress as of August 31, 2015
		PILLAR 4: BUILDING A SUPPORTIVE ENVIRONMENT[b]			
A. Sustainable Macroeconomic Framework					
B. Building Institutions for Trade Policy Coherence and Implementation					
Insufficiently cohesive policies to strengthen trade competitiveness	Adopt a visible Trade Competitiveness Vision to make sure all laws and policies contribute toward this Vision	Ministries of Commerce (Chair), Shipping, Road Transport and Bridges, Planning Commission, NBR (see Pillar 1A)	Inter-agency coordination	More coherent and coordinated policy to improve competitiveness	Cabinet approval is being sought for the Inter-Ministerial Committee on Trade and Transport Facilitation.
	Develop formal joint committee of MOC and NBR with transparent consultation processes in tariff setting	MOC/BTC, NBR, MOI	Buy-in by NBR	Clear agreed upon criteria established for tariff setting; reduced opportunities for rent-seeking	The proposed New Customs Act 2015 has incorporated mandatory consultation with related stakeholders, including the Tariff Commission, before enactment of any new legislation, self-regulatory organizations, rules, orders, tariff rates, etc. according to the provision of WTO TFA (but this falls short of joint tariff setting).
Strong analytical and research capabilities should underpin the policy formulation process	Mobilize key economists from Bangladesh's existing think tanks and policy institutes more formally to support policy making throughout the life cycle (build capacity at MOC and BFTI)	MOC		Improved capacity for designing and implementing trade-related policies	

table continues next page

Table A.1 Proposed Action Matrix (continued)

Issue to be addressed	Proposed policy measure/project/technical assistance/capacity building	Responsible government unit	Potential implementation challenges	Expected results	Progress as of August 31, 2015
	Train MOC staff on basics of trade policy, WTO, regional agreements	MOC			MOC and NBR staff are being exposed to the needs of the WTO TFA.
	Provide training-of-trainers to BFTI	MOC/BFTI			
Inadequate branding of Bangladesh	Build country branding	MOC, EPB, Ministry of Foreign Affairs		Development of a positive reputation for Bangladesh	
Inadequacy of robust research and analysis to support trade policy formulation	Deepen linkages with existing research/policy institutes and academia to support ex ante and ex post analysis of trade policies, and strengthen trade research capacity in Bangladesh	MOC, Planning Commission, Bangladesh Institute of Development Studies, Centre for Policy Dialogue, Policy Research Institute, and academia	Thin supply of quality research that is driven by short-term donor exigencies	More rigorous analytical inputs to policy making and evaluation	
Structure and effectiveness of EPB	Increase private sector participation in the board	EPB		Improved effectiveness of EPB	
	Improve funding and provide management assistance to EPB	MOC		Improving the targeting of fairs and markets	
	Improve statistical capability of EPB to monitor trade flows	EPB, MOC		Improving market information and branding	
Strengthening BSTI	Train people in standardization, testing, and certification	BSTI/MOI			The "Modernization and Strengthening of BSTI" project is being implemented by the government. A modern Energy Efficient Testing Laboratory has been established in the BSTI head office.

table continues next page

Table A.1 Proposed Action Matrix *(continued)*

Issue to be addressed	Proposed policy measure/ project/ technical assistance/ capacity building	Responsible government unit	Potential implementation challenges	Expected results	Progress as of August 31, 2015
					Several BSTI laboratories have already been awarded accreditation from the National Accreditation Board for Testing Laboratories, India. BSTI is taking steps to get its Product Certification Systems fully accredited.
Liberalization of market for testing and certification	Change in policy to allow private laboratories to certify shrimp and seafood exports General change in policy to allow private service providers to provide services for quality in areas under government regulation	Department of Fisheries, Ministry of Fisheries and Livestock	Resistance as revenues may be important and government may be adverse to give up control	Easier compliance with EU food safety legislation – avoidance of future costly extra requirements like 20% inspection	Government is considering more effective involvement of the private sector. Government has taken a PPP initiative to ensure quality of shrimp and other frozen food throughout the value chain by forming the Aquaculture and Aquatic Food Safety Centre, in collaboration with MOC.
PILLAR 5: SECTOR-SPECIFIC MEASURES					
Shipbuilding – inadequate quality of ships in the domestic market, with implications for safety as well as exportability, and a shortage of trained labor	Update and improve the domestic vessel code with stricter technical rules and standards	MOI, Ministry of Shipping		Higher quality vessels for domestic and export markets	
	Enforce the current rules and standards through appropriately educated surveyors employed by the government	MOI, Ministry of Shipping			
	Formal training for workers, managers, and engineers	Department of Shipping in Marine Academy, Ministry of Shipping		Productivity gains	

table continues next page

Table A.1 Proposed Action Matrix *(continued)*

Issue to be addressed	Proposed policy measure/project/technical assistance/capacity building	Responsible government unit	Potential implementation challenges	Expected results	Progress as of August 31, 2015
Jute products – lack of sustained demand for jute products, local and foreign; favored treatment to public sector that hurts the more competitive private sector	Jute Packaging Act 2010 and Jute Packaging Rules 2013 need to be enforced			More stable source of demand for the jute industry	
	Phase out subsidies to public jute mills			Increased market for private sector	
	Stimulate further research and development in the sector for the development of additional diversified fabrics	BJRI, Jute Diversification Promotion Centre		Reduced cost and increased fabric variety	
	Joint marketing, research, and branding with India and Nepal to expand domestic and international demand for jute	BJRI and government			
Bicycles – low technology domestically-oriented local producers	Large OEMs (manufacturers) support local producers' investment by guaranteeing the borrowings of suppliers on the basis of OEM	MOI, Bangladesh Steel and Engineering Corporation		To modernize and create potential for a more competitive parts and components industry	
ITES – insufficiently reliable Internet connectivity with latency	Install two additional international submarine cables to ensure minimal redundancy in case of failure of one of the three cables			Improve quality Internet services at affordable rates	

table continues next page

137

Table A.1 Proposed Action Matrix (continued)

Issue to be addressed	Proposed policy measure/ project/ technical assistance/ capacity building	Responsible government unit	Potential implementation challenges	Expected results	Progress as of August 31, 2015
Significant skill gaps in ITES, including soft skills and English language and management skills	Develop training programs, coaching, workshops, and certification for individuals and organizations	BASIS Institute of Technology and Management		Improved skills	
Inadequate access to finance in ITES is a major handicap, given the lack of physical collateral	Improve access to specialized credit facilities, such as the small and medium enterprises facility funded by the Equity Entrepreneurship Fund and the Japan International Cooperation Agency			Improved access to finance for ITES-BPOs in Bangladesh	

Note: ASYCUDA = Automated SYstem for CUstoms DAta; BB = Bangladesh Bank; BEZA = Bangladesh Economic Zones Authority; BFTI = Bangladesh Foreign Trade Institute; BJRI = Bangladesh Jute Research Institute; BOI = Board of Investment; BPDB = Bangladesh Power Development Board; BSTI = Bangladesh Standards and Testing Institution; BTC = Bangladesh Tariff Commission; CCI&E = Chief Controller of Imports and Exports; EPB = Export Promotion Bureau; FDI = foreign direct investment; ITES = information technology enabled services; ITES-BPO = information technology enabled services–business process outsourcing; LCS = Land Customs Stations; MOC = Ministry of Commerce; MOF = Ministry of Finance; MOI = Ministry of Industries; NBR = National Board of Revenue; OEM = original equipment manufacturer; PMO = Prime Minister's Office; PPP = public–private partnership; TFA = Trade Facilitation Agreement; WTO = World Trade Organization.

This Action Matrix was updated shortly before publication of this report. Some of the updates contained here are not reflected in the main body of the report.

a. Area C of Pillar 3 is Making Safety Nets More Effective in Dealing with Trade Shocks. This has not been explored in the Diagnostic Trade Integration Study.

b. Area A of Pillar 4 is Sustaining Sound Macroeconomic Fundamentals. Much of this agenda is covered by the ongoing International Monetary Fund program and is therefore not detailed here.

Environmental Benefits Statement

The World Bank Group is committed to reducing its environmental footprint. In support of this commitment, the Publishing and Knowledge Division leverages electronic publishing options and print-on-demand technology, which is located in regional hubs worldwide. Together, these initiatives enable print runs to be lowered and shipping distances decreased, resulting in reduced paper consumption, chemical use, greenhouse gas emissions, and waste.

The Publishing and Knowledge Division follows the recommended standards for paper use set by the Green Press Initiative. Whenever possible, books are printed on 50 percent to 100 percent postconsumer recycled paper, and at least 50 percent of the fiber in our book paper is either unbleached or bleached using Totally Chlorine Free (TCF), Processed Chlorine Free (PCF), or Enhanced Elemental Chlorine Free (EECF) processes.

More information about the Bank's environmental philosophy can be found at http://crinfo.worldbank.org/wbcrinfo/node/4.